Miles Franklin UNDERCOVER

The little-known years when she created her own brilliant career

KERRIE DAVIES

ALLEN&UNWIN
SYDNEY • MELBOURNE • AUCKLAND • LONDON

First published in 2025

Allen & Unwin
Cammeraygal Country
83 Alexander Street
Crows Nest NSW 2065
Australia
Phone: (61 2) 8425 0100
Email: info@allenandunwin.com
Web: www.allenandunwin.com

Allen & Unwin acknowledges the Traditional Owners of the Country on which we live and work. We pay our respects to all Aboriginal and Torres Strait Islander Elders, past and present.

NATIONAL LIBRARY OF AUSTRALIA

A catalogue record for this book is available from the National Library of Australia

ISBN 978 1 76147 093 6

Grateful acknowledgement is given to H.C. and A. Glad, Estate of Norman Lindsay, for permission to reprint extracts from Norman Lindsay, *Bohemians of The Bulletin* (Angus & Roberston, 1965), and an extract from a letter from Norman Lindsay to Lionel Lindsay, in Norman Lindsay, Robert Guy Howarth & Anthony Barker, *Letters of Norman Lindsay* (Angus & Robertson, 1979).

Set in 12.6/17 pt Bembo MT Pro by Midland Typesetters, Australia
Printed and bound in Australia by the Opus Group

10 9 8 7 6 5 4 3 2 1

MIX
Paper | Supporting responsible forestry
FSC® C001695
FSC www.fsc.org

The paper in this book is FSC® certified. FSC® promotes environmentally responsible, socially beneficial and economically viable management of the world's forests.

To all those who choose themselves over security

Contents

Prologue

Autumn, 1903

Blackboards chalked with 'Positions Vacant' hang against the wall. She feels like she has walked all morning to get here.

She hurries past loiterers with worn faces and sagging hats. They spit and slouch in her wake, watching. Inside, she sits on the nearest bench, as rigid as wood. A crowd of women seated on the other benches glance at her with curiosity and competition. Like them—for she wants to be like them—she is wearing a plain linen dress edged with a stiff, shiny starched collar and cuffs. Her long, dark curls are tucked into a bun under a sailor's cap, and her petite feet are in brown boots. On her lap, an open diary shifts with her nervousness.

The women stare at her. At her diary. At how she looks so refined, despite the plain clothes. Is she a governess who has come through the wrong agency door? The wrong life?

She tries to ignore the stares. Using a pencil, as ink will leak on her dress, she writes about her morning's experiences searching for work, knocking on terrace-house doors with her cotton-gloved hands.

Arriving in the metropolis by an early train from the country . . .

I had armed myself with the portions of the leading dailies headed, 'Servants wanted' and 'Situations Wanted'.

I left a purse containing a few shillings on the counter and tho' I returned within two minutes . . . I did not recover it . . .

He eyed me in the manner of a purchaser inspecting a horse . . .

One of the women, smaller than her in stature, inches closer.

Miles smiles at her. She edges closer again.

'Are you trying to get a place?' the woman whispered. Miles nods her head.

She pauses.

'I thought you might be a missus.'

'No, a servant,' Miles replies.

'You'll find it terrible . . . consequences of the drought and all are trying to cut down expenses. It makes dozens after every place.'

The woman says she is deaf, from typhoid. Because she can no longer answer the door, she has begun working as a laundress and cook instead. Now, having lost the strength to carry heavy pots and wet washing, she will do whatever menial task is offered to her.

Miles makes mental notes for her diary as she listens. Experience is to be milked daily, like a cow at her family's dairy farm, or what is now left of it after the drought.

The clattering carts and shouts drift in from the street. Miles feels nauseous from her constant nerves, rather than from the brew of tea she was served earlier in a tearoom that had advertised for a waitress.

To quell her stomach as much as to occupy the time, she bends into the solace of her diary again, and describes the agency staff ignoring her and the other girls lined up on the benches.

A very superior young lady sitting before a desk . . .

Through the back window . . . a hard-faced old dame, lumpily strutting around in a gorgeous blue gown of satin brocade . . .

She sits and sits. As the hours pass, she feels the weight of the boots on her feet. The pressure of her hair pinned tight under the cap, and what to do next.

She writes: *I changed the only individual over whom I have any control.*

PART ONE
Miles

1

The late winter of 1901. A burning frost, instead of rain. Her mother had named their property Stillwater for the ponds Miles once swam in among turtles and leeches, long shrivelled into shallow holes. The surviving cows stumbled beside bleached bones by the rim of the fading waterline. Crumbled wattle flowers blew across the farm like yellow confetti, the only colour beyond a relentless brown.

This deep into the drought, the two things Miles knew with certainty would arrive in the wasteland their farm had become were the flies and the mail, if the mailman was not too drunk to deliver it. She saw the mail as a channel of possibility, a 'sweepstake' that might throw up a prize.

She reached the kerosene tin nailed to the fence that served as their mailbox and pulled out an untied parcel marked with English stamps. The prize was so great, she was not irritated that the mailman had looked already to see what she had won.

Clutching the parcel close, she hurried back to the farmhouse and shut the door against what now seemed like a different world to the one in which she had walked to the fence.

She stared at the six copies of the book, titled *My Brilliant Career.* They looked as fresh as rain.

Nearly two years had passed since she had sent her novel to a poet she admired. He had also written short stories about an isolated drover's wife, about scrubby plains, and about drought as the 'red marauder'. She had felt a connection to him.

'I have lived such a secluded life in the bush that I am unacquainted with any literary people of note and too hard-up to incur the expense of travelling to Sydney to interview a publisher . . .' she had written. 'As for posting a story to them with a hope of it being read, unless one has swell influence, one might as well try to sell an elderly cow for a young racehorse. Perhaps it is a foolish notion as you will neither have time or inclination . . .'

She had dated the letter 19 November 1899, and signed her letter as 'Miles Franklin'.

The new century had turned by the time the poet wrote back that he had 'more than skimmed' her manuscript. He was intrigued.

'Will you write and tell me who and what you really are? Man or woman?'

The poet was generous rather than jealous and, after local publishers dithered, he took Miles' manuscript with him when he left for England with his wife and child. He gave it to his agent in London, and if adhering to some mythical literary law, the poet gifted his success to Miles.

In October 1900, Miles replied to the poet, blossoming with gratitude:

> Words of thanks are tame & flat in return for the trouble you take with me but I wish you could understand how I feel yr goodness . . .

> From the art world of London Australia must seem very crude & oh! so far away. The wattles are just done & the haze of the summer is beginning to once more veil the hills at sunset . . . I enclose a few gum leaves & sprig of wattle . . .

When the poet's agent sent her an offer of publication in January 1901, she did not send flowers. Instead, to their surprise, Miles had sent a sprig of instructions: that the title should remain with a question mark, as *My Brilliant (?) Career.* And: 'Please on no acct allow "Miss" to prefix my name on the title page as I do not wish it to be known that I'm a young girl.'

Now, after months of waiting and wondering, six books had materialised. Excitement cracked through her, like the whip the young woman rider on the cover was swinging as she mustered sheep.

Miles did like the cover, with *MY BRILLIANT CAREER* in capital letters. She felt the shock of paper in her hands. The sight of fresh black type, rendering words she had written in ink.

There was a mistake. The question mark, which she had specifically insisted should remain, was missing. She would question that, and any changes that had been made to her words for sense and sensibilities.

She peeped into the pages and paused at the preface, written by the poet:

> A few months before I left Australia, I got a letter from the bush signed 'Miles Franklin', saying the writer had written a novel, but knew nothing of editors and publishers, and asking me to read and advise. Something about the letter, which was written in a strong, original hand attracted me, so I sent for the MS, and one dull afternoon I started to read it. I hadn't

> read three pages when I saw what you will no doubt see at once—that the story had been written by a girl . . .
>
> I wrote to Miles Franklin and she confessed she was a girl . . . She is just a little bush girl, barely twenty-one yet . . . She has lived her book . . .
>
> HENRY LAWSON

Girl. It grated every time she read it. Her excitement frayed in frustration. Girl or not, she would keep Miles as her name. Miles meant miles away. Miles away from Stillwater, and at Stillwater she was still Stella. Her mother was too tired to call her all her given names—Stella Maria Sarah Miles Franklin—as mothers did when they were frustrated with their dreamy children hiding from their chores, lingering on the piano, escaping on horseback, talking back or refusing to go to church for prayers.

'You run about like a gypsy,' her grandmother scolded her. 'You have a froward heart.'

Miles' heart was wilfully contrary, obstinate, habitually disposed to opposition and not easily managed.

'You are idle like a boy,' Granny declared. A froward, gypsy boy. The scolding only filled her head with a caravan of dreams.

Her younger sister, Linda, now lived with Granny, because her heart was less froward. It was for Linda's health, Miles' mother explained, as she was delicate, but Linda had replaced Miles as favourite, while Miles remained at Stillwater helping her mother, pulling up cows stricken with drought, and helping with her younger siblings Tal, Norman and Laurel. She longed to stay another season at Granny's Talbingo Station, deep in the mountain country, where the eucalypts were dusted with snow and snakes lay beside creeks that still flowed. All she could do now from dusty, dull Stillwater was write about her Eden in her novel, for then it was hers alone again.

There was still a Granny in the novel, who ran her station like it was a grand abbey, and a kind aunt, like her Aunt Helena who lived at Talbingo. There was also a local grazier, whom she named Harold Beecham, who was 'big and sunburnt', had a 'chestnut moustache', and was 'six foot three and a half in his socks'. When Harold met Sybylla, her heroine, Sybylla was wearing a simple dress, perched on a ladder picking lemons from a tree. Harold's hands were so big, and she so tiny, that his hands encircled her waist. He admired her as a 'mighty well-shaped filly'. She wanted to flee. Gallop away.

Instead, Sybylla pretended to be one of the station's servants, for a game was the only way to play with men.

Spring was melting the snow away when Linda wrote from Granny's that she'd received the '*lovely, lovely* present' Miles had sent, and that it had caused a rush of 'great excitement in the camp':

> It wasn't altogether a surprise to me, as you said you were sending me something I could never be able to send you & of course I guessed then . . . I wish I was only clever enough to do it . . . Did you mean when you told me to keep it to myself, not to let anyone in the house see it, for if you did it was useless . . . First thing Grannie wanted to see it to see if the price was on it. She nearly has read it all & seems to like it. Nearly killed herself laughing at parts of it I can't get her nose out of it. Poor me I can't get a show at it at all . . .

Linda added that their cousin, 'the Lordly Phillip', was visiting the station, and eyeing the cover of the book. 'I can hear his melodious voice while I write. He is all anxiety to read it. I wonder if he will recognise himself *partly* in it,' she giggled, as if the two sisters were still sharing a bedroom. 'When I read it right through I will tell you who the characters I think are like. Who they remind me of . . .' Their favourite uncle Theo was also visiting, and had vowed to buy it because Granny wouldn't let him read it for free.

Linda's letter was the start of a deluge. Each postal run, the Franklin mail-tin was stuffed from rusted end to end. There were so many that the mailman could not keep up with reading them all. Ignoring the heat now piercing the paddocks, the birds sheltering in the tops of the eucalypts to catch any coolness, and the thunder that warned of another dry storm in the distance that could set alight what little was left, Miles sweated down the road and returned with her own kindling of mail.

She was surprised by how many more sisters she had gained. They were young women in the city, in country towns, or who lived on stations across the country, some of whom were destined to be drovers' wives. She'd already told them in her book: 'To weary hearts throbbing slowly in hopeless breasts the sweetest thing is rest. And my heart is weary . . . I see it and know it, but I cannot help you.'

And yet still they wrote.

The letters were addressed in guesses as to her real identity: 'Miss Sybylla Melvyn', 'Miss Miles Franklin', 'the authoress' and 'Miss Franklin'.

A correspondent named 'Stella of St Kilda' told 'Miss Franklin': 'How I have longed to do something glorious . . . I am 23 . . . I am an Australian girl like yourself & I have had the same longings & I think exactly the same things as you do . . . how I have revolted against being a girl and tried so hard to earn my own living'. St Kilda Stella was unaware that she shared her first name with the authoress, but still felt they were one.

Beyond her surprise that anyone wrote to her at all, Miles discovered that not all her new sisters were daughters of toil. They crossed class barriers, from threadbare cotton to silks, from factory floors and servant kitchens to English drawing rooms. One long letter arrived on embossed white parchment paper from London, addressed to 'Dear Sybylla Melvyn' from Martha Garnett, the wife of Richard Garnett, a writer, translator and lawyer. She congratulates Miles on writing a book that 'sets all the English world talking':

> I feel it is a very daring thing to write to an author whom I have never seen, yet I have been so moved I cannot refrain from trying . . . So many times I have said to myself just such things as you, & have vowed that I would make a name for myself.
>
> I am afraid you will lose interest in me, and put me down at once as an old frump when you hear I am thirty-two, married and have three children. But I have not forgotten what it is to be eighteen & twenty, and when I read you, I was just your age again.
>
> . . . I will sink the garnered wisdom of my thirty-two years and be one & twenty again with you, and tell you how I love & admire you, laugh & cry with you at the thought of all your gifts in the bush, slaving away . . . Dear you are as clever as they make them . . .
>
> I felt I was too young to write, & was going to write and practice more before I tried seriously to publish . . . Then an opportunity came for me to go to Wenham (you know, the ladies' college at Cambridge) & I took classics for a year, then my Harold Beecham arrived & I married him, since when, I have had no time to think of literature or myself when I am engaged in living happily ever after . . .

The letter was kept carefully in Miles' folder, along with the others who told Miles their stories. This one had a message: 'Happily ever after' wasn't a fairy-tale ending.

It was a warning.

Leaning against the pigsty fence, Miles talks to her father.

'It is absurd that girls all over the continent are writing to me and telling me I have expressed their innermost lives and emotions.'

He is tall, lean and thoughtful above his Ned Kelly beard. Like his daughter, he does not believe in prayers for rain.

Nor does he believe in regret: 'You mustn't spoil what you have done.'

2

Emboldened by her admirers, by her book's existence, by her father's advice, Miles sent a copy to the editor of a national magazine, *The Bulletin*, in the hope of a review, adding in her note that the title should be: '*My Brilliant (?) Career*, also any passages not orthodox and tame have been toned to a correct girly-girlishness. I am indebted, but without gratitude, for this.'

She signed the letter 'Miles Franklin' and, in a whimsical mood, added: 'residence: The Land o' lots o' time'.

The Bulletin's critic was already aware of her book and in his office, punctuated by ferry horns from the nearby quay, he was writing his review of *My Brilliant Career*. He was annoyed that the local publishers had dithered over it. In his view, new talent should be nurtured.

The preface to *My Brilliant Career* explained that it was about the harshness and heart of living on the land. True. Yet it was more than that. That missed the real story, especially the point that she was 'just' a girl. The critic realised that Miles and her heroine, Sybylla Melvyn, were 'New Women'. Perhaps that's why the local publishers had hesitated, and the Edinburgh publisher had inserted a 'girly-girlishness'.

He understood, with a critic's acute sense of the Zeitgeist, that the New Woman was about more than the right to vote, ride bicycles and wear daring 'divided skirts'. It was a lift of consciousness; a demand to be seen and heard in public life. It was a resistance to the world that corseted their ambitions as well as their waists. Young women at the sunrise of their lives saw the coming sunset of marriage that would dominate their days, and this book was their demand for a brilliant career of their own.

The critic titled his review of the debut 'A Bookful of Sunlight'. 'All over this country brooding on squatters' verandahs or mooning in selector's huts, there are scattered here-and-there hundreds of lively, dreamy Australian girls whose queer, uncomprehended ambitions are the despair of the household. They yearn, they aspire, for what they know not; but it is essentially yearning for a fuller, stronger life.'

In London, where sunlight was watery and weak, like the colonial painters' artworks, reviews of *My Brilliant Career* appeared. Miles was described as 'of the bush', like a new species discovered in the colonies. She was unknown. Vivid. Entrancing. 'Slipshod'. 'Egotistical but written with passion and power.'

Miles was the 'Brontë' of the bush, and the 'Marie Bashkirtseff' of the bush. A decade before *My Brilliant Career, The Journal of Marie Bashkirtseff* had been published, written by a Russian-Parisian teenager who wrote in solitude in front of the mirror and declared: 'It's perhaps silly to praise myself so much; but authors always describe their heroine, and I am my own heroine.'

Over a hundred notebooks had been filled, as fast and as full as the fluid in Marie's lungs from the tuberculosis that killed her, aged 25. After her diaries, in two volumes, were posthumously published three years later by her mother and an editor, there were pilgrimages by young women to Marie's grave in the Passy Cemetery in Paris. Her mother conducted tours of her daughter's bedroom and painting studio. Young men also were intrigued, and joined the phenomenon dubbed 'the Bashkirtseff cult'. And now the cult of Miles Franklin was beginning.

She was 'of the bush'. Her own heroine.

The Bulletin critic Alfred George Stephens, who was known as 'A.G.', sent her a private personal note, asking for a photo. He dismissed comparisons to Marie Bashkirtseff.

'Marie B was a self-conscious little prig.'

Instead, he likened Miles' face, and her story to the novelist Olive Schreiner and her semi-autobiographical *The Story of an African Farm*. Miles found a copy on a visit to family friends. It had been mistaken for a guide to farming and tossed aside. She seized it. Olive was living on another continent, but she seemed like a kindred literary spirit.

Olive had another warning about happily ever afters: 'A man's love is a fire of olive-wood. It leaps higher every moment; it roars, it blazes, it shoots out red flames; it threatens to wrap you round and devour you . . . The next day, when you go to warm your hands a little, you find a few ashes.'

Miles liked playing with fire. She had no intention of returning to the ashes.

~

At Stillwater, Miles' younger brothers—fifteen-year-old Norman, and Tal, only twelve—took little notice of the fuss and kept milking what little the last cows could give. The sunsets simmered over the paddocks as their mother prepared lamb and rabbit, which at the dinner table of hungry hands soon became carcasses, like the animals of the drought.

There had been more hands at the table until last year, when fair-haired Mervyn, Miles' favourite brother, had been with them too. Then he'd gone to work at Talbingo, until typhoid came for him and he'd died in the late summer, aged sixteen. Miles missed their closeness, the way they had recited ballads together.

Their mother hid her sadness under the same stoicism with which she had borne the short-lived life of her baby girl, Una, five years ago. Ashes, dust, bones. It was the way of the bush. Now the living were here, asking for a second helping—a husband, the boys, little Laurel, and a grown daughter.

Book or not, their mother snapped at Miles to help, for she was the eldest girl and her name was Stella, as much as she wanted to be known as Miles.

'Stella!' her mother would say, frayed by life on the land. With the same air of rebellion of her heroine, Sybylla, Miles jumped from the table and snatched the dirty plates from her brothers and father.

At Talbingo, Granny took the book with a pinch of saltbush. Linda was feeling scalded by what she'd managed to read of it, with the rest of the family around Talbingo pouncing on the copy.

'You are pretty hot on me in places not to say anything of poor father,' she complained in her letter to Miles. She was irritated by the heat and warned that the creek of the Snowy River had almost stopped running.

'The Lordly Phillip' was hinting he was Harold and was still trying to get a copy. But there were only limited supplies from London.

Miles did the maths and understood that no books meant no sales in Australia, where it was likely to sell the most copies. She wrote to her agent, fretting.

Another of Miles' uncles, George Franklin, had managed to find a copy, or had heard enough about its contents. He wrote in protest to Miles, and it was a jolt of criticism among her mail. He charged that her book was 'all malicious lies' and had disrespected the family, especially her parents; he'd also heard that she was writing another and warned her to stop it at once.

Miles knew why. Before writing the novel, Miles had been sent for a miserable six months to be a governess to his children, her cousins, who in the novel had inspired the feral 'M'Swat' children who Sybylla is sent to teach. Defiant, Miles snapped back at her uncle: 'Your letter to hand. Had anyone else written it I would have replied, "if the cap fits, you may wear it" but as it is you and I am mindful of all your goodness I am going to reply. I wrote a story of Australian life and if anyone thinks they see themselves in it I cannot help it as I did not mean any of the characters as real.'

She tried to reply to all her new sisters, and thanked A.G., the critic, for his 'A Bookful of Sunlight' review, but added her now customary correction: 'There is one dreadful mistake—*My Brilliant Career* is not my own life.'

She tried to correct the rumours. The community around Stillwater, in the specks called Bangalore, Thornford and Currawang, were gossiping and guessing identities, for they didn't believe it was a novel either. It was shocking. Uppity. How dare she write a book about them all? Still, she was famous, which made the district known for being more than a small inland city with a railway station, a gaol and a lack of rain. And who was Harold? The Lordly Phillip, and the graziers around Talbingo and Stillwater, checked their moustaches in the looking glass for tints of chestnut, and stretched to reach closer to six foot three in their socks.

Miles' next book, which her uncle had heard rumours about, followed another girl, whom Miles calls Ignez, a name Spanish for Agnes that everyone pronounced like 'it's spelt, and that's worse like a lizard of some sort'.

The Boer War was raging in South Africa over territory and gold. Colonial boys were cannon fodder; to Ignez's despair, they only saw the war as a shot at adventure.

Ignez wanted to be a singer. Her voice did not match her ambition, so she turned to writing a novel. And when a parcel of her books arrived, she stared at it in shock, and realised that, when she'd been writing the book, she had been 'shouting at the top of her lungs into an unhabituated silence'.

Now Miles knew her silence 'had all the time been full of listeners'.

3

The start of the Saturday afternoon hare runs was signalled by the ring of a bullock bell. Miles was at the front of the herd of hunters, who galloped on horseback, aiming shots at fleeing shapes in the scrub.

The grazier's son, Charles Graham, was chasing Miles as much as the rabbits, for which the Rabbit Board paid per skin. He admired her from his family property, which bordered the lake that mysteriously disappeared and reappeared independently of drought or flood.

In Currawang, Charles and Miles played tennis on grass that had hardened to clay. On the court, Charles admired her 'strokes' as Miles, in a white tennis dress down to her ankles and trying not to trip, whacked the ball using the same force with which she approached life.

Now the book's publication added another stroke to her game. He felt a need to up his.

In between tennis matches, he wrote in a longing hand to 'Miss Miles', 'I think I am jealous of your book.'

Who was the hero of her book, Harold Beecham, based on? Was it really the cousin, the Lordly Phillip, who visited

Sybylla Melvyn at the property that was obviously based on her grandmother's station in Talbingo?

There was no love interest in the scenes set in Possum Gully, which everyone knew was Stillwater and its surrounds. There was only a side of Miles that she hid under her charm, a hatred of her weary life in the backward bush unless she was on a horse.

Charles was annoyed. Since the book, every bachelor in the district had been lending Miles his favourite filly and risking his stallion to see her sitting on top. The neighbouring Baxter boys had allowed her to be photographed in equestrian dress on their best horse, and she'd raised her chin to look more regal for the photographer.

To stay in the frame, Charles wrote to Miles:

I would have seen you at the tennis court on Saturday, you ought to come.

I want you to have a ride on my grey horse . . .

. . . it seems to me you have a bad opinion. . . when I try to be kind to you it only gives offence . . .

Charles has also begun writing to Miles' sister Linda, still in Talbingo with Granny. He knew she would be going home for Christmas and, as the holiday approached, he asked Miles to 'try and do something for me':

I want you to try and keep Linda up here until after Christmas, I want to see a little more of her.

Linda teased Miles: 'Uncle Theo calls us the two Mrs Grahams.'

Miles is sure that there will be only one Mrs Graham.

4

The year 1902 began with a bang. In the early hours of one January morning, dark paddocks of dust lifted into thick clouds that grew as they gathered speed, propelled by a hurricane wind from the west. The clouds blew through the windows of Stillwater and the surrounding farms, left open in the hope of some cooler night air.

It was so hot a nine-year-old boy died a few days after playing outside for hours without his hat. His death was reported as a fatal case of sunstroke that sparked 'inflammation of the brain'. The child, named Bertie Baxter, was buried in the Old Goulburn Cemetery, a small grave befitting a short life.

Further north, on the coast, it was cooler in Sydney after another sudden summer squall. The waters of the harbour washed against sandy coves and rocks that climbed into gardens of houses graced with wide verandahs, french doors and drawing rooms, hidden behind stone walls and wrought-iron gates on the harbour edge.

At Lynton, her home perched at the top of a road that led down to the water, fanned by the coastal breeze, Rose Scott dressed in her bedroom, which was walled with books and ornamental fans. Her lady's maid buttoned Rose's blouse up her back, adjusted the lace collar with a Wedgwood brooch, and helped her secure her cashmere stockings under her skirt, with garters rimmed so tight they might bruise.

Dressed for the day, Rose could now address her work. She walked into her study, a room stacked with more clothbound books, more fans, and vases spilling over with tea roses and camellias from the garden. She settled at her dark-wood desk.

There were so many letters to read and reply to. A request for a donation from the Animals' Protection Society of New South Wales whose motto was 'We speak for those who cannot speak for themselves' since she was recognised as 'one of our most earnest reformers IN [sic] the interests of Mankind' . . . When the occasion presents itself, 'kindly assist the Society in its efforts for reform, as defenders of defenceless, dumb animals'. Rose perused the fines the Society had given out, including 10 fines for starving a horse, 10 for working horses with wounds, and five fines for 'brutally injuring a travelling sheep'.

Rose read a letter from a marvellous fellow suffragist and journalist in Melbourne, Alice Henry, saying she would be in Sydney, 'but please I want it to be as quiet as possible'.

Rose would try to be quiet, but quietness did not rest well with her. She was 54 and unmarried—she wanted 'men's respect, not their love', as she would wittily deflect to inquirers with the charm that softened her status among those who were suspicious of single women of a certain age.

She was often tired of writing letters, and sometimes she wondered if all she'd done in her life could be measured in stamped envelopes. She received such a volume of mail that the postmaster insisted she install a bigger letterbox. She was still trying to raise the age of consent, and money for the Women's College at the University of Sydney. There needed to be police matrons for prisons and watchhouses. She was on the National Council of Women and advised the Factory Club and the Widows' and Orphans' Fund. She advocated for shopgirls and women who had fled from the frying pan of domestic service to the fire of the factories. And then there was women's right to vote. They were so close to national suffrage. It would be soon now, and worth the sacrifices she had made to dedicate herself to equal rights.

Charities were not on her priority list because she detested the word. Charity should mean kindness, but so often it didn't. Rose preferred to use a word she believed in: justice. A single, strong word. If there was justice, there would be no need for charity.

First, however, she must write a letter to a Miss Miles Franklin, who had written *My Brilliant Career.* Rose had come close to the author's home in Stillwater when she'd addressed the town hall in Goulburn, the nearest city to the Franklin farm. The hall had been crowded with women dressed in long skirts and buttoned-up blouses, laced with resolve, and men who wanted to show their support or protest at such an affront as women voting.

Rose scrawled a gale of thrilling praise across the paper to Miles: 'I have just read your book . . . your book is *wonderful*, you have the gift of placing characters as well as scenes. I lived your book with you . . . I cannot disassociate yourself from the heroine . . . my dear fellow woman.'

After writing the letter, Rose added to her list for shopping and errands: 'milk, rosemary, postmaster'. There was her weekly Friday night salon to prepare for, and a regular garden party that hosted more influential people, where the occasional shop or factory girl was invited to talk, and represent the young women who worked. Rose had more time now that her mother had died but, in that sentimental way of missing what most irritates, she missed her mother singing 'God Save the Queen' from her bedroom to drown out all the guests' talk of radical reforms.

Writing the letter to Miles Franklin had meant putting off more letters and more lectures that were constantly on the to-do lists in her mind.

No matter. This 'fellow woman' deserved her time.

5

In the city, the Man from Snowy River's polished bespoke boots tap on the foyer stairs of the Australian Club. He glances with pleasure at the skull of a water buffalo with curving horns that he'd shot in the Northern Territory mounted on the wall.

He browses the Suggestions and Complaints Book. Among the complaints from his fellow members are: waiting for more than ten minutes for service, a 'repulsive' cockroach infestation, bad oysters, the treatment of French burgundy wine and the lingering smell of cooking. He himself has complained that the Club's copy of *The Times* is always late, and the cigars are inferior.

As always, he is immaculately dressed in a pressed striped suit. He looks more like the lawyer he trained to be than the celebrity writer he has become since the publication of *The Man from Snowy River and Other Verses*. His rhymes are read, recited and repeated everywhere. He is the man of the hour after returning from being a war correspondent in South Africa. He is in demand on the speaking circuit and appears before crowded houses, rapidly reciting stories about horses, for they are animals of war as well as peace. He talks of soothing their necks with calming strokes and whispering into their manes when they reared in a rolling swell around the 'Cape of Storms', or when they trembled, wobbled and kicked at troopers as they came down the gangplank after five weeks at sea. In action, he has seen 'trained horses like machinery'; ponies charging with men holding guns instead of polo sticks in the death match of war; and, under grey skies, rows of horses resting with drooping heads tied to picket pegs. He has seen the bodies of men lying beside still horses on battlefields. 'Don't look at them too closely,' he writes, 'they are dead men.'

His lectures have made him some handsome hay to pay for his expensive Club membership, suits, shoes and the horse he stables near the park.

Where is *The Times?*

Settling in the main dining room, he sits forward, spread on the cedar chair like he is astride a saddle, and takes a sheaf of paper monogrammed with the Club's emblem of a belted blue-ribbon loop. It is rare for him to reply to other writers he does not know; however, this author is different. He's already heard about her in conversations about her book, *My Brilliant Career*, although he has yet to read it.

A mutual friend has written to him to say that the author, Miles Franklin, who also lives in southern New South Wales, the same region as his childhood property, Illalong, asked whether he would help her with legal advice about her publishing contract. Now a letter from 'Miss Franklin' herself has come to him at the Club.

He is intrigued. He will arrange to meet her for lunch if she can be in Sydney, somewhere suitable and respectable, as he could not meet her here at his men-only Club. A woman in this sanctum of suits and cigars would fill the Suggestions and Complaints Book with outrage, even one with the name of 'Miles' who has written a book.

In the meantime, he will write to her.

He adjusts his saddle position on the chair and, in a leaning hand at the pace of a gallop, he invites her to write to him again. Then he inks his signature: *A.B. Paterson.*

6

Rose's letter to Miles blew into Stillwater. In the top corner of the first page was a paragraph written at a slant, so Miles had to crane her neck or turn the paper sideways. Rose had added the invitation: 'I should like if you will pay for a ticket + stay with me.'

Rose's letter was followed by another one, which was monogrammed with the blue loop of the Australian Club. Recognising the signature, Miles felt as tightly strung as a new banjo.

'Mother!' she called with the same force that she heard 'Stella' when she was hiding from her chores. The house was quieter; Laurel was at school at the closest village, Thornford, poring over her careful handwriting, with Tal shifting restlessly in his seat in the same tiny classroom. Tal dreamt of a life at sea or at least outside like his older brother who was on the farm somewhere. Leave the writing to his oldest sister.

In the kitchen her mother wiped her hands carefully on a cloth and nodded as Miles showed her the letters. She saw the problem.

Miles' clothes were of the bush. Her mother was drained like Stillwater's ponds from debt and the drought, and from worries that Miles never wanted. She turned to her only 'elegancy', *Weigel's Journal of Fashion*, a magazine of patterns that included a romance serial, which allowed her to retain a little of the haggard elegance that remained from her upbringing with Granny and a governess.

How serene Miles' mother looked. When she sewed her daughter's two new dresses, she escaped into a world of fabric, fine needles, buttons and thread. While her mother bent over the fabric, Miles read the serialisation. She was much better at stitching words together than dressmaking.

~

In early, cooler April, when fires were lit in the hearths rather than sparked by lightning in the scrub, Miles' father tied their tired horse to the cart and took his daughter to catch the Mail Express from Goulburn. Outside the railway station, she saw men who, like the white cockatoos they were derisively named for, pecked and clawed a living from the ground they had selected to farm. They lingered at the hotel, then afterwards slouched down the street and went into the church to pray for rain. The district's farms were built on the meeting place of thirteen First Nations people's lands. Miles only knew what had been taken by the settlers; a flock of white, colonising, poor cockatoos.

Birds flew in the sky as the train rattled north then east to the coast. She saw bursts of forest and flowers beside the tracks and glimpses of the sea. It was a thrill to see green again, to feel the sway of the carriage, and the loud shock of a train hurtling past in the opposite direction on the parallel track. To see the sights and hear the sounds of a different life.

Alighting at the terminus, with a small carpetbag holding her new dresses her mother had sewed, she negotiated her path through the traffic of trams, pedestrians and horse-drawn carts to a nearby city street, where her mother had arranged through friends for her to board for a week. From this safe place, she could meet the list of luminaries who had written to her at Stillwater and see if they were going to have more than a fleeting interest in her brilliant career.

7

In the city, the artist is in his studio with the door barred against intrusion, drawing pen studies he is obsessing to perfect.

He is lithe, little and restless. His fringe is brushed over to cover his forehead, as he finds the baldness, given that he is only 23, displeasing in the mirror. The shell of a boiled egg, his habitual breakfast, is on a plate, forgotten, beside a full cup of tea. He will not eat for the rest of the day. In the future, he will draw food in the shape of a magic pudding; for now, he practises the curve of a woman's breast, the flesh of a leg, the shape of an eye. Forms on paper and canvas.

He must remember not to leave scraps around in his studio; there are rats about. The streets still steam with bursts of fumigation from the efforts to sanitise against the plague, but the little bastards escape into building cracks and pipes.

He'd found one crawling out of a drawer, denuded of fur and rank with disease. He'd smashed its head, then wrapped it in newspaper, like rat and chips, and disposed of it in the nearest street bin. He is now wary of opening drawers.

His male model, Nat, is due to give him a boxing lesson, so he can be like Starlight, the star middleweight boxer. He has planned a ride in the city's Centennial Park with the writer of *The Man from Snowy River*, A.B. Paterson, whose flat is in the same street as his studio. Then there is a book to read by this girl everyone is talking about with the curious name of Miles. First, though, to finish these illustrations for a review by the critic at the national periodical, *The Bulletin*, which pays his studio rent.

Here, he is separate from his home across the harbour, in which his wife and two-year-old son, Jack, live. His studio life—his drawings, his paintings, the writers, the artists and the models—are a bridge apart from her, if one will ever get built. He feels regretful but not ashamed; he wonders why his wife does not murder him out of frustration.

He looks at his new favourite model, draped on a chair with her breast half-covered by a gown; around her neck hangs a key to the locked diary he's given her as a present. He has another key.

On paper and in his mind, in his sleep, she drips in ink.

The letter from the Man from Snowy River had instructed Miles he would be easy to find; she should look for a 'sad looking person with a very hard face'. She arrives on Wednesday at 1 p.m. at the A.B.C. tearoom in the city centre, searching for sadness. The smell of warm bread and sugar lingers from the morning's loaves and cakes being sold in the Aerated Bread Company's bakery next door.

Petite and curvy, shaded by her large hat festooned with petals, Miles looks like a flower herself. Men glance at her, wanting to pluck.

He waits, his suit as sharp as his cheekbones and chin. Seeing her, he suddenly doesn't look sad at all.

At their table, sitting on a gold-edged chair and alert with nervousness, Miles feels fancy. She notices the tearoom's rich red-patterned carpets that spread across the floor like jam on fresh bread, and the fountain spouting water like there is no drought.

He picks at his lunch, to minimise his chronic reflux. He has mastered hiding his discomfort. Talking rapid fire, as he does when he is nervous, he recites stories of the war, which he called the 'embodiment of destructiveness'. She is pleased, because too many glorify war. She is guarded, shy, and gives only hints.

He asks questions about her book. About her childhood near where her grandmother lives, riding bareback across ridges to see the range, until they moved to stagnant Stillwater.

Miles still only gives wisps of information. He realises he wants to know more, at least about her horsemanship. Or is that horsewomanship? She could ride for as long as her name. She could have ridden his horse, after which he chose his pen name, Banjo.

To business, though. She has asked for his advice about her contractual obligations to her publisher. Like the colt, he thinks that she is 'free as air'; she can seek other publishers, he thinks, because she was under 21 when she signed the agreement with her English publisher. But he will need to know the facts.

He leans closer.

8

In a flowered hat, shading her frilled white-cotton dress, with a bow in her ponytail that reaches down to the sash around her waist, Miles caught a tram to the harbour end of the city. Finding the laneway, she climbed the stairs to the office of *The Bulletin* critic A.G. Stephens.

He was 'charmed' to finally meet her. He told her that she made him 'feel young again'. She had heard that he incited fear in artists and writers, but to her he seemed like a second father.

The critic was curious about rumours he'd heard about The Man from Snowy River and Miles meeting. With a gully of curiosity in his voice he asked, 'Was it true he had you in hand?'

Miles was demure.

The critic tried again. 'Is there anyone you would like to meet?'

'Can I meet Norman Lindsay?' Lindsay was young, like her. She would have chosen the talent to draw like Lindsay if a fairy had given her a gift. In her mind, she added: *His drawings are more shocking than my book.*

She caught a flash of Stephens' infamous scowl. Her eyes followed his glare.

The artist Norman Lindsay had appeared with a portfolio of his weekly illustrations for the critic to review. Such impeccable, infuriating timing. The artist dreaded these meetings with Stephens. To the artist, 'A' was for arrogant, abrasive, autocratic. And 'G' was for the critic's ghastly red-pen suggestions that sliced across his artwork. A.G. Stephens was only at ease with words that hid his nervous ego.

Lindsay had written about the critic to his brother, Lionel, who was back in Melbourne and who Norman missed: 'Stephens—poof—crap—bum—I sheet on heem [*sic*]. Stephen's attitude to art—to everything—is the alterer. A poem, a picture—you give to him, it has to be altered; that's the beginning and the end of Stephens. He is the man with the big head—the cow in the front garden. I am the honest farmer who runs out with the pitchfork, but bless you, he only turns and tramples on the cabbages.'

Today, though, as he looked up to the top of the stairs, Lindsay saw, standing beside the critic that he wanted to 'sheet' on, a vision draped in a summery, ankle-length frock and a flowered hat. He assessed her 'pert nose', and hair that cascaded to a 'pert rump', as he was later to describe them in a memoir. It was as if her bottom was a saucy, literary steak. He mentally drew her as the critic glowered beside her at Lindsay's unexpected entrance.

He hurried up, and looked to the critic, daring him to make an introduction.

Politeness was victorious and the critic, bristling under his beard, snapped names.

Lindsay was up in the air. She was, he thought 'another Marie', the local version of the Russian in Paris teen sensation. He and the other artists and writers had all fallen for Miles, and her heroine, Sybylla, and now here she is. He wanted to invite her to dinner at Sydney's fashionable restaurant, The Paris House. She was shy, but he could sense her excitement. She stepped forward.

'I would . . .' the artist began. The critic glowered.

'I must be going,' Miles said, tensing.

'I will go with you,' the artist offered. He hoped they could make an exit together that would be as unwelcome to Stephens as Lindsay's arrival had been.

'You come here,' the critic ordered Lindsay.

The artist wanted to duck and parry, displaying the skills that Nat had developed in him during their weekly boxing lessons. A hat of flowers fled down the stairs.

Lindsay peered over the banister as the flowers floated away. He was annoyed, and wondered if he would ever see her again except in print. Bloody Stephens. Poof. Crap. Bum.

'Damn it, I was only going to see her to wherever she was going,' Lindsay protested.

'You leave her alone,' the bearded critic ordered. 'I will not have you interfering with her, or any other young girl.'

With a derisive jerk of his thrown-back head, the critic shut the door of his office.

Outside, Lindsay seethed. This was about the critic's own attraction to Miles, rather than a protection of her virtue, he was sure of it. A.G. was old enough to be her father. If Lindsay had known her birthday, he would have celebrated that they were only six months apart in age.

Despite the insistence in her book's preface that she was just a girl, it was obvious she did not need protecting. Miles was a raw drawing, a free spirit. Like him, an artist, she sought freedom in form and in life.

He stomped back to his studio, where his always-full cups of tea and his full-cupped model waited.

A well-worn Latin tag came into his mind: *Dis aliter visum.* The gods had other plans.

Years later, full of other plans, he and Miles would meet again and sigh about this day and what might have been. He would write, 'The best love affairs are those we never had'.

In Sydney's bohemian circle of poets, artists and writers, the Man from Snowy River rode a dignified, different route. His world was one of exclusive clubs, suits and wealthy landowning friends, rather than all-night revels in pubs, and poverty. He made an exception for Lindsay, the exceptional artist, who—like Miles, who kept trotting back into his mind—could ride as well as create. So, in a grand green park that evoked the heaths of London, the two men would regularly meet for a ride.

Today they entered the traffic of horses around the park's circle, nodding to those they knew. Always drawing, with or without a pen, the artist noticed how Paterson—he did not call him A.B. or Banjo—sat tall in the saddle, his dark hair barbered short under his riding hat. Paterson's dark, hooded eyes observed beyond what they saw. He was 'saturnine', Lindsay decided. Serious. Cold, but he could run rings around you.

Talking was difficult. Lindsay's new thoroughbred fought for its head, veering towards the fence and nearly unseating the artist. Always seduced by a beautiful build, he had recently bought this horse in a rush of impulse and vanity.

Paterson watched dispassionately from his saturnine mount: 'I'll buy that horse at your funeral, Lindsay.'

9

The week Miles arrived in Sydney, Rose Scott had other matters on her mind, which she was following closely as they unfolded in the federal parliament. With the site of the national capital still a sheep paddock, the parliament sat in Melbourne.

Rose read daily reports of the word 'women' being loudly discussed by politicians. Women thronged the viewing gallery, fluttering their fans and watching their futures unfold. A light April rain fell outside.

'I see no reason in the world,' the leader of the Senate, Senator Richard O'Connor, continued in his introduction to the day's debate on the Commonwealth Franchise Bill, 'why we should continue to impose laws which have to be obeyed by the women of the community without giving them some voice in the election of the members who make those laws . . . It seems to me that the question of reform in the direction of women's suffrage has already won its way in Australia.'

Another senator, his moustache and eyebrows in a permanently disapproving droop, interjected: 'Really!'

O'Connor was amused. 'I say again that everywhere in Australia this reform has won its way practically to the front.' A gallery of glares stared in his direction and nodded.

The debate resumed in the afternoon. The gallery returned too, shaking the rain from their umbrellas.

A senator from the Wild West rose on the parliament floor. He was a very forgettable third baronet, a minor aristocrat who had built his wealth as a banker on the dreams of goldrush miners in Western Australia; he wanted to create a separate 'goldfields' colony to quarantine the state's wealth. He had a young, pinched face, with an elderly cravat, top hat and cane.

The question of women's franchise was favoured, that was clear, he said. But he proposed that the franchise be withheld nationally from anyone who was not as white as he was.

The following day, Senator O'Connor stood up again to address the Senate. 'It would be a monstrous thing, an unheard piece of savagery on our part, to treat the Aboriginals, whose land we were occupying, in such a manner as to deprive them absolutely of any right to vote in their own country, simply on the ground of their colour.'

The parliament was stunned, and then debate erupted once more.

That Friday evening, the franchise bill dominated discussion at Lynton, where Rose reigned over her weekly salon. She bantered with the barristers in bow ties. Her favourite compliment was that she had a knack for saying 'the nastiest things of men in the nicest way', and tonight was no different.

She moved among the politicians, judges, artists, activists, poets, editors, novelists, musicians, journalists and critics.

Unlike Paterson, she liked to mix them all, like a bouquet of flowers from her garden. Different varieties created colour.

'Where do you dig us all up?' a lawyer once asked her. Tonight, she'd dug up someone new, who should be at the salon soon. Miles had promised Rose she would come before she returned home in coming days.

Miles' horse-drawn carriage halted outside a house half-hidden by shrubs and shaded by the silhouettes of fig trees. The darkness was perfumed with roses, as she followed the lamps on foot up the garden path.

In the drawing room, she glanced at the art, books and guests. She refused a glass of wine; drinking disturbed nerves and morals. Poets, with no such reserve and without evening dress, hovered near silver trays of champagne. But Miles could not see the Man from Snowy River.

'Dear girl!'

Holding her hand, a triumphant Rose turned Miles towards her guests so as to present her latest protégé. Miles noticed her embroidered shawl curled around her bodice, and her breasts looked like 'white puddings' dressed in cream.

10

The Man from Snowy River had decorated his city bachelor flat with reminders of Illalong, his family's property. A white sulphur-crested cockatoo perched on the mantelpiece and the rug was made of possum fur. Somewhere, a banjo played.

He'd read Miles' book now and admired its photographic detail of bush life. He'd also read some of the new short stories she'd sent him to review, but some of them were 'sheer drivel'.

Of course she would write like a schoolgirl at times; after all, she was barely 22. Yet her book showed what Miles was already capable of, and she was little more than half his age.

Paterson had survived war and celebrity, and a broken engagement after he co-wrote a song about a jolly camping swagman one flirtatious evening in Queensland with his fiancée's best friend. His fiancée had waltzed angrily away.

In his flat, he'd written his regimented output for the day, and he was tired. He picked up his pen again.

Dear Miss Franklin,

Your note & mine must have crossed. I am so weary of pen-pushing it is a relief to write to you. That is a poor compliment you will say but it is not a compliment that I would pay to everybody . . .

I am in my flat & doing 2000 words a day so you see I am hard at it. Very unambitious work it is, racing & humour of a sort. I wish you were here to run your eagle eye over the stuff and tell me whether you think it is drivel or not. Also you could come and play and sing to the piano which I haven't yet got. Is there any chance of you coming down again. My writing room is quite swell now. Good pictures.

. . . pay me a visit . . .

I hope you will have a run down before I leave for the islands.

It was not yet winter. In Stillwater it was snowing with letters to *Dear Miss Franklin* from Paterson. They wrote to each other so often that their mail overlapped. They were mail-crossed.

Miles always felt more daring with a pen in her hand. He was at a distance now. One hundred and twenty miles between his Sydney flat and Stillwater, and soon there would be hundreds more as he was intending to accompany an expedition of new settlers to the South Pacific for a series of articles for *The Sydney Morning Herald*.

She teased with her pen:

Dear Sir,

You lucky fellow to be going to the islands . . . I would dress up as a boy and be your valet. Are you a good boss? I fear your invitation is just out of my reach. Is that why it is so tempting?

In the evenings, Miles refills her empty fountain pen from the clay inkwell that is round and comforting in her hand. The summer storms have quietened. She is not afraid of thunder; she enjoys the drama of it.

She writes at a time of the day when her mother cannot interrupt her, when long days become hours of starry quiet and her restlessness is soothed by words. She writes letters and her next novel.

Her new heroine, Ignez, is a version of her once more, though she keeps telling herself and others it is another story. She writes her drafts in school exercise books and on scraps of paper, impatient for the story of the young singer from the scrub to reach its climax. She names it 'On the Outside Track'.

As she writes, Miles sees visions of the snake that has lived with her since she was a child of the bush, when she used to explore her grandmother's Talbingo property, and she glimpsed it stretched out among ferns by the creek. She had stared at its glossy blue-black skin, the pomegranate slash on its underbelly and its flickering forked tongue. Despite the clear and present danger, she had remained rooted in fascination rather than fear.

In her head, the snake shadowed her home, and has since stayed in her imagination. It slithers into her dreams and curls in her mind. She doesn't know when it will reveal itself, only that it is always there.

On the evening of his departure for the Pacific, having packed his lightweight suits and Panama hats and locked up his flat, Paterson paused at the Club, from where it was a short walk to the ship, the *Mambare*, docked in the harbour. He had time to write one more letter to Miss Franklin. He could wait until he returned in six weeks, but Miles was worth the hurry. He explained his request, sealed the letter, dropped it in the mail bundle to be sent and hurried down the hill to his waiting ship.

On board Captain Todd, a burly New Zealander, gave him a tour of the SS *Mambare* and told him the ship had a kink in its keel from scraping a coral reef so that, without steady steering to keep it on course, it wavered between north and south.

Paterson inspected the cargo hold, into which the animals for the expedition had been loaded, as if into a colonial ark. The group of chosen men was aboard and anxious, and so were the animals. The ewes and a single ram swayed in their pens. Pigeons, chickens, canaries and a cockatoo cowered in their coops and cages. A monkey called Kruger that didn't answer to its name clambered about in its cage. The ship's dog barked and cockroaches crawled into taps and gaps. Stacks of wooden boxes were packed with bananas, onions, potatoes and strawberries.

Whaleboats and dinghies were lashed to the ship's sides. In their cabins, the missionaries kneeled in prayer, and the men who had signed up to farm the new land prayed for profit. By midnight, the *Mambare*, weighed down with its cargo of hope, sailed beyond the Heads of Sydney Harbour.

Miles followed its trail across the South Pacific in newsprint. Paterson's articles to the *Herald* were sent back from resupply stops on Lord Howe and Norfolk islands, and then from Noumea, where they made port near a copper and nickel mine that split open the volcanic landscape with its stains of rust. His pieces appeared in sporadic order, at the mercy of the winds and the whims of the mail.

He reported that he was accompanying eighteen settlers, who 'all have little capital to lose', and who had left their wives and children at home with relatives, until they might one day join them on an island they had only seen as a blot on a map. Underneath their ambitions was the fact, rolling beneath them, like the waves under the *Mambare*, that the islands were not theirs to claim and many of the island's men had been blackbirded to cut snake-infested cane fields in Queensland.

Once the boat was at sea, the crossbreed sheep climbed out of their pens to wander about the decks, as if they were goats; a pig escaped the hold and then squealed in shock when it bit into a baited fishhook left lying around by a passenger, bored of fishing. Stepping around the sheep rolling on the deck and the squealing pig, Paterson observed the settlers restlessly looking out to sea. They trusted the Man from Snowy River's words rather than the words of marketing, which hailed them as the 'Pilgrim Fathers of the New Hebrides'.

They, and Paterson, knew who they really were. If they were pilgrims, it was for profit. They had won their places on board out of 300 applications with their own all-or-nothing investment. Paterson sized them up as adventurers driven by desperation rather than higher ambitions.

'There are farmers, prospectors, labourers, bushmen, and tradesmen among them,' he reported. 'Nearly every one of them on being asked why they left Australia, told the same tale. They have been driven out by failure of seasons . . . One man said, "Even if seasons are good, you can't make much, and if they are bad, you lose all you have." They want money now, not glory here-after.'

Back at Stillwater, Miles' family had no such capital to lose on the promise of paradise, and so they risked the ruin of one more season. Rain or not, Miles could still write her new book for glory, and hopefully money, if only her royalties weren't worse than a drought-afflicted tap.

She had received a curious letter from Paterson too. It had offered her a new source of income and had been written with a sense of urgency—he wrote at such a slant that every word seemed urgent—just before he boarded the ship to the South Pacific:

> I am leaving . . . tonight . . . My sister has instructions . . .
>
> Now there is another matter. I have written a racing & sporting yarn which I am telling her to send you . . .
>
> It is full of good stuff . . . It is too flat . . . it wants a crime or a rival . . . a villain. Do you feel like supplying these things. Read my chapters and see if you can make a historic bold villain . . . it might be a good story for both of us.
>
> Don't write back, I won't be back for six weeks.

When Paterson's sister, Jessie wrote to Miles to expect the manuscript, Miles archly replied: 'He desired my collaboration'. She did not add that she sensed that he desired more.

Jessie understood, because she knew her brother, and how he did not flow as smoothly as he wanted everyone to believe:

> Dear Miss Franklin . . .
>
> I quite agree with you about the suddenness of my brother's action in sending his manuscript . . . I only did what I was told . . . I can assure you it is sharper than a serpent's tooth to have an unbusinesslike brother.

Still, Jessie hoped that Miles could improve the text: 'I agree with you that there are weaknesses, and it seems to me that they are in the social & conversational parts, and wherever women are brought in, lovemaking & so on . . . if you could improve on those parts it would be a great thing . . . I think with your life-like style of writing, could do much to make wooden people real.'

Jessie was persuasive. A sister whispering in her ear. She was pleased Miles was considering the collaboration, and approved of the name Miles rather than Stella, 'being rather fond of masculine names', she will use the 'one by which the world knows you'.

Miles was flattered, but flummoxed. She was used to being her own heroine; heroes complicated the story. She wrote to Linda about her dilemma, as Linda liked heroes.

For once, she received from her sister a reply that did not talk about dresses, about Charlie, about the disappointing local show or that the creek was distressingly nearly dried up. She sounded sharper, like Granny.

'I don't know what to think of Paterson,' she wrote. 'One thing he must think a lot of your brains. After you have all the trouble, he will very likely take all the honour & glory on himself . . .'

She passed another aunt's advice, having discussed it with her at Talbingo. 'Aunt Sara's advice is to write all on your own & then you will have all the glory for yourself, and not have to share it with somebody else.'

~

Another Paterson was in the news. Off the coast of Papua New Guinea, there was an explosion aboard an engine-driven cutter laden with a cargo of gold that sent out waves of metal and fire. An oil slick slid across the turquoise surface of the sea as the crew rowed frantically away.

The engineer moaned at their feet while their treasure sank to the ocean floor. The reports named the injured engineer as the famous Paterson's younger brother, who had sought his own glory through gold.

Upon arriving back in Sydney, after six weeks in the South Pacific, Paterson left the *Mambare* which, for its return journey, had replaced settlers and sheep with crates of coconut copra.

He returned to his club. He wore a black suit, and politely accepted the handshakes, condolences, whiskies and cigars, and promised to share stories of the South Pacific once he could think beyond his younger brother's death.

At the Club, he read the latest letter from Miles, which she had sent in anticipation of his return. She disappointed him. He was irritated by her elusiveness about the book collaboration, and her suggestion of co-writing poems instead. Poems were his domain. That was no matter compared to the death of his brother. He did not need any disappointment or coyness. He did not have time for her games, if she was playing them with him.

Now it was not a relief to write to her. He inked a pen.

> Dear Miss Franklin,
>
> I have just got back from the island to hear of my brother's terribly tragic death. My sister tells me that you have not been able to decide about collaborating, which is just as well, as . . . I have been working at my book while away. I get very despondent at times & at those times feel like burning all the stuff . . .
>
> Send the stuff back at your convenience. I am in great trouble with my brother, and it will be a blessing for this to work out.
>
> With best wishes
> Yours truly A.B. Paterson

When the letter arrived, Miles held it, and then wrote one word near his signature: *finale.*

11

She heard the beat of bush birds on her morning walk to the mailbox. It was the still of winter, and she huddled in on herself because of her mood as much as the cold.

Among the new envelopes was a letter from Fred Maudsley, with whom she now regularly corresponded and confided. She regarded Maudsley, a member of the Book Lover's Library in Melbourne, as one of her literary doctors, dispensing both editing advice and diagnoses.

She flicked open his latest prescription, which he had marked 'Private' in case her mother or the nosy mailman read it first:

> I know all about your 'temperament' now, I can only wonder why I did not see it before.
>
> You are troubled with what has been called 'the artistic temperament', there never was a better definition of it than the one you accidentally gave in your last note. You say, 'I must write. It is like a fever which comes on me and worries me day and night 'till I sort of murder it by putting it on paper & then it is like a corpse; I don't want to see it anymore.'
>
> That last phrase is one of the characteristics of the highest artistic temperament—dissatisfaction with your own work.

> Well, you must let others judge of that. Now, the artistic temperament is a blessing to some & a curse to others. To some it brings happiness in work achieved, fame, . . . wealth . . . to others disgust, disappointment, wretchedness, & all sorts of unpleasantness.

~

The handwriting of Paterson's sister, Jessie, was slanted at a canter rather than a gallop. She thanked Miles for her sympathies, knowing that 'you too have lost a brother'.

'A young, strong life suddenly cut off by violence,' she grieved, and Miles felt her familiar heaviness.

Jessie said the eldest Paterson was taking it the hardest. Fame was no shield from grief: 'I don't think my brother has replied to you yet, but he was not at all well when he first landed . . . He was prostrated by the shock of hearing the bad news.'

She still hoped that Miles and he would collaborate in some form. That would be good news, and her brother needed a new story.

~

Miles decided there was going to be a sequel after writing *finale*. She wrote Paterson a letter, offering him a literary olive branch: instead of his story with its weak women, or poems that she composed, they could write theatre. A new, blank page to play upon.

When Paterson received Miles' offer of a play, he felt something other than grief for the first time since his brother had died the month before. He'd been unable to write or think.

She was alluring. He read between the lines. He took the lead, for he was like a stallion who couldn't follow. He was 'very taken with the idea of a joint play'. It could be 'a plot which I found among the old Arthurian legends'. It would be a new twist on King Arthur, Lancelot and Guinevere. A 'serious drama', but it 'must be a play that the public will come to see . . . It is no good doing an academic high-class thing . . . There must be a chance to rant & sweat & weep & curse.'

He knew how to play to his public, who wanted action. None of this 'drawing room comedy, with light & shade & cynicism & repartee doesn't hit hard enough. We want a villain . . . I feel certain we can do well at the drama, you can do the thrills plus tears & I can do the villainy and the fighting . . .' Join me in my Camelot, he implied.

Somewhere, a banjo was playing faster than Paterson could write. He got up from the pain that had left him prostrate. He was impatient. He had buried his grief with work. Soon, he would be away on a tour of the drought for the *Herald*, then for a lecture tour of Fiji.

Faster and faster the thoughts came.

'It is queer that you let yourself [write] unreservedly (almost) in letters and talk guardedly, while I write guardedly & talk at large . . . you err I think in saying that I am too sane,' he wrote:

> I mean to take a spell of work up the country somewhere. If we can meet it would be a good thing. Is there any place where I can put up near you? I have lots of friends in the district, but If I go to them I will be hampered by them wanting to amuse me instead of leaving me free to the task of connecting with you. It would be much better if you could come down for a week or so . . . seeing that we are friends though, not acquaintances, to say that I would be glad to lend you any cash you might want for expenses as I know I will get it all back when your ship comes in. Try & arrange this.

> The best of all possible ways would be for us to meet at some place in the country where we both would be free of local worries . . .
>
> I think I understand your temperament. You will be in great glee in one minute, & thinking the blackest of thoughts the next. I am willing to believe that you are honest with me and expect you to give me the same credit.
>
> I write this feelingly . . .
>
> Write to me & say if you can come down or if we can get a week together, no matter how humble . . .

He sent another letter within days, enclosing two plays he'd borrowed for 'stage-craft' guidance.

'We can do our work all night.'

When his letters arrived at Stillwater, five pounds fell out. The mailman had left it in the envelope. He was nosy, but not a thief.

Miles clutched the note, and Paterson's assurance that it was a loan. She owed him nothing except the return of his manuscript, her thoughts on the play and five pounds. They could write all night.

Linda had advised: 'Have all the glory for yourself.'

'When are you going to be Mrs Banjo?' Linda asked, changing her tune.

~

There were arguments at Stillwater about the Man from Snowy River. Her mother would not accompany her to Sydney and feared his intentions, and the intention of anyone in the city.

Her father rolled his eyes as mother and daughter argued and fretted. They were fighting like cats again; he couldn't stand it. He could not accompany her because of his work for other farms in the district now that their family finances were as withered as Stillwater's garden.

However, there was a single rose.

That night, in a rush to make the next mail, and hoping her letter would arrive in time to meet Paterson, Miles wrote:

> Dear Miss Scott,
>
> I am sorry to worry you now when I see by the papers that you must have a lot of business & worry but could you come to my rescue. Mr A.B. Paterson (this is a secret yet a while) . . .
>
> I am such a silly about the city and Mother is in a state for fear I will come to some harm so I have written to you dear Miss Scott.

She signed the letter, 'in haste'.

Rose waited for Vida Goldstein at the wharf as the passengers streamed off the *Ventura* steamer from San Francisco. Later, at Lynton, she hosted reporters who wanted to interview Miss Goldstein about her trip to America, and about how she had attended the First International Women's Conference in Washington as the inaugural Australian and New Zealand delegate.

Vida was on her way back to Melbourne, where she edited *The Australian Woman's Sphere*. Her magazine eschewed fashion and cookery; yet, like Rose, she continued to dress with an unassailable elegance because it was easy for a lack of style to be attacked as unwomanly. They both chose to be like pearls made of steel.

'I think American men have a much higher opinion of their women folk than the men have here,' Vida told the press. 'In every way, except politics, women are much freer.'

When Miles' letter arrived, Rose didn't hesitate. There was room for Vida and for Miles—her marvellous fellow women, who could orbit around her while they were in Sydney.

Rose telegrammed Miles: 'Welcome, welcome.'

A fearful rush of packing her two dresses, and a hurried train trip to Redfern station. Alighting, she did not feel as unnerved by the city as she had feared she would be when she wrote her letter to Rose asking to stay. It didn't feel familiar yet, but she was not as startled by the surge of peak-hour traffic, by the collision of hats and umbrellas waiting to cross the streets, or by the news that a prominent Chinese merchant had been assaulted with an iron bar in Chinatown and robbed of twenty pounds.

At the station, no screams were heard at the height of peak hour, as there had been recently when a woman had fallen from a tram. The tragedy had seeped into the final pages of Miles' new book, in which Ignez witnessed a body lying on the tracks, her face upwards, white and tranquil, while a stray dog sipped at the blood until she was taken away.

Miles climbed into the protection of Rose's cab, and they joined the throng.

Arriving at Rose's home, there was a red-and-white telegram waiting for 'Miss Franklin', dispatched from Coonamble station, deep in the shearing country that stretched across the central western plains of New South Wales. She recognised the writing before seeing his name.

'Sent up here hurriedly . . .'

She sighed. The rush had been for nothing.

12

Over three hundred miles from Sydney, Paterson walked warily into the shearers' camp. He had shed his stylish suit and instead was wearing sturdy pants, a shirt and a hat dusty from his days touring the drought-stricken region before his editor asked him to detour to Coonamble to report on the shearers' strike. He was the closest correspondent they had, and the best.

Shearers emerged from their humpies and tarpaulin tents. Few would have seen his face before, so he talked faster than he ever had before to explain. He leaned on the goodwill of his famous ballad that that they would have recited around a drunken campfire on cold nights out here on the plains, and his song about a swagman.

He heard the distant, sudden rumble of a train. The shearers immediately became soldiers, as tightly formed as those he had seen in the war. On bicycles or running hard, they raced towards the railway track, where trains were forced to slow because of the as-yet unfinished line. They swung onto the train and fired warning shots in the air to frighten the shearers on board who had been brought in by the graziers to break the strike.

On the road, he had seen the shearers bail up coaches, as if they were bushrangers. They'd slashed the harnesses of the horses, and hauled the drivers and passengers from their seats. He had been shocked at their ruthless efficiency.

The new shearers were marched like hostages to the camp, where they joined the strike. Then the men relaxed again and played cards through restless hours. Dogs fought over scraps; fights among the men broke out.

Police on nervous horses trotted in. 'If any man wants to leave, we will escort them,' an officer shouted.

The shearers and their frightened, reluctant new recruits were silent.

The police retreated. Later, Paterson was one of the few able to leave without an escort. In town, he watched locals' eyes dart about to see who was listening before they spoke. The shearing sheds were empty and the squatters were locked inside their homesteads, guarding the doors.

He felt once again in a war zone. The soldiers here were shearers, and the war was over wool. It was a town besieged.

He was still in town when a hardened police inspector rode 100 miles in 24 hours, from Dubbo to Coonamble, to take charge. He was followed by reinforcements.

That night the police rushed at the striking shearers with blinding lanterns and revolvers shooting at the moon. The shearers scattered like sheep, and one fell into a fence.

Paterson filed his final report and packed up for the long train ride home. He had missed the Fiji boat, which was now steaming towards the South Pacific. He wanted a bath, a whisky and a suit, and to see Miles.

13

Near the disappearing lake, Charles Graham, the grazier's son, should have been writing to Linda, who replied to his letters with a warm and loving heart. But as he looked at the sky for the promised rain, and thought about going to church, he was preoccupied by a recent, odd request. Miles wanted him to use the bush telegraph of boys to find out about Paterson's time at Illalong.

She had asked him if 'he be a cad or a lad'.

Charles replied to still his feelings. He couldn't sleep:

> I was thinking over something that you wanted me to find out about Paterson. I don't think I could do it. Or if I did learn anything . . . could I tell you . . . I think you can find all this out yourself.
>
> First you want to learn if he is in earnest and not trifling with you . . .
>
> If he is a man and has the true & right feelings for you, he will soon show them.

Miles stopped to smell the roses climbing the verandah posts and entwined around the wrought-iron balcony rails. After the slow death of Stillwater, she marvelled at the luxury of growth and greenery at Lynton. The garden was better dressed than she was, for once again she was wearing one of her two simple white dresses, which, in a delicate dance of washing and wringing, she had managed to keep interchanging throughout the week. Her mother would approve.

She felt plain next to other women—a common, sturdy wattle among blooms—when she was presented once more at Rose's Friday-night salon. She noticed how they sat beside their husbands or in chic cliques, poured into their corseted dresses that shaped them as the Venus de Milo. Miles also noticed that they were not content to be statues on display. They waved graceful, braceleted arms as they talked and offered opinions about more than fashion. There were no empty-headed vessels here; Rose made sure of it.

Miles felt the pressure of being Rose's latest acquisition.

14

A reunion. She follows the Man from Snowy River to his flat in the city with its possum-skin rug. Before they work on their play of *thrills* and *villainy*, he asks her once more to look at his book that he has been struggling to progress. He is diffident and sheepish as he lays the manuscript before her to take another look. She agrees to read it again.

'How about . . .' she suggests.

He is annoyed, so she stops. She puts down the manuscript, and retreats into her chair.

She looks at him.

He comes over to her.

~

After returning to Lynton from their rendezvous, Miles keeps herself close.

She moves through the motions of the day and night and lingers in the bath. She will later write about that afternoon. That she was in no mood *for revelations* afterwards; In his flat, he *shrivelled all inspiration*, her *shell sealed up firmly*, and he tried to prise her shell open.

Rose does not need to ask all the details, although of course she will. One day, Miles will let slip: he was *the most sophisticated man that has so far attempted to woo me sexually.*

Rose stretches out her arms: 'Dear girl.'

~

On the ferry, travelling to the other side of the harbour, it is unseasonably humid. The boat ploughs towards the community of Manly, behind the cliffs. For once, she is glad she is dressed in her steadfast cotton dress.

The swell gathers in speed and size as the boat sails across the Heads, and spray scatters water across the decks. Miles feels the boat pitching forward against the forces gathering underneath, and she holds on.

From the wharf, she heads along the harbour to a modest cottage where Lawson, the writer who first helped her publish *My Brilliant Career*, and his family are now living after returning from England. When he greets her, she can smell stale beer.

His wife senses Miles' subduedness under her smile, and so can Lawson. After she left their cottage she sent a thank-you note, and Lawson can read the subtext.

'Mrs Lawson just received your letter and is busy washing. Now I want you to write to her by <u>return post</u> and tell her exactly what is troubling you. I need not see the letter. You did not ask me certain questions for nothing, and I hold myself responsible for your future welfare and happiness.'

He added a hastily written footnote: 'You don't know Sydney well—I do.'

~

At the A.B.C. tearoom where he first met Miles, Paterson is attending a midnight feast for a departing actor who is returning to England to claim an inheritance. He walks home through gaslit streets.

Over the following days, he plays golf on the undulating course across from the park where he rides his horse. At the Australian Club, and at his flat, he studies the proofs of his new book of poetry, which is due for publication before Christmas. His publisher is anxious to receive from him its last additions and proof that it will be as good as *The Man from Snowy River.* It has now been seven years, as long as the Federation drought, since his debut.

He dwells on one of the smaller poems. It is not in his usual style; he wrote it in a mood:

> The long day passes with its load of sorrow:
> In slumber deep
> I lay me down to rest until to-morrow–
> Thank God for sleep.

While Paterson works, Miles fills her time with Rose.

'You are my fairy,' she says.

'You are my spirit child,' Rose says, and waves her wand of influence and invitations once more.

They attend state parliament and watch from the gallery. Women are now able to vote, but they are still unable to stand for election to the New South Wales parliament. They can stand for the federal parliament and Vida is considering running in the federal election next year.

Miles picnics with the family of the Secretary for Public Works. His wife, Agnes, is addressed as Mrs E. O'Sullivan, her name reduced to her husband's initial after their marriage. She tells Miles to call on her if she ever needs advice or assistance. Rose is not the only one with a wand.

She meets a 'Special Correspondent' for a women's gossip page, who writes that 'Miss Miles Franklin' was in Sydney, staying with Rose Scott. The waspish critique reduced her to a few paragraphs.

'She is most shy and has a habit of saying nothing for a few seconds, and then bursting out into something brilliant,' the correspondent declared. 'Her personal appearance is very much against her, as she is short, insignificant looking, and has a square face implying very little character until you begin to know her, and then she seems to light up . . . She certainly does not dress to the best advantage . . . Her hair is jet black . . . Still she is crude, but sufficiently interesting . . .'

It was mortifying. How can wearing a simple dress, with hair in a long plait, be worthy of comment in a paper? Why had Rose not warned her about journalists and how to be *sufficiently interesting?* She only understood that she needed to maintain her momentum so as to encourage more sales, because she had yet to receive any significant royalties despite now being a household name, at least among those who read books.

There was comfort in the passing acknowledgement of her brilliance, and that the columnist did not highlight her turned-up nose that wasn't aristocratic like Linda's. Whenever she was photographed, she was conscious to angle her head to a slight profile, so her nose would be more aquiline like her sister's. Brilliance was not an attribute that photographed well.

Another columnist reported, more kindly, that Miles had been 'holding daily receptions of admirers', but wondered if the constant attention might turn her head.

Miles turned away from newspapers and mirrors. The columnists had missed her secret that was still a memory.

She still had something left.

At garden parties, soirees and dinners, Miles smiles among the silk. She doesn't care anymore that she's not dressed to meet a columnist's critique.

She frolics and flirts to forget. Long days passing with their load of sorrow.

Thank God for sleep.

She struggles to close her eyes.

15

The sunset was longer, and the days warmer. New lambs should be birthing at Stillwater and at the Grahams' in Currawong.

Still in Sydney, Miles sent her newborn novel about Ignez, 'On the Outside Track', to her agent in England. She was reluctant to let any book of hers go so far again, but she was not as free as air as she had once thought. Instead, she was tethered to her English publisher by the contract the agent had brokered for her debut. She should not listen to poets.

Still, she did have rights. In the package containing her neatly written manuscript, Miles added an explanatory note about her new book, a book she thought was 'superior' to *My Brilliant Career.* Still simmering about how her first book had been edited for sensibilities rather than sense, she wrote that the novel was still bold, but she would not permit 'toning'.

It was a burst of bravado. She trembled as she handed the package over to the postmaster, who swamped it with stamps.

She gave her manuscript a secular blessing of safe journey, because she doubted prayer. Then she prepared to return home to Stillwater.

Bertha, Lawson's wife in Manly, was thinking of Miles amid her own worries of a wife's heart. She had learned enough from Miles' mood when they met, and from her guarded thank you note, to guess. There had also been gossip among the poets. She decided to be direct:

> Dear,
>
> Am I wrong when I think it was, 'Banjo'? If so, I am so thankful you rejected him. You know, I never like to speak about anyone unless there is need, and somehow, when you came to see us, there was something wrong, that's the reason I told you what I did. He did not want your love but your brains.
>
> You will be loved and will love.

She paused. A moment of the self to share:

> But be very careful you do not make a mistake. I understand your nature, and it would be a death blow to you and your work to find out the mistake when it was too late.

In the weeks after Miles returned to Stillwater, the sisterhood joined the poet's wife in reaching out to her, for they also knew her well enough to know even what she was not saying.

Rose was missing her 'dear girl' too:

> I am sad that you are sad . . . dear, dear little girl cheer up . . . Perhaps I could help you feel better if I knew all your heart. [It's] not always easy to show, for like the sea our hearts are sometimes calm, and sometimes turbulent. When the wind is near, I like to be quiet with books . . .
>
> I wish I could have you with me always.
>
> Goodbye, goodbye, write soon.

A surprising addition to the sisterhood was Jessie Paterson, who talked about books and veiled her thoughts under her regret that the collaboration between Miles and her brother had not continued. 'I believe that you and my brother could have supplied each other's deficiencies . . .' But she sensed that 'there must always be a lot of trouble in writing with another person unless if one is subordinate to the other'.

Miles stiffened at the suggestion of being subordinate. Yes, there would have been trouble, and she was troubled enough by him as it was.

Rose was troubled by more matters than Miles' mood. She was preparing for an upcoming lecture tour; there was pressing correspondence to attend to, and she had thrown herself into a campaign to save her latest 'fellow woman', Selina Sangal, the mother of four children who had recently appeared in a Melbourne court heavily pregnant under her prison smock and convicted of murdering her husband. There was a public obsession with a trial; editorials and letters rushed into print.

Rose's critics had been quick to take issue. So: women could have an equal vote, but not an equal execution? She 'represented the rebellious portion of femininity'.

No, Rose argued. Miss Sangal should be 'saved from the death penalty under laws which her sex had no voice in making'.

16

At Stillwater, Miles has lost interest in the world beyond the farm, or in the fate of Selina Sangal—except for the barest, necessary news. The creative fever that she once described to the critic has come upon her again, and fast. She can feel it.

She feeds the chickens and the pigs, scattering their seed and swill while writing in her mind and putting pen to paper at night.

With her mother she sweeps and wipes the dust away after yet another hurricane wind, but she is quiet, compliant, distant. Miles distractedly takes away her sibling's dirty plates at the table.

Her family has now learned to recognise this mood, and to leave her to her imagination, as long as her chores are done.

~

The fever does not break. It creates dreams of Sybylla, of Possum Gully, and what happened to her young heroine after *My Brilliant Career.*

As Miles writes through the warm spring nights, Possum Gully locals sway around Sybylla. They are either hissing, or they bring her presents and proposals. To escape, Sybylla accepts the invitation of a wealthy, influential widow to stay in Sydney, where she finds she is only more notorious, and the snakes are only more sophisticated, and famous. One of them is a cobra, who strikes. She writes:

> Sybylla asleep in the big chair.
>
> One ankle of the lace stocking protruded from drapery of the small curved figure.
>
> Sybylla was awakened by kisses . . .
>
> Slap.
>
> Heart pain
>
> He asked for forgiveness.
>
> 'Forgive us our trespasses, as we forgive those who trespass against us . . .'
>
> She quotes a poem by Ambrose Pratt, 'The Woman Speaks':
>
> So you think because I'm a woman
> I was made but for pleasure and tears—
> You! Who smile and sneer at the sex I claim
> With the *savoir faire* of your forty years

Miles' fever lasted for four weeks. It only ebbed away when she wrote 'The End' to the novel that had manifested itself to her in that time. Exhausted, she stayed in bed.

She gave her fever-driven manuscript the title *The End of My Career.* There'd been no word yet from her agent in England, to whom she'd sent 'On the Outside Track'. By rights, she was supposed to wait until that ship of mail came in.

Above her, the sky was bush blue. She decided to free her own air.

She didn't need an agent, or an introduction from a poet anymore. Or any poets. She could write on her own two famous feet.

Outside in the paddocks, there were still no spring lambs.

17

The publisher's home in the Blue Mountains was his retreat after a week working at his office above the bookstore in the city that still smelled like a stable, from the former coach-house next door. Uninterrupted by questions and meetings, he had space to think in the mountains.

A new manuscript had been sent there, from Miles Franklin. He knew her name now. She'd been the sensation of 1901; her original submission of *My Brilliant Career* to his firm had been dithered over while he was on business in England. By the time he'd returned, her agent had sold it to an English publisher. He had been so annoyed he'd written 'serious mistake' on Miles' submission letter in the file.

Now here was his chance to redeem that mistake. Her manuscript had arrived addressed to him, George Robertson, and she'd written an anxious letter:

> Dear Mr. Robertson,
>
> Re some stuff I've written . . . Will you read it? If despatched next week will you be there, as I want it to fall into no hands but yrs.? It is intended for a satirical skit . . . takes the form of a take off sequel to 'M.B.C.'

He had to keep a steadier eye on spotting raw local talent, as well as his stars like Paterson, whose new book would be a Christmas cracker.

He took out the manuscript. He frowned at the title: *The End of My Career.* No matter, that could be changed, although he'd heard she was still upset about the editing of *My Brilliant Career* and the question mark that had gone missing, without her consent, in its title. So he'd need to be delicate and persuasive.

The sales for *My Brilliant Career* had not reflected its celebrity, so perhaps people preferred to talk about her, rather than read her book. But the book was never properly distributed in Australia by the English publisher—that was *their* 'serious mistake', not his—and the drought meant new books were a luxury for many outside the cities.

The haze of the Blue Mountains sky appeared in the distance outside his window. He settled into his study and began to read.

Above Stillwater's paddocks, haunted by shapes of trees, the starscape seemed brighter as a celestial wanderer streaked across the southern sky. In the cities, crowds strained to see its small glowing head and wispy tail; they whispered that comets herald coming change.

'No need to fear' the news reassured. 'Do not be afraid', an astronomer soothed.

The year was closing. A literary comet, A.B. Paterson, published his new book, *Rio Grande's Last Race and Other Verses*, in time for seasonal shopping. It was an anthology of poetry, rather than the intended novel draft from which Miles had retreated, while at the same time retreating from him.

The *Herald* was loyal to their correspondent and championed the anthology's Boer War poems, 'for the war has changed us all'. But Paterson was annoyed by the review in the Melbourne *Age*, which reduced him to a folksy popularist—'a favourite among the extremely horsey section of the Australian public'. Their critic had been searching for depth in the rivers of his rhyme: 'Occasionally the writer drops the banjo, letting the reader see more of his serious self and understand something of the longing which the successful rhymester feels.'

Paterson longed for what he did not have. But, to his relief, his book was briskly selling at bookshops across the country ahead of Christmas. It was splashed across advertisements, in reviews and on shelves. In the festively decorated shops in Goulburn, Miles could not avoid seeing it or reading about it.

His was a constant stream of success, but Miles reminded herself that she would have her own glory soon. Two books in one year would be truly glorious. See how he matched that.

At the Blue Mountains retreat, Miles' manuscript was on the publisher's desk. He looked at the marks he had made on its pages. He could see where she had tried to cleave people in two to mask their inspiration, but the mask was made of chiffon. He could see straight through it.

There was Rose Scott. Making her a widow helped, but her high-profile guests were a giveaway. Her alter ego, who was the elegant and serene hostess of garden parties and who hosted Sybylla in Sydney, did not compensate. Rose Scott did not like to be made a fool of.

The glamorous war correspondent and poet character who asked, 'What do you think of a poet as a lover?' and figured in the slap scene was obviously inspired by her romance with Paterson. Was this a clue to what had happened? There were rumours. Gossip. Writers talked.

Miles had included another Australian writer, blurring recognition; he was generous, kind, married and had a sister. Maybe that was a fusion of Paterson and the poet Lawson, who had championed *My Brilliant Career*, but he could not risk Paterson. Apart from being the biggest author in his stable, Paterson was a lawyer down to his polished boots. Robertson had no wish to be confronted by Paterson's lawyerly writing.

He ticked off more threats. The demanding lord was most likely the former governor-general, Lord Hallam Tennyson, who had so publicly praised Miles, and whose father was the famous poet, Alfred Tennyson. Lady Hobnob was no doubt Tennyson's wife.

And the whole book wallowed in sex. Even if he—and Miles as the author—weren't sued for libel, and possibly gaoled with hard labour, the book would at the very least be banned.

He put the manuscript to one side, disappointed.

If he published this sequel, it would be the end of his career, as well as hers.

~

In London, the agent was annoyed with this girl from the colonies who showed promise but not profit. One book does not make an author; it had not done so for the likes of Joseph Conrad and the other famous men on his list.

However, after the publisher of *My Brilliant Career* passed on this mess called 'On the Outside Track', he had tried to place it elsewhere. He'd given it to a new publisher who was looking to build a reputation.

Their reader had admired the 'dark brilliancy' of Miles' debut but concluded that this new manuscript was not brilliant. The reader was blunt: the manuscript needed more sense, modesty and style: 'She takes no pains with her expression; she is only desperately anxious to throw her thoughts & feelings at the reader's head.'

A thin letter, covered in English stamps, arrived at Stillwater. It may as well have been covered with scalpels. The agent did not bother to cushion the faceless assessment of Miles' novel about Ignez with consoling points. He advised her that a total rewrite was necessary before it had any hope of being placed. Ignez needed to be reborn.

Within the week, there was another bulky package tied with string, this one with local postage marks. Her family was now used to the stream of post, and how she prioritised ones that had English stamps or elegant handwriting.

Miles prised the package open and read the note. The submitted sequel to *My Brilliant Career* was unpublishable, George Robertson wrote with regret. He was kinder than the English agent, but still was piercing in his point.

'I had no difficulty in spotting most of the people—they are to life, and you've made me jolly well glad I didn't meet you . . . people prefer a novel with a sweet, good woman in it—when they cannot get one with a very, very wicked one.'

He promised to send her a copy of *Rio Grande's Last Race*.

18

Across the NSW southern districts, a violent thunderstorm splintered trees and dropped dozens of hailstones the size of eggs. Then, rain. Thick drops echoed on the chicken coop's tin roof and soaked the stringybark cowshed. The limping livestock that had survived the drought now inhaled the puddles pooling in the paddocks and waited for green shoots. The wooden house was damp and hot.

Elsewhere, a log washed into the path of a train; the cricket was interrupted; a circus cart was washed into a river. Frogs chorused; snakes sped to higher ground; the birds shook their wet feathers.

The weather reports declared the rain was 'splendid', 'glorious', a 'monsoon'.

Miles' father watched the rain. It was indeed splendid and glorious. It was too late.

Rose's handwriting rains once more in Stillwater:

> My dear, dear, little Stella,
>
> It is over two months since you last wrote . . .
>
> I feel the whirl of travelling. I really do not know how many letters I owe. I am too tired for ideas!
>
> My dear little Stella, I long to hear from you again . . .
>
> A happy, happy Xmas.

She has much to tell her 'dear little Stella'. She has more time now. Vida has returned to Melbourne.

Christmas tidings have come early. In the weeks after Selina Sangal gave birth in a Melbourne prison, and her baby girl, Myrtle, was hurried out of the cell and prison gates by a wet nurse, an emergency meeting of cabinet convened.

Public opinion was a sensitive barometer, and it was declared that Selina Sangal's death sentence would be commuted to imprisonment for the term of her natural life. Politicians did not want to risk their own necks by necking a murderess mother.

Rose is relieved. Justice has been done. Let others arrange charity for Selina's children.

~

When she is calmer, Miles replies to George Robertson. 'Alas, Alack, My gift or curse of impersonation seems to be fatally real. Last venture I had on an average three people to every character hunting me for my scalp. I didn't mean the characters for real in this last affair but if they struck you so emphatically as such I owe you a deep debt of gratitude for rescuing me from a tragic end.'

Miles sends Rose a lyrebird tail feather for Christmas. It is light, long and flutters like a fan.

Later, she will keep a newspaper article about the first pet lyrebirds to lay eggs in captivity. She feels an affinity to lyrebirds for, like her, lyrebirds mimic their immediate surroundings. They shared her gift of impersonation.

The district's new year church services are advertised as a 'thanksgiving for rain'. The Reverend dedicates his homily to the downpours that have broken the drought, at least for the month of December. He adds to his prayers the 'wisdom and necessity' for future conservation of water, 'which should be carried out by government and municipal councils as well as individuals'.

In the pew at her church, Miles sits with her family, who have insisted she come and give thanks for the rain. She listens, listless in the humid heat.

It is nearly the end of the year, and she is conscious of unfinished business, like the loan from the Man from Snowy River.

Miles finds five pounds from her meagre sixteen pounds of book sale royalties to pay back the money he had sent her in August to 'fetch her down'. She rankles now at the words. She will not be fetched.

With the five-pound note, she sends a formal notice of the reconciled account and, as a slap, she adds interest. She sends this care of his club, hoping the money will not be stolen en route as she would not be able to find another five pounds.

He is not rude, so he replies:

Dear Miss Franklin,

Many thanks for the cheque & interest. I gather from your letter that you are going out of the State, if so, I wish you luck.

> I have been constantly travelling lately . . . I am weary to death of sleeping in railway trains and bush public houses. With best wishes yours A.B.P.

~

The manuscript of her Sybylla sequel is now like swill. She carries it to the privacy of the pigs and hides it behind the mud-splattered pigsty. She would have hidden Ignez there too, but her agent did not bother to spend the money on returning that manuscript.

The pigs snort and sniff around her, looking for food.

Miles' mother runs in the rain over to the pigs. They are surprised to have so many visitors who leave wet prints in the mud.

She finds the manuscript—Stella should really find new hiding places—and brings it back to the dryness of the house. She stores it safely in a suitcase, sure her daughter will one day want it again on a rainy day.

~

Miles does not throw Paterson's letters to the pigs, or burn them. She does not like to burn someone's work, even if it is only correspondence, so she stores his letters away.

Among them she keeps fragments. Slashes of sadness that she never sent, and a shred of the *Rubáiyát* by Omar Khayyam, the astronomer-poet from Persia:

> Strange, is it not? that of the myriads who
> Before us pass'd the door of Darkness through,
> Not one returns to tell us of the Road,
> Which to discover we must travel too.

She adds to the shred in her handwriting: *Your little beautiful Miles.*

19

The new year began with fear.

Dead sheep were discovered, with their hearts missing. A predator stalked the paddocks. A teetotaller schoolteacher, while riding home, claimed to have escaped the tiger, that 'came bounding at me with gaping mouth and eyes which glared like bulls eye lanterns . . . growling fiercely' in the dark. His horse, scarred with claw marks, seemed to confirm his story.

It was claimed the creature was a pet leopard that had escaped from its owner, an officer who had brought it back from the South African war. It had disappeared into the bush while he was visiting the district. The officer was lying low, fearing the consequences of his murderous pet.

A local clergyman who had lived in India examined the tracks and he was convinced it was a tiger. A southern tiger, which in myth is red and once ruled over India's south.

It was last seen near Marulan, north-east of Stillwater; it became, in whispers and printed news, the 'Marulan Tiger'.

Farmers gathered their guns, and drovers' wives warily looked outside for strangers, snakes and tigers.

At Stillwater, there was a clearing-out sale. Everything must go.

The local cockatoos braved the tiger for a bargain. Miles watched them pick over her family's furniture, farm implements, calves, sheep and dairy. Underneath their roughness and opportunism, their chests ruffled with feeling. Like cockatoos, they bonded for life and survived the hardship of the land. *Death do us part.*

Later, the cockatoos gathered at a farewell picnic for the Franklins. It was fond and festive. Charles Graham, a grazier's hat covering his balding head, joined the festivities, but his fiancée, Linda, was still with Granny in the mountains.

There will be only one Mrs Graham. Linda and Charles too will rise above the cockatoos.

Miles wanted to fly away.

Miles helped pack up the dray that threatened to tip over under the burden of furniture and wooden crates. She then climbed up beside her father and brothers. The horse, barely recovered from the drought, strained forward. They will camp along the way, her father said. It will be an adventure. Another beginning: he liked new starts because it was easier to start again than to stare at the future.

Her father talked of opening a butcher's shop. Miles nodded, accustomed to her father's schemes, which had previously sent their accounts into debt and her mother into despair. He had originally quarrelled with his brother over the family highlands property, near their grandmother, and that dispute had brought them from mountains to still ponds when she was a child. At Stillwater his ambition to trade livestock had collapsed, and then so had the dairy when the cows were too weak to milk because of the drought.

At least the butcher's shop was dead meat already; there were no live animals to feed and fret about when no rain came.

Linda fretted in Talbingo. 'He's <u>no</u> businessman. Poor you would have all your time taken up pulling him out of pubs.'

Linda remained with Granny. She was the reluctant companion to the family matriarch, even though she would have preferred to be with Charles or her family while she waited for her wedding day.

Granny was suspicious that there was no wedding date yet. The union was not yet complete and, until then, Linda was wedded to her grandmother. Granny complained to Miles: 'How is Graham getting on? . . . he never comes to see Linda, but don't tell him I said so.'

Her mother waved the dray off with the resignation of a woman married to a man with mad ideas, then retreated inside the empty house to worry about what lay ahead. She and their youngest daughter, Laurel, were to catch the train, and would meet them at their new home in Penrith, on the outskirts of Sydney.

Miles felt the road bumping underneath them as her mother, Laurel and Stillwater disappeared. At Marulan, they caught fish for their dinner and camped under the stars.

Somewhere, the Marulan Tiger roamed in the night, and roared.

20

Jessie Paterson was surprised and amused that her brother had taken a desk job as editor of *The Evening News*. She laughed every time she thought of it.

He was tired of roaming. Paterson reminded himself again that he was nearly 40, and men younger than he were dead on a battlefield or, like his brother, from a senseless explosion at sea. He'd lived so many lives already and fortune only favoured the brave for so long.

He turned to the typeset page of the newspaper. This Marulan Tiger was a story. He placed it next to the robbery of the mine in the goldfields. It was just like he'd told Miles: the public wanted *villainy. Fighting. Tears. Thrills.*

He bent over the story again, hunting with cat's eyes for a mistake.

He did have one more safari planned. He planned for it to last a lifetime. Soon he would visit Tenterfield Station, a cattle property stretched to the horizon for 300 square miles, irrigated with dams and a river fringed with weeping willows that drooped over the current. Pockets of eucalypts reached with deep roots in the fertile soil, spreading shade for the herds of fat cattle and thoroughbreds grazing on green grass. There, on the homestead's grand verandah surrounded by a well-watered garden, a woman was waiting for the Man from Snowy River.

Alice Walker was 25, two years older than Miles, and she had an aristocratic nose. Paterson was a family friend, and had regularly come to Tenterfield Station to hunt with her father and to talk over cigars about the intricacies of breeding horses and cattle.

Her father had died; her mother, now a widowed matriarch of the station, was readying the staff of the homestead for Paterson's arrival. If Alice hadn't already realised, she soon would.

~

Rose, hearing that Miles was moving, sent a frantic postcard to Stillwater to catch her before she left: 'Am very anxious to get address. Don't know where to write now.'

Later, Jessie too wrote to Miles, sympathetic that 'you were breaking up your home'. It was as if they were divorcing Stillwater on the grounds of abandonment, or cruelty. But it was the drought that had been cruel to them, and they had now to abandon hope, after three years and upwards of no rain.

The mailman's nosiness was for once useful. He packed up these letters with other stray mail for Stillwater and sent it all on to the Franklins' forwarding address. He would miss Miles' mail.

~

In their new home in Penrith, Miles heard the train clattering regularly across the iron bridge, and it rattled her nerves. In town, boys slouched around the railway station. The heat soaked into red iron roofs. The dawn brought a hot dullness. She longed for a cool change and reinvigorating circumstances.

At sunset flying foxes formed black mists over the orchards. Farmers rang bells to startle them and save their crops. Half-eaten apples dropped to the ground, and vines were tangled with fruit.

Along the town's high street there was a line-up of carts, loaded with crates of peaches and melons, bumping their way to the station. A watermelon teetering on top of one crate tumbled to the road and lay in the dirt, smashed apart in the crash. It leaked pink juice in the heat and the boys dodged the horses to pick up the pieces before they spoiled.

If Stillwater was 'the land o' lots o' time', as Miles had once dubbed it, their new locale was 'the land of melons'. Melon fruits and melon heads.

Some, however, had heads full of dreams and looked to the sky. A local astronomer spotted a meteor the size of the moon throwing off flakes of fire.

Her father groomed his beard and put on his best suit to ready himself for appointments. The dream of a butcher's shop had been replaced by a gentleman's aspiration. No sausage fingers and smelling of rank meat in the heat. Instead, he announced, he would be an auctioneer. He had a business partner and henceforth it would be a gentleman's life. Her mother raised her eyes to the meteor in the heavens.

Her mother needed Miles' help; she had no more time or patience for her daughter's dreams than for her husband's schemes. Spiders spilled out of corners of their dilapidated new cottage, crawling ahead of Miles' broom. Laurel slapped a mosquito that had smelled new blood in the house. Her brothers were already making plans to leave; Norman to be a station hand at a property neighbouring their cousin's, the Bridle Family property near the goldfields, and Tal, 14, as soon as he left school.

With her mother, Miles swept a broom at the spiders, ripping down their webs, and despaired at the dust that had built up from neglect rather than from a hurricane westerly. Her mother muttered about poisoning the corners and the air. Granny was alarmed and intrigued when she heard about the size of the mosquitoes: 'Be sure and catch one . . . send it in a little box so I can measure and weigh it to see if you are correct . . . I don't think you need to be afraid of seeing me there [Penrith] if you are correct, for they will soon kill me; the second thought perhaps they may draw the bad blood out of me.'

Granny was stout and small; but made of iron, like a little teapot. Granny wanted a word with Miles' father, for 'selling what does not belong to him, why did he not take things with him? . . . I hope your Father will be able to keep bread to eat.' She wanted to know what was not sold and what would be earned.

Granny was buzzing about more than the mosquitoes and father. She'd heard about her granddaughter's romance with the Man from Snowy River; but she was more concerned about the young men around Stillwater, with whom Miles was scandalously corresponding from her new home in Penrith. They missed her riding their horses on the rabbit hunts, and racing them to the top of the range.

Granny once more scolded Miles' *froward* heart: 'Now Dear Stella, how can you be so base writing to 2 or 3 at once? Keep up your character . . .'

In another letter Granny wrote, 'No, I would not advise you to marry a man you did not like . . . if you do not like them why do you lead them to believe you do . . . I hope it will please God that you may change and trust in God while you have a chance to do so . . .' She abruptly changed the subject, as grandmothers do: 'It has rained.'

Dawn brought little more than another day. Stillwater had seemed small after the wilds of their mountain property, near Granny's, but compared to Stillwater, this was just a plot, and the only plots Miles liked were in novels.

Their new cottage had a grand name—Chesterfield, like the luxurious leather couches that furnished the libraries and drawing rooms she had visited with Rose Scott. The city of lush gardens and harbour breezes, of literature and love, of elegance and education, that she had come to know through Rose was now just two hours by train, but it felt out of reach. Sydney was another world, into which she had fallen down a rabbit hole for an enchanting few months.

Now Miles could feel herself falling again. This time it was into a shrinking, shallow world.

21

A bachelor party, then a wedding in Tenterfield. Paterson's sister Jessie sat in the family's pew in the little wooden Presbyterian church, smiling at her brother at the altar.

The bride, in a dress of crepe with a chiffon flounce, and a veil—fastened with a diamond star—that fell over her aristocratic nose, glided down the aisle, which was decorated with arches of flowers. Locals and admirers crowded outside the church to see the bride and her celebrity groom.

The sisterhood was shocked by the suddenness of the marriage of the heiress Miss Alice Walker to the editor and poet A.B. Paterson. They wrote with exclamation and question marks.

Rose wrote to her: 'a queer man'.

Linda huffed: 'I always thought you might have him.'

The bachelor from Snowy River had married, seemingly out of the blue bush sky. There were no hints that the bride was wearing a flowing gown to hide a bump. It was perfect. Proper. Pretty.

But Rose and Linda had a theory. They both noted that he had married into Tenterfield Station, one of the richest landholdings in the state.

Linda was blunt, and jealous. She had already waited for over a year with no date on her bridal horizon; but the Man from Snowy River and the Tenterfield heiress had been engaged barely four months. The bride was Alice in Wonderland. 'What a life his poor wife will have when he only has married her for her money,' wrote Linda.

Jessie was more diplomatic. She and Miles were friends by this time, but Alice was now family: 'His wife is very nice, and she is a good housekeeper, which is after all the main thing in wives.'

~

In Penrith, bats clouded the sky and the train rattled the iron bridge in a monotonous routine. Miles tried to think. There were other ways to be in Wonderland without having to be a very nice wife. Rose had shown her that was possible.

She knew that she only needed to ask to stay with Rose again; but she also knew that books only last a season, and *My Brilliant Career* had its debut. Her new manuscripts had the bad blood of rejection on them now.

Miles did not like receiving charity. If she went to Lynton, she would be like the mosquitoes that plagued the house in Penrith, feeding on Rose's goodwill, wealth and wonder.

She needed to find a way back on her own.

PART TWO

Sarah

22

It was Easter 1903. Rabbits had been transformed from pests and carcasses into chocolate decorations. Crowds thronged with their children through the gates of the Royal Agricultural Society's Easter Show, which was proclaimed to be within the reach of even the very poor. Away from the Show's festivity, in the back alleys of the city, another report: that poor women and children were fighting with dogs for garbage and begging for discarded food outside restaurant doors and hotels.

Rose Scott was not in a holiday mood. She was miffed. Worried. Her darling girl had disappeared. Surely she couldn't be happy at that straggly new property in Penrith? If she was, at least she could write and say so. There were rumours that she'd slipped overseas, but the only slipping away was performed by stowaways, and she surely wasn't one of those.

There was no scandal surrounding her, only that flirtation with the Man from Snowy River, which had ended before he married money. Perhaps she was writing another book. Rose knew how Miles got when the fever took over. And she'd had enough disappointments with the last two manuscripts being rejected to be quiet about starting a third.

But this would not do. This was not the girl she knew.

The first reviews and reports of *The Autobiography of a 'Newspaper Girl'* by the American journalist Elizabeth L. Banks began to appear in Australia in January 1903. They chronicled how Banks, newly arrived in London and down on her money, had left her pampered poodle, Judge, with a friend while she worked 'downstairs' to research the life of a servant, and the investigation had made her a celebrity.

Miles began to think. An investigation was an alluring idea. Banks herself had imported the idea from America, where for years women had been making their names through daring and dangerous undercover investigations of asylums, abortion clinics, underfunded public hospitals, factories and servant life. If Elizabeth Banks could do it in London, Miles could do it here, in the Southern Hemisphere.

She could go miles undercover. The research would be a real-life play. Miles and the Man from Snowy River had flirted with theatre, but it had all ended in his flat, and there would be no third act.

This was her own show. She would create 'Sarah Frankling' as its star.

Miles did not have a poodle to discuss the idea with, as Banks did. While staying with Rose during her Sydney heyday the year before, she had picnicked with Mrs O'Sullivan, the wife of the NSW Secretary for Works. Miles thought that, of all the people she knew, Mrs O'Sullivan would be the most open to the plan that was now taking shape in her head. She and her husband supported the minimum wage, and Mrs O'Sullivan had told Miles to come to her if she needed anything.

They sipped tea in china cups.

'How could one truly understand the servant question without experiencing it for themselves?' Miles asked.

Mrs O'Sullivan was thoughtful.

Miles gauged her reaction, and then unveiled her plan: would Mrs O'Sullivan be prepared to be her 'fairy' and give her a character reference, so she could gain work as a domestic servant and write a book about the experience? Miles would be Cinderella in reverse. She did not want a prince, and no longer wanted a poet. She wanted words.

Mrs O'Sullivan was cautious. 'What do your parents think?'

'Mother and father are in some trepidation for my safety.'

'The idea of a hospital nurse, governess, writer, missionary, milliner or tea-room waitress might have received calm consideration. But to be really a servant maid aroused considerable horror among my circle,' Miles said.

'And your name will be?' Mrs O'Sullivan asked, intrigued.

'Sarah Frankling.'

Sarah was one of the multiple middle names that stretched across her birth certificate: Stella Maria Miles Sarah Franklin. For extra anonymity, Miles dangled a 'g' off Franklin to become Frankling, a happy joining to make a familiar name for an unfamiliar life.

She had not told Mrs O'Sullivan everything. That her plan to be a reverse Cinderella—Sarah Frankling—was born of desperation. She was rotting like a summer melon at home. She was an author whose name was known, but few authors could live on a name; living ran on a harder currency. Miles would be a melon head to think she could.

As she had said, her mother was anxious. Her father, no stranger to wild schemes, was dubious. Miles had tried the more respectable route, governessing to her wild cousins for six awful months, and that experience had only inspired her to savage them in *My Brilliant Career* as the feral M'Swats. Their relatives were still angry about their portrayal in the book, especially her cousins' father, Uncle George, who had warned Miles not to write another book, and still howled 'all malicious lies!'

Except for her excellence in riding a horse, in writing and in outraging relatives, she had no other skills, outside those learned in forced domesticity as an eldest daughter. The Man from Snowy River had made some profit from his poetry, yet even he had taken a side job as an editor, and now had a wife—and rolling green hills of money and land.

Had he really married her for the money, as Rose and Linda believed? If that was true, she felt pity for him and his wife. She couldn't be that cold.

If Rose Scott had taken her carriage onto the main road that led from Lynton into the city, and travelled past the rows of leaking, peeling terrace houses and the shops cluttered with wares, she might have entered a grotty tearoom on the edge of the city centre, and found there a girl wearing a plain linen dress and a sailor's cap answering to the name Sarah Frankling.

Sarah had seen the tearoom in the 'Waitress Wanted' ads of *The Sydney Morning Herald.* When she arrived, it was assumed she was there for tea, and she had been taken to a table. She now felt too tired to ask about their vacancy for a waitress, so instead she sat down and considered her position.

She'd been responding to vacancies advertised all morning, but her inquiries had been dismissed as brusquely as the lines describing these jobs in the newspaper: *A THOROUGH general. Small family. Housemaid. Good wages.*

The ads were all the same. They began with a shout: *SMART. YOUNG. FIRST CLASS. RESPECTABLE. USEFUL. SOBER.* She had all these attributes. She was young, given that she'd dropped her age from 23 to 18. After each inquiry at a half-opened door, a faded room or a tawdry bar she was told that the positions were already filled. She wondered if the reports about a shortage of servants and the vexed articles about the 'servant question'—the fear that girls were filing into the factories, rather than cooking and cleaning for a family other than their own—were an exaggeration.

There was anxiety upstairs too, about a call for a revolution of kitchen equality downstairs as 'girls' demanded more respect, or at least humanity. Mistresses were said to 'lose sight of the fact that servants are women like themselves, women with thoughts, feelings, habits, bad and good, with weaknesses mental and physical, with aims and hopes'. A former servant also proposed that maids should be allowed to ask for character references from their future mistresses before agreeing to a new position, but then she acknowledged the reality: 'The mistress may be a she-dragon or worse, but no question must be asked. That would be the first sign of intolerable insolence on the part of the girl, and would be resented.'

Sarah Frankling, a young woman of thought and feeling, possessed Mrs O'Sullivan's essential character reference; she also had in spades the personal attributes demanded in the advertisements. She would not ask intolerable, insolent questions that would cause resentment.

In the tearoom, she stirred the muddy brew, brooding what to do next.

She ignored the suspicious glances. Perhaps she looked like a fine and dainty cup in her plain dress, and everyone else in the tearoom seemed cracked by life. She didn't look as tired and washed up. Or perhaps they had heard her educated accent, softened by a mother who was brought up by a governess, and a grandmother who corrected vowels and posture.

She had a realisation. The other diners saw her as someone who had wandered in by mistake. But, she thought, 'it was imperative I get work to sustain myself'.

She stirred her tea. 'Perhaps I was more hard-up than the waitress.'

She looked again at the column of advertisements. After the morning's frustration, she now knew the ads would only bring her more pain.

The employment offices looked more promising, if only because they emphasised the job, rather than the personal attributes required. They also listed multiple positions. One particular agency, Hittman's, seemed to offer a lot: *COOKS and L'dresses, country and city (3). Cook for Station. Waitresses (2). Housemaid and assist bar. Generals (5). Mother and Daughter for Station. Cook and Laundress. H.P. maid. Nursegirl. Housemaids. HITTMANN's, 49a Castlereagh Street.*

That address was quite close. Yes. This would be a new plan of attack.

Leaving, she could feel her ankles rubbing against her boots as she negotiated the traffic of horses and carts, then tramped across the park to the city centre. As she approached the cluster of buildings, she kept her head down in case she was recognised.

The city was the domain of the Man from Snowy River, and of the critic, who had had that strange standoff over her with the artist Norman Lindsay at *The Bulletin* office. That had been an exhilarating day for Miles Franklin.

But on this day, she was Sarah Frankling. Just another girl in the crowd.

It is evening by the time she leaves the city. For 30 miles, her head sags against the seat on the Penrith train, then lolls with the clip of the pony for the final three miles home.

Her youngest sister, Laurel, is asleep with her doll, and her mother is wearily awake, waiting to make sure she is home safe. Miles nods that she has a position as a general maid, who cooks, cleans and serves meals. Her mother sighs in resignation and goes to bed.

She lays her linen dress over a chair and puts on her night-gown. Outside, the moon hangs over the orchards.

She feels too over-strung for sleep, so she writes about her day instead. It is her soothing habit of absorbing the quiet. She has resolved to keep a diary, for authenticity, so she will have a record.

She recalls the afternoon at the employment office, waiting on the wooden seat to be picked, like produce on a blackboard. How she heard the terrible story of the deaf domestic servant, desperate for anything that offered shelter and a shilling.

Later she met a doctor's wife, laden with jewellery, who asked her if she could use a telephone and worried whether she had the strength to wash four little boys. Finally, the tram ride to a coastal suburb to meet a Mrs Finlayson, who wanted a general maid to cook and clean.

She remembers arriving there in the late afternoon, when the light had turned to a dusky glow, and the sea air blew colder. She sees equestrians in spotless white suits riding in the sunset, but for once the sight of riders does not please her, for she can only think of the women who, for the smallest living wage, made their suits so white.

She writes herself to sleep, counting words instead of sheep.

23

It was Monday. Putting on the linen dress and fastening her sailor's cap, Miles hugged Laurel goodbye, and caught the pony to the railway and the train to the city. She stepped off the train as Sarah Frankling, with nerves that climbed with the tram to the cliffs, and a throat full of panic.

As her new employer, Mrs Finlayson, had instructed, she left her luggage at the grocer outside the tram stop, where she got off and walked around the curves of trees to a large terrace house. Her hand froze on the gate latch and she gripped her parasol to steady herself.

When she had sipped tea with Mrs O'Sullivan in her drawing room, her plan to be a servant had seemed such a grand scheme. It solved her financial fix and her need to escape the dullness of suburban orchards; she could research her book. Now her hand was on the latch that opened up the reality.

'Come right in, Sarah!' a voice called. 'I think you have done very well to get here so early . . . You've come so far, you must be in need of a cup of tea.'

'Sarah'—Miles—sat down in the neat and, to her relief, clean kitchen. Panic stuttered her words. The house-dog placed its paws on her lap. Mrs Finlayson, with her sleeves rolled decorously up, placed the tea and bread on a snowy cloth, and left her new maid alone.

She did not have to return to Penrith that night via train and pony, for she was now a live-in maid, with a little bedroom next to the kitchen and laundry. It had a candle, a looking glass and a bed with worn blankets. She remembered, longingly, her bedroom at Rose Scott's, where she had slumbered in a four-poster bed in the best guestroom. In a fit of fastidiousness, she checked the room for dirt, which would later become a ritual at each new position.

Miles calmed herself. She could write by the candlelight, and she didn't mind the simple surrounds of her crib; apart from around the window, her check had found it clean. She didn't have to do the washing because one of those laundresses she had thought of when she saw the bright-white riding parties at sunset had already come and soaked the family's clothes in suds; the vapours drifted into her room and clung to her nostrils.

The arrangement meant Miles received ten shillings per week, instead of twelve; the laundress received three shillings for the five hours' work it took to do the washing. The disparity disgusted her more than the smell did.

Her stomach churned with fear of failure. The candle flickered over her pen, and she wrote: *My nervousness beats classification, did the Mistress come home intoxicated or insane, I could deal with her without a tremor of fear, but how gracious altho' she is, I have not courage to ask her about my bath, and for the present am confined to a bowl.*

She blew out her candle in her servant's room by the sea.

The 'Master' of the house was Mr R.W. Finlayson, an engineer. She had never called a man 'Master' before; men were fathers, brothers, friends. Charles and the Man from Snowy River had wanted to be something more.

When she polished his boots, she found that he had small feet. Seeing the back of his head at the breakfast table, she made mental notes for her diary: he was *aggressively bald*, and had a *self-important voice*. When he tested the piano and sang, she was surprised his voice was passable, given how odious his normal speaking tone was to hear.

As she worked, she made more mental notes about the family. They were characters in her real-life show. She watched the confident 'Mistress', the person who gave out the orders, become a meek wife. The two teenage daughters quietened around Mr Finlayson's unspoken authority, then laughed at his jokes and nodded in agreement. He was *boss of his backyard and lord of his little suburban dining room*. She couldn't stand it, and escaped without permission to breathe something that wasn't the cloying air of the house.

When she saw Mr Finlayson walking towards her on the cliff walk, she wondered if he would nod or stop her and question why she was out; but he strode by her, and she felt like a *beetle on the fence*.

She would write all these thoughts down later.

Yes, she would write.

But first, she beetled home to make the roast lamb for the family's dinner. She was the maid who watched, and who wrote down everything she saw and heard.

22 May 1903. Addressed to Sarah Frankling, care of Waverley Post Office:

> I was glad to hear from you—but dear one—do you only have *an hour* on Saturday? Have you no arrangement for an afternoon & Evening out? A day a month? or any outings? Because if so you will hurt the girls you want to help—They will think if you do not want times out, why shd [*sic*] other girls! Think of this point—for the sake of others, you must not be a slave only going out for an hour once a week—I do not say this out of pure selfishness & because I want you—but because I think it is bad for other girls & for yr mistress—not to have proper & established hours off.
>
> Mrs O'Sullivan told me, she thought I knew! – I shall not of course tell a soul—not even here . . . This is only a hasty scrawl just to say <u>come soon</u>. I am just dead tired tonight. Can't you get out <u>next</u> Saturday week, or after work one Evening? & then come to me. Do, do, <u>do</u> dear little girl—
>
> Your ever loving
> Rose Scott
> alias Rachel Soot!

~

It was May. The envelopes stacked up on Rose's desk—her life of correspondence. Among the replies she composed was a letter to the *Herald* in response to accusations by a reader that she was 'blindly' leading women, and that the suffrage organisations excluded country women so the city could rule. She was surprised this letter had been from a fellow woman. Where was her solidarity?

Rose's pen scrawled, but the *Herald* editor was used to her handwriting by now. She protested that there was no plot to exclude country women or lead them blindly to the voting booth: 'They were asked, as I would ask all women, to be led only by the thoughts of others, to think for themselves.'

Rose notes that the complaining woman was from Goulburn. What a shame her dear little girl still wasn't there to advocate.

As a woman of the country and the city, and admired as the author of *My Brilliant Career*, she would have been able to convince this complainant there was power in unity.

Miles had told her in a letter about her life that was measured in ten shillings and an hour and a half off each Saturday.

'Ye Gods!' Rose had written, horrified. No wonder domestic service was not a 'popular profession'. Rose did not say how much she paid her cook.

'That next Saturday is mine,' Rose vowed.

She was still miffed. But she was no longer worried about Miles' whereabouts after meeting with Mrs O'Sullivan, who had dropped Miles' secret, like a cube of sugar, into her tea: 'Oh, I thought you knew.'

She had not let Mrs O'Sullivan know how she felt. Rose was airy. Confident. Her purring voice always kept her feelings private.

She had stirred her tea: 'How clever of our dear little girl to investigate the servant question.'

24

In the suburb by the sea, Mr Finlayson read the newspapers at the breakfast table, and his new maid peeked over his 'aggressive baldness' at the precious printed words.

Other precious words came by mail. She invented excuses to run up to the high street on errands so she could collect her letters from the post office.

She found Rose's letter waiting. A secret her Mistress didn't know; another life. Rose would not forget her.

Rose's letter felt like a reprimand, even though she was relieved to know where her little girl was.

Yes, Miles knew she should object to the hours demanded of her, which saw her working from dawn until late in the evening. But she would be just one maid on strike because she did not know other maids and there was no union, like there was for the miners.

If she glanced again over Mr Finlayson's head, she could read that the miners were picketing again, and six of their wives had been arrested for stoning their evicting landlords. The miners banged on the side of the train carrying them to court. The wives waved to them like queens, and their children cried.

There had been some shaking of the status quo in 1901, when a group of domestic servants sent a polite petition to the Victorian Government that 'asked for a maximum working week of 60 hours'; for every second Sunday off; and for 'proper sleeping accommodation', as there were many reports of servants being required to sleep on kitchen floors or verandahs with little privacy. The petitioners had been brushed away and now their requests were somewhere in a government file, gathering dust.

Miles did not have a picket or a petition. She did have words. She would cook up a book.

Every morning Miles cooked breakfast for the family. In her first week, she was still serving her nerves as well as their meals. The Finlayson daughters made their school lunch as she prepared the eggs, bacon, potatoes and toast. She was glad of the girls' laughter and chatter, for it reminded her of when she and Linda had made their lunches together in the kitchen. Like Rose, Linda now knew to write to the Waverley post office, so they could again correspond.

It was nearly time. The bacon was stripped, the eggs ready to fry, and the potatoes cut to boil. Used to a bush pot-belly oven, Miles eyed the newfangled gas stove with nervous perspiration. She wiped her hands on her apron and pushed down the pilot light.

She felt searing skin and the slaps of a wet towel against her face. She smelled scorched hair. Her eyes clouded with hot smoke.

She heard the girls screaming. Or was it her?

She stumbled and sat down. But there was still breakfast to prepare, and ironing to finish. She had to get up.

The girls took the breakfast tray. They were sweet, she thought. Bless the girls. Curse the house.

Mrs Finlayson rushed in and dabbed olive oil on her face, and it felt like a frying pan.

'Dear me, how terribly your face is burned,' Mrs Finlayson said. 'It must have been the length of your eyelashes that saved your sight as I never saw anyone so much burned around the face without the sight being injured.'

That night, quiet in her misery, her room took on a haze of yellow. Her eyes were swollen from smoke, and balded without lashes. Her eyebrows were singed and smoky, and a chunk of her hair at the front was clumped like coal. Oil-covered blisters slicked across her cheeks, forehead, chin and fingers. It was painful to hold a tray or a pen without feeling a blister threaten to pop and weep.

She was surprised that she had endured it and kept going all day. Mrs Finlayson's sympathy only went so far. When she had finished ironing the clothes, she had sweated and winced as the steam warmed her injured skin. Somehow she'd managed to make the dinner.

At the memory of it, boiling tears slid down her blisters.

On the Sunday, the family observed the Sabbath, so she cooked fish and roast lamb. The heat made her blisters steam. The family posed for Sunday photographs and entertained guests, but she felt like the day was honouring Mr Finlayson rather than God.

She loathed the sight of him. She despised his small boots and his bald head, and his ego whenever he strode in from work, like the night that he came home from a NSW Engineering Association meeting, where he'd pontificated on 'the absence of economy in manufacturers in Australasia'.

Hearing the front door open, the rustle of him dropping his coat and taking off his hat, and the adoring hellos from his wife and daughters, Miles grimaced then forced a smile; it still hurt to move her mouth. She was terrified of the stove exploding again and shrank away from its flame. Instead of fixing its knobs for her, Mr Finlayson complained that there was no sauce.

After dinner, she'd heard his passable voice at the piano, and realised that Mr Finlayson had not yet touched the loose gas taps that had caused the hobs to explode in her face. It was not one of his daughters who had been burned.

~

It is June. The southerly is colder now, and she feels the chill. She notices her linen dress is hanging more loosely on her. She looks more worn, like her dress. Her eyes still feel glazed by the burn but she can see again, and her eyelashes are growing back as spiky slivers. Her face feels stiff, and her lips crack when she opens her mouth to eat.

She feels numb now and moves noiselessly about her chores. She worries about scars. She must apply more oil.

Among the mail at the Waverley post office, she is cheered to finally find a letter from Granny, forwarded from home—'my dear girl where are you and what are you doing, I have not told anyone you left home'—and from her loyal Linda. Her smoked sight struggles to read her sister's amiable list of demands.

Be sure to tell me how you like the place you are in.

And what the Mistress is like.

And if you don't like it.

And when they find out they have a great Australian writer in their midst.

And that you are making a study of them.

Miles closes her eyes, and the smoky blur turns to black.

25

When she woke, the winter rain was washing the roof of the terrace and running down the window of her little room. Her blistered fingers had healed, so she would be able to hold a pen easily again. The fireplace was smouldering downstairs, and her candle was a warm comfort.

During the morning, she put the washing out, but it was useless in this weather. Both she and the laundress knew they would have to repeat the cycle, or the clothes would smell like they had never been washed at all and a mouldy steam would rise from them when she tried to iron them flat.

The laundress attacked the suds, which boiled blue as a result of the whitening agent that bleached the clothes and corroded her skin. The laundress's hands were permanently chapped red, white and blue. She asked about Miles' burns.

'It's easy to see you've never been "out" before, you're so eager,' the laundress scolded. 'They'd run you to death in a hard place.'

The laundress told Miles her story. She was widowed, with nine children, and supported the family with washing and other domestic work. As she talked, Miles helped her heave the heavy, steaming and dripping cottons out of the tub and onto a wooden rack, where she torturously cranked them through the mangle rollers to wring them out, before rinsing and cranking them again. The wet clothes seemed to swallow the laundress's fragile frame as she hoisted their weight about.

Miles wondered if the laundress earned enough to survive, when she only made three shillings a week for ten mouths, if she fed herself as well as her children. Since the drought, the cost of food had been piling up in pennies.

Hearing the laundress's story about her life, and the nine lives she was responsible for, Miles felt grateful she only had to think about herself.

Mrs Finlayson was often at lunch, morning tea, afternoon tea and charity events, while the girls were at school and Mr Finlayson at work—not that he would deign to talk to her. The house, she noted in her diary, was a *reflection of its mistress: exemplary, clean and dully commonplace.* She assessed Mrs Finlayson's intelligence as ordinary; still, her time, brain and energy were worth more to the world than worrying about how to get a better shine on the silverware, or that the grocer had slyly charged her five pence more for a cauliflower.

She had decided the terrace was like *playing cubby house*, with small-sized deliveries of steak, bread, vegetables and ice. Throughout the day, a carousel of tradesmen and delivery boys came to the door. As they arrived with their packages, cans and tools, Miles opened the door without a smile or hello, because she felt too shy and embarrassed about her burned face, and her grandmother had taught her not to be common. So Miles was icy to the iceman, haughty with the grocer, and distant with the gas-fitter who came to fix the gasolier rather than the stove.

They all invaded her new habitat. She was in a forest of class, and she couldn't see the person for the trees.

Slowly, as her loneliness loomed each day, except for the occasional conversation with the laundress, she began to shed her stand-offishness with those who came to the door. She realised that she liked the overcharging greengrocer, although he smoked as he talked; and she became warmer with the iceman, who carried icebergs in pincers to keep the fresh food cool.

Rupert, the milkman, used to friendlier maids, came each morning in the dew-laden dawn to pour fresh milk into the jug that she was tasked to leave out beside the gate, and he would return each afternoon with a second delivery. Until the night when, deep into her diary writing, she fell asleep and forgot to leave out the jug.

She woke to a tap at the window. It was soft, then insistent. Drowsily she put on a gown. In the pre-dawn glimmer she saw the milkman through the glass, smiling with his dazzling teeth. It must have been the milk that fed his good looks, for such excellent teeth were rare.

She opened the window, and the frigid air cooled her awake.

'Hullo! You forgot your jug!'

She mouthed her thanks and, half-asleep, found the jug, thrust her arm with the morning jug in her hand out the door—just enough so he could fill it—then watched his shadow negotiate the slippery path back down to the gate.

That afternoon, Rupert returned and came into the kitchen, to fill her biggest pitcher with milk from the can that he shouldered into each house. Miles smiled in gratitude. She really must try to be nicer.

When he'd finished, she turned away, but he moved behind her and caused her to drop the jug in fright, splashing milk across the floor.

She apologised and despaired at the pool of milk. Since the gas accident she'd been starting at the slightest sound, she explained.

He picked up the pitcher and refilled it, smiling with his milk-white teeth.

The milkman was curious: had someone hurt her, to make her so jumpy? He spoke like he knew what it was like to live in a house of fear.

She appreciated his concern. 'Oh dear, no. I don't know why I'm so silly, perhaps it is because I've never been away from home.'

It wasn't quite true. She'd lived away during her ordeal as her cousins' governess, and when she stayed with Rose Scott. And she'd spent a summer at her grandmother's station.

Her white lie bolstered the pretence of being Sarah Frankling, a young girl from the country who did not know the world. But what she'd meant was true.

She had never felt so alone.

The following afternoon, she was holding twopence for the two quarts she'd spilled; but Rupert waved it away, and instead asked her out.

Miles murmured that she was too busy. It was too hard for her to get away from the Mistress, she explained, and her last hour off had been abruptly cancelled. He echoed Rose Scott, if only for his own self-interest: 'You make her give you a day. No wonder you look so scared.'

The milkman's overture rattled her, like the coins still in her hand. It was a complication. She made sure she left the milk jug by the gate the next night for the dawn delivery.

She left the coins for the spilled milk again by the door for the afternoon delivery but then the doorbell rang and rang, and she knew Mrs Finlayson would be cross if she did not answer it.

She opened the door, bracing herself for Rupert's smile. Instead, another boy was standing there, who explained to her that Rupert was ill in bed.

He hurried away.

Miles picked up the two pennies and put them back in her purse, disappointed but relieved.

Finally, Mrs Finlayson grants her new maid time off. It can be any afternoon, she decrees, so long as it is not Sunday. Miles knows she should be given a whole day off, but she isn't Rose Scott or a striking miner, so she doesn't argue.

She has dinner ready by three o'clock in the afternoon so Mrs Finlayson can heat it up later. Then, hurrying into her mackintosh, Miles rushes out into the pouring rain, nearly skidding on the path.

Skipping over puddles, she sprints to the tram. Glorious rain. It still feels marvellous, after all those years of empty clouds and dead paddocks.

She swings herself onto the departing tram. 'Miss, be careful!' the conductor admonishes.

Miles nods, but she is unchastened. For six, maybe seven hours, she can leave Sarah the servant by the gate, like a jug of milk.

In town, she first goes to the employment agency office, because Mrs Finlayson has reminded her that they should refund her a shilling.

The agency lady has a square jaw that dips in disapproval when the receptionist asks her what to do about Miles' refund request.

'Give it to her. I said I would. You can see the girl needs it.'

The money is grudgingly given over.

Thanking them, Miles leaves the agency and, in a fit of revenge, puts their shilling into a homeless man's upturned wet hat on the street outside. This will go into her diary. And when she writes the book—wait until she writes the book—she will make it clear what she thinks about employment agencies, and how they treat the servant girls whom they feed off.

She skips back into the rain. She could sing.

26

When Rupert the milkman returned from his bout of tonsillitis, he immediately asked her out again as he filled the milk pitcher during the afternoon delivery.

She told him her mother had warned her to be careful of town men.

'Very good,' he said. 'But you needn't be afraid of me.'

The house clanged with the piano. Beatrice, the younger girl, was trying to play Mendelssohn. Miles was annoyed by the hacking of the notes as much as by Rupert's earnestness.

He was as wholesome as his milk, he promised. He could take her to church if she was hesitant. And he wasn't a 'bounder'. She looked puzzled by the word, so he explained it meant a 'take you down' type of man.

Oh, she realised. Take down your reputation. You would fall into their arms. Fall pregnant. Fall from grace. So many ways to fall. She stood so her petite frame was a tiny bit taller. She had no intention of falling for anyone.

His request for an evening out—a church outing, a walk, anything—now became part of his daily delivery. 'By Jove,' he grinned, as she greeted him at the door. 'I wish a fellow could have two girls.'

'Every fellow is at heart a Mormon, eh?'

He cajoled her in the kitchen and blocked her way with his can of milk.

She was wearing thin, like her body, and her dress.

'Don't begin to invite me out at night as I've made an inflexible rule not to go out with a man.'

He suddenly soured. 'You'll be an old maid at that rate.'

She thought of Mrs Finlayson, simpering around her husband and teaching her daughters to do the same.

'There are worse fates than that in matrimony.'

~

Linda writes again and this time she has news. Her fiancé, Charlie, has finally visited.

Granny will be pleased, Miles thinks.

Linda has more questions she doesn't ask. They lie under her chatter, and in Charles's locket with its strand of Miles' hair.

'Charlie was thinking he had insulted you because you haven't answered two of his letters,' she writes. 'It was all Stella from morning till night when he was here. He has a hair guard that he wears right across the front of his waistcoat. He wouldn't tell me for a long time that it was your hair. But I knew from the first he has your photo fastened onto the end of it.'

In the privacy of her room next to the laundry, with Linda's letter on her bed, Miles lets down her hair. It grazes her bottom and brushes her back, and its weight makes her feel like herself again, apart from the singed fringe she's lost.

The memory of the smell of burning hair still makes her shudder. But it will grow back. She can feel a little bit of fuzz.

It is her hair, and Charles only ever got strands of it in his locket. She hopes Linda knows that.

27

At the end of June, she ticked off the date. She had nearly completed eight weeks in the house. Her plan was to cycle through two months at six houses over a year, to get the full range of domestic-service situations for her book. It would be much bigger than what Elizabeth Banks, the American journalist in London, had attempted.

If she was careful, she could save the little money she earned for when she was writing it up the following year, because she had few expenses as a live-in maid. She rarely had time off to spend on treats anyway. She could live frugally; her mother had taught her that.

She approached Mrs Finlayson, who had her sleeves rolled up even though her maid did all the work, and told her of her desire to leave.

'Very well. I can easily get another girl.' She looked irritated by the inconvenience.

'Thank you, ma'am,' Miles said, and backed away.

The laundress rolled her eyes that the new maid was already leaving after just two months. The clothes rolled through the washing mangle as she cranked it. Her Irish accent thickened as she scolded Miles for leaving such an easy place.

Miles wanted to wring a bit more character out of the laundress before she left. Her backstory.

'Did you ever have a row with a Mistress?'

The laundress nodded. 'Did I not! I up and told her that I was as good as she was—there was only the difference of a bit of money that she could lose any day between us. I said it, and what's more, I meant it. I had a better figure than she had . . . I had more brains too.

'Now don't you think you are as good as your Mistress? If you don't, ye're a weak-minded little fool.'

Miles knew she was not weak-minded, or a fool. But, as she wrote in her diary, she did not know who she was, *who walks about so noiselessly*. She did not know this *suppression*. She too was a new character, who she had to understand.

It was a game of cat-and-mouse as she made herself scarce when Rupert was due to deliver the afternoon milk. But on the Tuesday of her last week, he insistently rang the bell on the back door until she came out of hiding and answered, salty like the lamb she was readying for dinner.

For once she was taller than he was, because she stayed poised on the top step while he waited at the bottom of the stairs.

'Here's the bill, you ran away without it,' he said, and she relaxed. But as she held her hand out for the bill, he grabbed her by the waist and lifted her to the ground.

Miles exploded into threats. He was no Harold Beecham, who had done the same by the lemon tree in her novel.

'How dare you interfere with me!' she snapped. She did not add 'sir', like in Victorian novels. 'You try it again, and I will throw all the milk in your can over you.'

He looked hurt and let go of her waist. He just wanted to know, he explained, why she wouldn't have anything to do with him. That was all.

'Is it a case of another man?'

She softened. He was a boy, really. They all were.

She verged on telling him the truth. That her name wasn't really Sarah, it was Stella Miles, and she was a writer. He may have heard of her.

But she also needed Mrs Finlayson's reference and, if Rupert spilled the truth, she doubted Mrs Finlayson would appreciate that she was to be in a book.

She must think of a pseudonym for the family. *Tomlinson* would work. She would decide later. For now, she faced her besotted milkman, who was sure she was secretly engaged.

He was a lot less sophisticated than the Man from Snowy River. She still blushed when she thought of the afternoon in Paterson's flat. And Charles had now accepted that his life would be with Linda, except for his locket.

'Has someone got a claim on you?' he asked again.

'No one has a claim on me. I am my own property.'

He asked her again to go out. To church. To tea. A walk. Anything proper for a proper girl.

She paused, thinking, then made an offer.

She needed more time for her burns to heal, she explained. By next week she would feel better about being seen, and he could invite her then. She warned with a waggling finger, it did not mean she would go out with him. In the meantime, he was not to mention anything but milk.

She waved as Rupert went off with his can of milk, whistling.

~

A deal had been done at the bottom of the stairs between the milkman and the maid. As promised, Rupert did not mention his invitation for the rest of the week. He was playing by her rules, and so did Mrs Finlayson, adding her reference to Mrs O'Sullivan's.

> Sarah Frankling was in my employ for somewhat over two months. I found her obliging, clean, quick, and honest, and feel sure she will make a competent servant in any capacity. It was her own wish to leave.
> Mrs R.W. Finlayson.

Sarah Frankling now had two references attesting to her character.

On the Sunday, Miles took her luggage box to the tram, and she had tucked away inside her final pay, and her new reference in an envelope, and her diary that revealed more than Mrs Finlayson could ever know.

The next morning, Rupert skims through his dawn deliveries to fill dew-frosted jugs. In the afternoon, he rings the bell, having rehearsed the invitation that Sarah said he could offer to her today, as it is now a week since he made his promise.

Her face is so pretty, he thinks. That cute little nose.

But Mrs Finlayson answers, irritated that she is having to talk to a delivery man and arrange the milk.

Sarah won't be hard to replace, she thinks. That much was true. There was something about Sarah that was unusual, apart from the delicacy hiding her strength. A curious girl.

Seeing Mrs Finlayson, Rupert is confused, and asks after Sarah. Irritated by the mention of her name, Mrs Finlayson is short with him. Registering his shock, she adds: 'Her choice.'

No, Mrs Finlayson says, she didn't leave a forwarding address, nor any goodbye notes.

The sound of the piano tinkles through the house.

Rupert's smile curdles as he realises. He's been played.

Far from Rupert's milk run, at Mrs O'Sullivan's, Miles glances at a clock and knows that it is the time when Rupert would be delivering the afternoon milk. She feels a pang of guilt, but his feelings are a casualty of her undercover research. All's fair in love and writing.

28

It was winter 1903. In the west of the state, authorities discovered a baby girl, Ruby, emaciated and close to death. Her mother, a servant, was charged with neglect and fined two shillings. In an inner-city suburb, a servant, Nellie, was found dead, holding her employer's revolver and with a bullet wound in her neck. And it was reported in *The Book Lover* that there had been an 'accident to Miles Franklin':

> THOSE of our readers who appreciated the great promise contained in the first literary effort of Miss Miles Franklin will be sorry to hear that she has recently been the victim of a painful accident, having been burnt by a gas explosion. The chief injuries she sustained were about the face; her eyes, though injured, were fortunately not permanently so.

The city read about Miles and the suffering of others, and moved on.

Miles wondered how the newspaper knew. Either Mrs O'Sullivan or Rose Scott must have mentioned it in passing horror. It was probably Rose at one of her salons, explaining why Miles had disappeared. Or perhaps she slipped it into a conversation and it became literary gossip.

There was no photograph of her accompanying the article about her burns. Photos of her remained a relative rarity but she still planned, before she finished the year, to find a photography studio and pose in her maid's uniform, to add to her book.

Most of all, she was relieved that the article about her burns didn't say why it happened, or where she was.

Sarah Frankling was safe.

~

From the Finlaysons, Miles had taken a ferry to Mrs O'Sullivan's, who fretted at the sight of her when she arrived. She was a ghost of her former self. Alarmed at her weight loss, Mrs O'Sullivan had a guest room prepared for her, and fed her a comforting bowl of beefy Bovril, prepared by her cook, who eyed the new guest curiously.

In the evenings, she sat at the dinner table with the O'Sullivans in a ladylike frock, then retired to her room. Yet during the day, the same girl donned a plain linen tunic, and cotton gloves like servants wore, and disappeared. The cook and maids wondered where she went.

~

At each employment agency, Miles heard the same refrain. It was a tight winter, because of the lingering effects of the drought. The rain had come, but the money was still not flowing after years of stock losses and crop failures. The agencies seemed more crowded than they had been in the autumn.

God help anyone with grey hairs, Miles thought. It was survival of the fittest, and the youngest. Some of the girls who waited for work seemed barely older than her little sister Laurel.

Hours passed, then a day. And another. She sat, watched and wrote, until 'Sarah Frankling' was finally offered a position in a villa in another splendid suburb, this time by the harbour rather than the sea.

It was with a Jewish family, the agent said.

Miles remembered how the laundress had advised her to go to a Jewish house if she wanted a good place because they were the cleanest. It was also close to Miss Scott; she could pop up the hill on her afternoons off.

The position paid eleven shillings per week, including washing. It was a small family, the motherly agency lady assured her. The villa was one of her pet places to send new girls.

Arriving at the villa, Miles stepped back from barks at the door. A dark-haired, blue-eyed Mistress greeted her, and introduced the dogs: a Great Dane that was almost as big as Miles, and an Irish terrier that sniffed around her boots.

Miles eyed them warily. She liked dogs. But these seemed untrained, and had the run of the house, although their kennels were outside. The Dane was like a horse. Perhaps she could ride it.

She shivered in the hall. It was a winter's day yet there was no fire. A damp coldness spread throughout the house. The son, 'Levy', showed her around the kitchen and she smiled at his enthusiasm for pointing out where the pots and utensils were kept. A little genius, she thought. And sweet.

The nanny came in, with a personality like mildew. A rising damp that chilled any friendliness.

'What's the Master like?' she asked the nanny, to make conversation.

'A contemptible little old fat cock sparrow of a thing.'

Mr Finlayson had been a cock too. He'd crowed in the morning for his breakfast. Then strutted in front of his hens, who sat docilely laying eggs. She had wanted to wring his neck, and it seemed here the Master of the house would be the same sort of rooster.

Miles tried again, complimenting the Mistress's good looks.

'You won't think much of her looks after you get a taste of her temper,' the nanny snorted, then disappeared with the little boy trailing behind her.

That afternoon, the Mistress of the house—it was still so strange to refer to another woman as her 'Mistress'—demanded a hot water bottle put under her feet for her daily afternoon nap. Miles had never heard of a siesta, so she assumed it was laziness rather than a custom.

Closing the main bedroom door, Miles seized the free moments, and headed to her own room to unpack and inspect.

Inside her new space, she looked around in dismay. Cobwebs were spread across the chest of drawers. When she sat on the bed, she began to itch, so jumped up again and stripped the sheets.

The Irish laundress had been right about the Finlaysons' house. The family had been irritating but, once she recovered from the burns, she found it so small and organised that it was easy to clean. Most of all, it was a healthy home.

Here in the damp villa, she was sure she was going to get sick. The laundress had told her to expect cleanliness. She was sure other Jewish houses were immaculate, but she did not know what to make of this family. Only that she would have to make up a name for them in the book. Perhaps *Michelstein*.

~

After a restless night. Miles woke, fretful.

There was no laundry help, so she washed alone in the corrosive suds in zinc tubs and hauled the clothes and linen out herself to rinse. There was no mangle to wring the clothes, so winter-cold water dripped over her as she wrung them by hand until she feared her wrists would break. Her nose became numb and her hands wrinkled.

Outside the laundry room, dogs lolled in the sun in a constant rest then were underfoot eating the scraps and treats from the kitchen as she made dinner. She was not to shoo them out, the Mistress ordered, as she lovingly patted each one.

Now Miles understood what the employment agency lady meant. It was a pet place.

The 'contemptible cock' arrived home from a business trip, and he lovingly kissed his wife, son and little daughter. Miles eyed him surreptitiously. He was shorter than his wife, fat, and wore spectacles.

As she washed, she peeked outside, and was astonished to see him cleaning out the dog kennels. Later in the day, he looked after the children when the nanny left for her afternoon out.

Miles realised that, in this house, he wasn't a rooster. He was a lovable chicken.

~

After another night's restless sleep, Miles woke again in a mood. She decided that two days' experience was worth two months', so 'Sarah' gave a week's notice.

She was freezing. When she wasn't shivering, she was itching.

Miles burst out of Sarah. She was feeling fretful again. Bratty.

The house was a muddle, Miles told the Mistress, explaining her sudden resignation. Dirty, she blurted, forgetting it was a maid's job to clean without complaint. The laundry washing room was next to the kennels, she added.

Insolence.

Silence.

Miles waited, hoping for an instant dismissal.

'You said my house was dirty. I'll make you clean it,' her employer snapped.

For the rest of the week, the Mistress followed Miles as she scrubbed the house from top to bottom. The Mistress tested windows for dust with her finger, and wiped her foot on floors and carpets for grime.

The nanny watched Miles work. She'd never seen the house so turned out, she told her later in amused astonishment. Miles winced when she remembered the nanny's warning about the Mistress's temper. She should have listened.

Miles, however, had her diary, and the book she would write from it. 'Wait until I write the book,' she thought. Then she'd show readers how cruel women could be to one another. It was going to be ugly.

~

At the end of her notice week, Miles lugs her trunk a mile up the road. Her nerves are jangling, and the palm of her hand is blistered again from when, tired and stressed, she slipped as she struck a match when trying to light a candle.

She is grateful to be able to go to Rose's home, Lynton, acutely aware that some girls have no home and endure excruciating circumstances until they find a new placement that will provide them with a roof. No refuge of roses and salons for them.

After a rest, she returns to the agency to let them know she has resigned; they have already heard the news.

The Mistress has told the agency she had to let her new maid go, because she was 'not quite strong enough for her work. But she was very quick and dainty and nicely mannered.'

Miles is dainty and, yes, she is quick. She will reserve her strength for somewhere else.

29

It was now midwinter. Miles' criteria for a new position became more stringent. She wanted warmth, and safety in numbers. She would avoid lonely cubbyhouses, and damp villas where she was the only maid. She needed some kitchen solidarity; she would only accept positions at bigger places, where they had more staff.

The agency lady whispered in one of the waiting girl's ears.

'No fear,' the girl said.

The agent called out. 'Perhaps some other girl would like to try this place? It is a parlourmaid position in a "first-class" boarding house.'

Miles was intrigued by the chorus of 'no fear' and girls looking away. Boarding houses were renowned for being hard work. Full of demanding travellers, or long-term residents who did not want the fuss of a house and their own servants, or people who were in the midst of establishing their own cubbyhouses and castles. Boarding houses were for the elegant homeless.

Miles agreed to be interviewed by Mrs Vance, the boarding house owner, who surveyed her with approval.

'Let's try each other out,' said Mrs Vance. Miles thought that she seemed kind.

The following day, Miles was optimistic as she got on the ferry and alighted at Kirribilli wharf. She walked along the water to the boarding house, named Elsiemere, which was shaded by ferns and by frangipanis bare of flowers in the winter wind. It looked welcoming. Smoke floated from the chimney, promising cosy fires.

With four others, Miles, a junior parlourmaid, was expected to help serve all meals to the guests in the dining room, and attend and clean the library and sitting rooms, as well as help turn down the beds in the rooms at night.

Miles presented herself in her uniform, a black-and-white frilled tunic that she had been asked to buy. The other parlourmaids laughed at the demure lace cap she had added for effect.

'Look at her pretty cap, and just take stock of her manner,' Alice, the head maid, said. 'It's like the blessed toffs themselves. I bet the old lady will be delighted with it.'

Alice told Miles that they tore off their caps at night and she warned her not to wear her maid's uniform outside work, as it was a 'badge of slavery'. Alice had dark rings under her eyes and premature lines, although, like Miles, she was only in her twenties. Miles watched her lean against the banister for mini-rests, shifting from limb to limb. She noticed that Alice watched the guests like she did, observant rather than subservient.

When Alice told her, 'These women have nothing to do but just be kept in ease and luxury, and dress themselves like dolls for the pleasure of men. All rich women seem to be toys, and the poor ones slaves,' Miles knew they would be friends.

As dawn broke over her first day, Miles went into the drawing room to clean and dust the large grate of dead coal and coke ashes; to set the pantry in order; to clear the early-morning washing up; and finally to light a spirit lamp to heat coffee and boil water for tea. She was now immune to the flames that shot up with alarming unpredictability out of every kitchen stove, lamp or match. How many maids had been fatally or grievously injured in workplace accidents, only to be discarded like soot in a fireplace? The papers only reported the deaths, never the injuries, unless they happened to a famous writer who was secretly working as a maid.

As breakfast time arrived, she readied herself for the 'zoo', as Alice and the other girls dubbed the dining room. It doubled in size when they opened the white folding-door partitions that stretched like an albatross's wings. The dining room was lined with mirrors, which faced the windows overlooking the water. As the light caught her reflection, Miles looked like she was walking on broken glass.

The girls named the guests after animals, because they were too tired, and the guests too annoying, for them to learn their real names. There was The Old Goat. The Sharks. The Wild Bull. The Birds' Nest. The Donkey family, and their elderly relative The Old Ass. They would be joined by the Stuffed Monkeys, and later by The Dog and The Giraffe.

Miles rushed from table to table.

Beyond the harbour, an albatross flew, with white wings as big as partitions across the ocean sky.

The days became the same. She woke at dawn and finished at ten o'clock at night, only to wake again at dawn in a cycle of murmured exhaustion that began and ended in the glow of distant ship lamps on the water through the bedroom window.

Miles had been given a bed beside Alice. Every night, she opened their window a crack for air, and then crouched over her diary on her narrow cot across from Alice. As she wrote, Alice watched her curiously from her bed. Miles considered Alice. It was only a matter of time before Alice asked about her diary. She missed nothing; it was a survival trick she'd learned after being orphaned.

Miles whispered.

'I knew it!' Alice exclaimed. 'I knew from the start by your funny little ways that you weren't a common slavey.'

Miles put her finger to her lips and Alice quietened: 'You can trust me.'

Her tone of self-congratulation, for divining that Sarah was not who she seemed to be, now became serious.

'It's to be hoped you succeed, for God knows, poor slaveys want someone to speak up for them.'

For once, Alice didn't look tired.

Miles held back her name from Alice, because that would have been too much of a risk. But it was a relief to share her secret with someone who was not shocked, horrified or afraid about her working as servant.

It was the life of Alice and the other maids that Miles knew she was living. Alice herself did not have the time or energy for drama. It was enough for her to get through the day.

It was a routine day when Miles, pretty in her parlour uniform, opened Elsiemere's door to greet a new guest. A gangly woman threw a fur coat at her, and Miles stepped back under its soft weight and the shock of recognition.

'Ma'am,' she greeted the woman, who strode past her, leaving her luggage at the door. Miles checked herself, as well as the coat. As if the new arrival would recognise this girl in a servant's uniform as someone she had met at an Admiralty House function last year. That young woman had been a celebrated author; she had swanned in on Rose Scott's arm and the other guests had gathered around her to ask about her book.

The woman who ignored Miles in her parlour uniform was a naval officer's wife; Elsiemere was to become an unofficial barracks for a group of navy officers attached to Vice-Admiral Arthur Dalrymple Fanshawe, who commanded the *Royal Arthur*, and was Commander-in-Chief of the Australia Station. The Giraffe, as the girls gleefully dubbed her, was the first to arrive and join the zoo.

It was after midnight. The harbour and the boarding house on its shore were still.

Later, Miles wrote that she woke with a noise and saw *a head and shoulders—brawny shoulders they were, and a close cropped bullet head and heavy moustache silhouetted against the silver of the sleeping night* at their open window.

She feigned sleep. She glanced over at Alice, who slumbered on, unknowing and uncaring.

The shadow came into focus. Miles was still. She felt strangely unafraid.

The intruder fumbled through the window. She heard him pant and puff, and saw through her regrown lashes that he looked anxious that he might have made a noise.

She should be the one feeling anxious, but Miles instead was irritated. She needed her sleep, and he was so clumsy and amateurish at this robbery business.

He looked confused about which way to go. Her annoyance turned to pity. She thought he must be desperate to be attempting such a difficult entry. She resisted jumping out of bed and telling him that there was an easier way to break in, through a broken lock on the drawing-room window. From there it would be a quick steal to the silver.

Instead, she remained still. Alice slept on. She waited to see what his next clumsy move would be.

But he did not bend over her or Alice's bed, or creep into the other girls' section of the room. He vanished out of the room.

It is breakfast after the burglary. The guests with animal heads gather, with the maids as their keepers, and news spreads through the zoo. The donkeys, sharks, wild bull, giraffes, birds, monkeys and goats rush to their nests and dens and lairs to check that there are no missing valuables. But the burglar has, as Miles had anticipated, stolen the silver and disappeared.

A silver snatch and grab. Except it all happened so slowly and was so fumbled that it will only be a matter of time before the burglar is caught at someone else's window.

When the police arrive after breakfast to investigate, they line up the maids like suspects. Miles stands with Alice and the other maids as the officers leer at them and appraise which maid would make a better prize than the boarding house silver.

Alice snaps at the officers, and Miles admires that her friend is so fearless. She itches to slap the police officers' faces.

A few months ago, she would have. But in her uniform, she is invisible, and her slap would be a puff of air.

30

It was August. A royal commission into the decline of the birth rate was announced because women were not falling pregnant at the rate they used to, and something had to be done about these females who weren't doing their duty for the new nation. At his *Evening News* desk in the city, the editor selected a letter from 'Mother'.

She suggested the commissioners could easily find out the reason for the birth rate decline. All they needed to do was to visit the Infants' Home, the Foundling Hospital and the Benevolent Asylums, where 'they will find 50 per cent of the children are fathered by married men'. 'Mother' added that it was up to the wealthy to have large families, for they could afford to feed them.

The letter stirred the editor. He was the Man from Snowy River. He enjoyed his Australian Club comforts, his horse and his wife. They were now contributing to the birth rate, for his wife was with child. This baby, and another one, would be enough.

In the harbour, a steamer carrying a Sultan collided with another ship near Goat Island, and the sounds of crashing steel and blowing horns drifted on the wind to the boarding house that sat on the harbour's northern shore. Inside, Miles and the other girls fed the zoo and cleaned their rooms. The girls were Miles' new sister keepers, and together they would not fall.

The burglary had rattled Mrs Vance and she ordered Miles to keep her window closed. Miles missed the harbour breeze at night and wanted to break out, rather than worry about someone breaking in. She was in a mood again. Restless. Bored. She would move on, soon. Meanwhile there were new guests to look after, as the officers had arrived; they had taken over the cottages attached to Elsiemere, and its upper floor. On the boarding house's flagstaff, the navy flag caught the wind.

'Oh, fascinating brass-buttoned uniforms and naval caps!' Miles wrote.

Apart from their senior officer, who was married to The Giraffe, the other three officers were young, single and brassy. This would be fun.

That evening, when the officers joined the zoo in the dining room, it was overflowing, with hungry guests stretching in every direction. The white-clothed tables became a blur of signals and beckonings, of calls and whistles for Miles' attention.

Holding plates of beef and lamb, Miles didn't know where to look. She felt her heartbeat surge and her arms seize up. She struggled not to drop the plates. With a silent smile, she put them on the nearest table of officers and rushed outside to the stairs.

As Alice did sometimes, Miles leaned against the banister. It was quieter there, although she could hear the hoots, cackles, growls and roars from the zoo.

The sickening paralysing of the limbs, and stopping of the heart.

Alice came out.

'What are you doing!' We are . . .'

Alice stopped her reprimand, seeing Miles with her eyes closed and holding her chest.

'Worry, worry,' Alice said gently. 'You'll be grey before you are 25. No one dare say a word to you while I'm on the warpath, and Tessy is going to take the officers.'

She took Miles' hand. 'Come on in. You're not afraid of burglars, and yet a few young boys and some harmless old women nearly make you faint.'

One of the other maids, Cassandra, asked Miles to join her on the nightly turn-down service before dinner. Cassandra wanted to have a companion; since the break-in, shadows in the darkened hallways had made her jump.

They knocked on the door of one of the officers, the flag lieutenant, Arthur Bedford.

'Can we come in?' Cassandra called. The longer they stood in the dark hallway, the more she felt jumpy.

'Wait till I throw on a dressing gown,' he said from behind the door.

Miles blushed. She wanted to faint again. She would much rather be in the dark. She turned away from the door, and suggested instead they leave it until later, after dinner when the guests were hopefully not yet in their rooms.

'I tried that once and they complained to the Missus and she gave me rats,' Cassandra said. 'Don't blush so. Love, they don't take any notice of you. You are no more to them than an animal.'

The door opened. While they turned down the bed, the officer waited in his gown outside.

Miles burned, but this time it was not from a pilot light. The navy officer, who was lounging in his monogrammed silk, was not much older than she was. He lingered by the door with a lazy, flirtatious smile.

Cassandra was wrong; he did notice them. Miles felt like now she was the exhibit in the zoo. A flighty deer.

She helped Cassandra hurry through their turn-down duties.

'Thank you,' Cassandra said to the lieutenant.

'Don't hurry, ladies. I'm at your disposal for any length of time.'

They shut the door on his silky back.

Over the next days, the larger zoo became easier to manage, and Miles found enough breath between servings to pause by the officers' table for some Shakespearean banter to ease her nerves.

Bedford asked for vegetables, and Miles gave him cauliflower.

'Hold the siege,' she flirted, 'and I'll ply you with potatoes.'

'Your tongue, I perceive, hat [*sic*] a turn for wit,' he replied.

'As yours for satire—Sir!'

As she darted to the next table, he watched her, amused and bemused. He'd grown up with servants and none of them spoke with her educated wit. He was sure she had a secret.

Miles wanted to share more of her secret. She had a plan; if Mrs Vance found out, despite her kindliness and calling her a dear little girl like Rose did, she'd be dismissed for unacceptable familiarity with guests. But, as Alice said, she was a 'game little kid'. She had no idea why everyone called her a child. Perhaps it was her nose.

That night, while serving dinner, she left a note for a friendly American honeymooning couple under their plate.

The couple would soon be leaving the country, so she felt her secret would be safe with them. Plus, the husband was the only man she'd met so far as a servant who would open a door for her or throw an arm up to grab something she could not reach. Equality wasn't at arm's length with him.

The couple immediately whispered an invitation to their room for supper the following evening. At the appointed time, Miles slipped into their room, quieter than the bungling burglar. It was a relief to be herself again.

'You must be wonderfully brave,' they congratulated her. 'Tell us about your book? Will we be in it?'

Miles nodded, laughing.

'Have you finished now?' they checked, not wanting to get her into trouble.

'Yes, I'm early tonight, and Alice has let me off and I do the same for her at other times.'

'Say, how can you stand it? How much do you get for this?' the wife asked.

'Ten shillings a week.'

'How much is that?' the wife asked, turning to her husband.

'About two dollars and a half,' he calculated.

'My God!'

On payday, Mrs Vance always gave the maids a pay cheque addressed to 'Miss', which they appreciated and later exchanged for a half-sovereign coin, worth ten shillings. It was a day's wage for a skilled tradesman, or a week's pay for a maid.

Miles studied the small gold coin in her hand. Perhaps Cassandra was right: working as a maid made them so invisible that this light coin was the only weight they could carry.

The girls noticed that, with each passing week now, Mrs Vance was handing each maid their ten-shilling cheque more reluctantly and was eyeing each maid as she did so, evaluating their worth. Mrs Vance had taken on an extra after one of her regulars, Amy, had collapsed and been sent on holidays. No holiday pay accompanied Amy's ordered leave and now she had returned; there were six maids, and they knew Mrs Vance would soon be looking to pay five.

Cassandra felt the mood. As she and Miles talked about it, she began to cry: 'I haven't got enough money to leave on and have no home or friends to stay with.'

Miles took her hand. 'I have business that will take me home,' she explained.

It was a half-truth. She had a home, and she had her mother, as much as they fought. She had her father and his mad plans; and she had little Laurel, now 11, who had sent her a letter about her schoolteacher.

'Her name is Mrs Free. She might be free but she does not let us be very free, and the cane is very much used since she came,' Laurel complained in her careful yet wobbling handwriting.

'My little pig is beginning to grow nicely and he eats a terrible lot,' she added. 'I am in the School library and I get a book out every Friday . . . One of the little calves died, that one who used to follow us everywhere we went.

'This is all, goodbye, heaps of love . . .'

Then she remembered how she had been taught to formally finish a letter:

'Your loving sister, Laurel Franklin.'

Miles was delighted. Another writer in the family.

The calls and letters from young women to the single officers were incessant. It was especially irritating as they often called at lunch or dinner time.

'Answer all my messages,' Bedford instructed the maids.

When the maids did the nightly turn-down, they noticed the invitations to balls and parties that hung from the mirrors in their rooms. There were lists of dates, with notes such as 'divinity', 'fat' and 'little fairy' scribbled beside their names.

'They are a pack of cads,' said Alice. One of the other maids looked up the girls' names in the telephone book.

Miles would have liked to go to a winter ball, but she had asked her fairy to turn her into Sarah Frankling, the maid, who worked for sixteen hours a day and often felt too tired to walk, let alone to dance. Cinderella was a fairy story and, as the dance cards hanging on the officers' mirrors showed, only fairies went to the ball.

Until, on a winter morning Miles was in the entrance hall. She stopped, and listened. A guest was playing a waltz on the piano in the drawing room.

She looked around. She was alone.

She would go to the ball.

Putting her left foot forward and holding out her arms to the air, she began to dance down the hallway.

As the front door at the end of the hall opened, she danced into a breeze, and she saw a body with brass buttons take shape, and an offered hand.

They waltzed together in the hall that had become a winter ball.

'I'm surprised! Mr Bedford!'

They stopped. Mrs Vance was standing in the hall, hands on hips and aghast over her spectacles.

'I assure you . . .' Bedford began, 'I really assure you.'

'Sarah! I will speak to you!'

Miles, the dancer who was Sarah the parlourmaid, had been caught dancing the waltz with a guest. An officer. Meekly she followed Mrs Vance as Bedford watched, worried about what would happen to his Cinderella.

The music stopped.

In Mrs Vance's office, Miles stood with her head bowed. She braced herself for a dismissal, reminding herself that she would be resigning soon so Cassandra would still have a home.

'I'm surprised that you let a young gentleman take such a liberty with you.' Mrs Vance scolded like Miles' grandmother.

'I had a tight rein on him, ma'am, and he's only a boy.'

Mrs Vance tried to stay stern. The girl was so charming and smart.

'Of course, I forgot you were a grandmother,' she quipped. 'I know there was no harm in your frolic, dear, but a girl in your position has to be so careful, lest a wrong construction be put upon her actions.' She paused. 'Gentlemen are apt to treat a girl in your position lightly.'

Miles felt the verbal slap.

The words stayed with her. She had to write them down. *Always that slur: A girl in your position.*

Bedford was still in the hall when Miles came out of Mrs Vance's office. He relaxed with relief when he saw she wasn't crying and that she had not been dismissed.

'I believe you had to be corrected for dancing with one of the maids,' she teased him. 'I'm surprised, sir!'

She would decide her position. Not Flag Lieutenant Arthur Bedford, nor Mrs Vance, nor anyone who chose to tell her what she did not choose to hear.

~

During her last days at Elsiemere, Miles felt regretful. She had stayed the winter, and Mrs Vance had pressed her to stay on for spring. 'Sarah' was not the maid she had had in mind to let go, but she understood that a deal had been done between the girls in the spirit of kitchen solidarity, and so she promised Sarah a place if she ever wanted to return. She asked Miles for her Penrith address, and Miles gave it. She must tell her mother not to return-to-sender letters addressed to Sarah Frankling.

Alice watched as she packed her bag. Early the next morning, Miles could hear the other maids getting ready to feed the zoo.

At the front door, Alice leaned wearily against the post. Miles was startled to see tears. Alice never cried.

'You did give me hope to struggle on,' Alice said, kissing her goodbye. 'But without you . . .' She faltered.

~

A train, and a pony ride from the station. Miles hasn't been home since Easter, and she is now back in the land of melons.

Her mother coughs as she opens the door. Laurel is feverish in bed. Miles realises that her half-truth that she was needed at home has now become wholly true.

It is called the Influenza Fiend and the Kissing Peril. It has spread in the last of the cold snap of winter. Miles keeps the fire high, and brings steaming tea to her mother and sister. They struggle to sip between fits of coughing that leave them gasping for breath.

Miles' mother recovers. Laurel's cough turns green; her fever is not an artistic rush but a dangerous spike. Miles strokes her sister's head, gives her broth and tells her stories.

Laurel sleeps. Miles thinks how innocent she looks. A child, whose spirit is bright and clear as the bush sky.

Miles writes to Linda at Granny's Talbingo station. Clutching Miles' letter, Linda rushes to find paper and ink:

'Dear little sister. If only I could be with her . . . If only I could help you . . . Where there is life, there is hope. Is Laurel conscious? Tell her I am coming to see her & give her my love.'

On the first Sunday morning of October, two children in Melbourne who have been missing since Wednesday, turn up alive at their home, explaining they've been living on berries and leaves, and slept in paddocks. In New South Wales, where a giant cat was mistaken for a tiger, a circus lion tamer rests after being bitten by his prize lion. In her cell, Selina Sangal, the mother murderess, thinks of her baby girl. Rose Scott has left Sydney for a lecture tour; the artist Norman Lindsay goes for a ride in the park with the Man from Snowy River. In the splendid suburb by the sea, the Finlayson family gather around a meal that their new general maid has cooked; and in the boarding house on the harbour, Alice and the maids feed the zoo their Sunday dinner, wishing Sarah was still with them.

In Penrith, Miles sits beside her young sister as she passes, bright and pure, beyond the Sabbath's night.

31

Granny's local paper, *The Adelong and Tumut Express*, reported the death of her granddaughter, Laurel, sister of 'the authoress'. In Penrith, Miles began to cough; then she collapsed, ill with influenza and sick with sadness.

It was weeks, nearly the summer, before Miles was well enough to travel again. Rather than return to Granny, Linda remained to help their mourning mother, who had lost two daughters now: one to stillbirth, after Miles was born, and now Laurel to pneumonia. She feared losing a third, the daughter who seemed so determined to live a life of risk.

The remnants of the flu clawed Miles' throat. Laurel did not have a chance to live many experiences. A tiny body, a tiny life, buried in the Anglican Cemetery, where Miles' brothers try to remain composed, because boys shouldn't cry, and they knew this struggle too well.

The book could not wait.

Their faces are like a funeral when Miles tells them she's returning to the city, where she will find another place as a servant.

Her mother sighed once more in resignation, but this time it was also a sigh of grief.

In the city, around the corner from A.B. Paterson's *Evening News* office, Miles booked 'Sarah Frankling' into the Working and Factory Girls' Club, near Sydney Town Hall. It was an anonymous place for an anonymous existence, and this suited her mood. The noise of the city startled her, and she shrank from the crowds. As was now her ritual, she inspected her new accommodation for cleanliness. A not-for-profit place, where women working in factories, shops and domestic service could sleep, it had its own wealthy 'patroness'. The club was safe, but in the bath she felt slimy, and she hurried through her wash. However, she appreciated the generosity of spirit to working women it represented. The Ladies' Needlework Guild donated clothes to the factory girls and the government gave blankets. The Arnott's factory donated their biscuits; the Fresh Food and Ice Company gave fish.

Yet, when Miles ate in her room, her food turned in her stomach. She was acutely aware she had only saved some half-sovereign coins, so she must find work soon. First she had to sleep—if only her nerves would settle and the sleeping cook next door would stop snoring. She stuck her fingers in her ears. She tried to sleep on the verandah chair for quiet, but it was too cold, so she woke the cook up, who then turned over and snored again.

During the day, Miles returned to employment agencies for a new position, holding her diary as a lifeline. She went to the home of a clergyman's wife, who said she could not pay normal wages as they were poor. Miles eyed the thick carpets and crystal glasses, and thought that the woman's claims of poverty were as likely as her prayers being answered.

Instead, Miles, still with a lingering cough, accepted a maid position at Keston, the grand Kirribilli home of the family of Richard Edward O'Connor, who had been an original member of the Australian Senate and was now an inaugural judge in the High Court.

'Come home,' her mother urged Miles in vain. 'No necessity to work so hard for the information.'

Rose Scott was pleased at this placement, as if Miles was the distinguished judge's guest rather than his maid, for O'Connor was a favourite of hers. Progressive and dynamic, he had led the support for women's suffrage when it was inching its way through the Senate.

Mrs Sarah O'Connor was more stringent about rules. She said she would call her 'Jane' instead of Sarah, so they wouldn't have the same name; so, just for Keston, Miles added Jane to her list of names.

Linda wrote to Keston, relieved to have another address to send her letters to, lest her sister disappear again. They organised to meet in the city on one of Miles' rare afternoons off.

Linda was still staying with her mother. She was now unwell too; her mother fretted over Linda and insisted on doing the ironing.

'She is a perfect wreck,' her mother told Miles.

Linda was more concerned about her sister. 'I am glad to hear you are alive and kicking but sorry you aren't well,' she reproached. 'It is dreadfully lonely without you.'

Keston's Irish cook, Honore, whom Miles assisted, helped with soothing Miles' loneliness away from Linda and her grief at losing Laurel. She called to Miles with affectionate commands: 'Come here, little chicken!' and 'Little doll!' She had names for the rest of the family too; she called the Mistress of the house 'Old Demon', which, because of her thick Irish accent, Miles heard as 'Auld Daymon'.

Honore explained that the eldest girl, Kathleen, was quiet and not a 'tattler'; she was learning to cook, which was a faddish thing for young socialites to do. So Honore tolerated her attempts at making a cake in the kitchen, and she pretended to agree when Kathleen blamed the oven when her cake burned or didn't rise. The young girl would walk out, shaking flour off her bracelets and leaving the mess for Honore and Miles to clean up.

Honore had no time for the eldest son, Richard, who, like Miles, was in his early twenties. He wore a monocle for effect; Honore looked irritated whenever she saw him, and complained that, during his father's frequent absences, he assumed the role of the master of the house.

'Have you come to grief with young Richard yet?' Honore asked Miles.

'Was he the gentleman at dinner?'

'Gentleman! He wants a boot to be introduced to the seat of his pants! He'll be telling you to do this, or that, but you ignore him. Say, "Are you the Missus?" The Old Demon is the boss.'

Before breakfast was served each morning at the table, Miles had to clean and set the 'morning' room, moving heavy furniture and rugs that were longer, and heavier, than herself, so it would look like the room had slept without a wrinkle. Then she would serve up tea and toast to the judge and his wife, and their six children. She sometimes wished she could snatch their early-morning offering away, as it was, she thought, *disgusting* to eat two breakfasts, especially if the first of these was partaken in bed.

But the little boys' exuberant sweetness was like Laurel's, and they tumbled out and ran to the garden and toys as soon as they were up. Little chickens. The youngest told her that he was writing a book.

'I am too!' Miles whispered, because nobody believed children.

Like cats who sense pain, the boys, Desmond and Roderick, ran to her like she was their nanny whenever they saw her, and snuck into the kitchen to chat with her and snack.

'I heard Mother say she didn't like to crow too soon but that she thought she had a decent girl at last,' Roderick told her, promising not to shoot banana skins around the pantry anymore, because 'Jane' kept it so clean.

'I say, my story is about the Argentine Republic. What's yours?'

As she helped Honore with the lunch preparations, Miles explained it was about the life of a servant.

'Pooh! That won't have any fun in it. I don't think I'll read it,' Roderick said.

'You might like to read it when you're a man, Master Roderick.'

The second-youngest daughter, Winifred, who Honore said was the family favourite, came in as the table was being set for luncheon.

'You're going to stay with us, aren't you?' Winifred asked. 'I'm so pleased; you manage just lovely and I'm afraid to enter the pantry lest I might upset it.'

'I'll stay if I can get through all the work.'

'Do you think there's much work here, Jane?' asked the girl in surprise. Miles glanced at her. She was unusually tall for a young woman—a willowy five foot ten, Miles estimated, with a strong-featured face like her father that suggested power. Winifred leaned over Miles, in height and status.

'I say, were you just saying about writing a book to interest Roderick, or is it real?'

Miles looked up. 'Do you think a servant girl could write a book?' she asked, feeling provocative. The silver she had polished gleamed next to the china plates.

Winifred was thoughtful. 'Don't be afraid to tell me. I'd be most terribly interested. I've got enough sense to see it's not those who have the most opportunities who have the most to show for them.'

It seemed to Miles that Winifred was like her father in more than looks.

Miles and Honore worked from the spring sunrise, at 5.45 a.m., to late evening most days, with a few hours off a week to breathe and feel the rain. As the lady's maid would not lift anything heavier than a hairbrush, and the nanny would only look after the two little boys, Miles and Honore did the main slog of the housework.

There were not enough staff to support the family of eight, Honore complained; but she was a widow, like the laundress at Miles' first house, and had two children to support. She said that her hope was that her 'sweetheart', the police officer who patrolled the grounds and the wharf, would propose by Christmas.

'I think the government ought to pension me off,' she said. 'They make a devilish fuss about the birth rate decreasing.' She looked around the kitchen, at the pile of dishes from the family's breakfasts, and the row of chickens and more piles of vegetables to prepare for lunch and dinner. 'And where's the inducement to be a mother when it won't save you from this if your man dies?'

Despite the long hours, Miles was determined to stay clean and well-presented; she thought Mrs O'Connor would expect her to be so, and would 'upbraid' her, as the saying went, if she appeared dirty. It was already an ingrained habit to keep herself and her room clean. Since she was little, her mother had taught

Miles about purity of appearances, no matter how strapped their circumstances were.

Her mother had never envisioned her daughter as a maid in a uniform. Still Miles kept herself spotless while she cleaned pots and served dripping food. She ironed her washed aprons late at night so they were ready for the morning and, when she woke each morning in the pre-dawn pale light of her room before she started her day, she curled her waist-length hair around her cap with pins in a makeshift smart style that her mother would have approved of, even if she did not approve of her being a maid.

One morning, after breakfast, Miles was passing by the Mistress on her way to the kitchen and nodded respectfully, her hair bouncing under her cap. Mrs O'Connor stopped and scrutinised her cap. Miles touched her cap, wondering if some hair was out of place.

'Your hair,' Mrs O'Connor said abruptly. 'It's untidy. Fix it.'

'Ma'am?' Miles replied, confused. Mrs O'Connor ignored her and walked off.

Miles fled to the comfort of the kitchen, where Honore gave her a sympathetic, knowing nod. That dainty step and small waist were bound to cause trouble too. But she confined herself to consoling Miles about her hair.

'Sure, I knew your hair was too smart to last long,' she said. 'I've seen ten girls come and go in your place during the six months I've been here, and every one of them was picked at about their hair. She pretends your hair is untidy—she wants you to make it unbecoming. Your cap looks too much like a butterfly.'

She scrutinised Miles like Mrs O'Connor had in the hall. 'You don't look enough the real slave, with your toy figure and fairy face.'

It was time for some more advice. 'Little chicken, you'll know when you've travelled in service as many weary years as I have that your body and soul don't belong to yourself, and the upper classes if they dared would like you to shave your eyebrows and hair to distinguish you from them. You must be clean and neat as a machine but not take the shine out of them in any way.

'Do your hair unbecomingly. That's what the Old Demon means by tidiness. Take the advice of an old dog on a hard road, and see how it works.'

Miles did her best to make her hair 'unbecoming', glad her mother was not there to see it. She trudged through the rest of the day, and that night, after ironing her apron, retreated to her diary, which she still kept, no matter how close it was to midnight.

Tonight she channelled Honore, and Alice, who was around the corner at the boarding house. After eight months as Sarah Frankling, she could articulate with cold eloquence what was required to survive as a servant. A girl *must have magnificent health for there will be no mercy on her once she sinks.* She needed *patience,* and a *sweetness of temper.* She must *have none of the ordinary girls' normal desire for pleasure because she will practically have no time to gratify it.*

She must never forget any of her employer's commissions, orders, or requests, tho' be delighted to have her own quite unheeded.

She thought of her hair and imagined if Linda was a maid. The mistress wouldn't bear her prettiness.

She must be sufficiently comely to be smart, yet not so attractive as to win any stray admiration from the male members of the family she serves. She must be refined and clean but be so much a common person that she may with impunity be crammed away in an ill-aired dirty little room behind the laundry, eat in the kitchen and creep out the back gate.

There was one more thing:

To be sensitive will be unfortunate for her.

By the light of every dawn, Miles throws her hair into a messy, discreet bun, which she hopes is suitably unbecoming. It gives her a few more grateful minutes' sleep in the morning and, when Mrs O'Connor passes her, she does not notice her butterfly maid, for Miles has turned herself into a moth.

She has her own quiet rebellion. She makes excuses to go to the house's library, which is lined with books and law journals. It is another ritual of her service at all her placements: to inspect the house's library, and quietly borrow books. The books are not hers but they comfort her, and soothe her hidden sensitivity.

She notices that the days are becoming longer, matching her work hours with the light. When she wakes at dawn, it doesn't feel so dim and cold. She feels the warmth of the evening and decides that in the summer, she will move on to another position. She does not care for Mrs O'Connor. Honore is right: the judge, she thinks, deserves better.

She is thinking she will do her final season, which will take her to Easter, in Melbourne. Then she will reconnect with Vida Goldstein, and once more do her hair any way she likes. For now, the library is enough.

32

The summer was unseasonably wet and cool. A Melbourne columnist declared the weather was like the stripes of a zebra, but to Miles the Melbourne employment agencies felt the same as in Sydney. They wanted the same girls with the same attributes. The same stripes of experience, and character.

Over the past year, Miles had added more attributes to the capitalised traits demanded by the advertisements that she had first read in the grotty tearoom a year ago. To *SMART, QUICK* and *CLEAN*, she could now add *TIRED*. And *HARDENED*.

The other domestics who waited for hours on wooden seats gave her a cursory glance rather than a suspicious stare. Or if they stared, she no longer cared.

She barely noticed the men loitering outside, or the women accompanying them, who rustled their skirts and leaned forward. Their faded silk, exposed legs and their painted faces had once shocked her. If it was raining, cold or searingly hot, or they needed other work, they would come into the agency for shelter; but they would be shooed back onto the balcony, the outside room. Anywhere, so long as they did not sit with the girls inside.

She remembered Mrs Vance's reprimand at the boarding house, when she was caught in an impromptu waltz in the hallway there with Bedford, the young naval officer: 'A girl in your position has to be so careful,' Mrs Vance had admonished.

She was not in the position of the women who were trading their bodies. But she was, in a way, trading her body too by offering herself for positions of domestic service. After all, nobody wanted her mind.

Miles was placed in a grand home in Melbourne's richest suburb, Toorak. It outshone Justice O'Connor's palm-tree-fringed residence in Sydney.

'It's society. One of the best homes in Melbourne,' she was told at the agency.

By now Miles cared little for what an agency said. She knew that to them she was a walking commission, to be traded for a profit. But she had to admit that the mansion in Toorak was more than grand.

At the dinners and balls, she watched in distaste as waiters refilled glasses with champagne—*nauseous fluid*, she wrote—and as the guests digested drinks and meals in their soft stomachs. As she washed up their plates, dishes and flutes, she felt like Mrs Finlayson's laundress, up to her arms in suds, but she was washing crockery instead of clothes.

On one of her afternoons off, Miles went into the city to meet the appointment she had made with a photography studio in an arcade. Defying the advice of Alice at the boarding house to never wear her uniform outside the house, she posed, in her starched white apron, with a frilly lace cap pinned on her piled-up bun, as proof of the life she was leading.

Instead of her preference for an aristocratic side profile, this time she stared directly at the camera, nose straight on. Sarah needed to be seen.

Miles sent a copy of the photograph to Granny.

'I received your letter with likeness and thought it resembled Linda,' Granny replied. 'Now for a scolding. You know well enough what I wrote last . . . I often wondered what had become of you, and I often fear something will happen, you away amongst strangers, and under an assumed name . . . What in the world are you doing?'

Granny knew there was one thing Miles still wasn't doing.

'When you are young, get a good offer. It would be better for you to accept, and settle down. When you get old there will be no chance. You could write all the same.'

Granny admitted that Miles' letters made her laugh, if only she wasn't so worried and scandalised about her behaviour. 'I don't know how you can act that deceitful, I could not and would not for all the books in the world.'

Granny wasn't finished yet. She worried about the impact of Miles' flightiness on her sister and mother, as Granny had heard rumours that Miles was considering moving to New Zealand: 'I suppose poor Linda will soon enough be married before you wander the earth . . . Your poor mother must be lonely.'

Poor Linda. Poor Mother. Poor Miles, having to read Granny's letters.

The Mistress of the Melbourne mansion was gracious and wrote polite notes to 'Sarah' and her staff about the daily routine. On her afternoons off—a whole afternoon—and when the family were holidaying in the country, Miles lay on the grass surrounding the mansion, under the magnolia trees, or if she was returning after dark, took advantage of the permission to enter through the front door rather than the usual less well-lit servant's entrance at the back.

Apart from 'those dinners' that half of Melbourne's society seem to attend, including the new Governor-General and the cricket team from 'home'—England—there was no reason for Miles to leave other than she'd completed her customary eight weeks. Time to move on to a new 'experience'.

The Mistress would not hear of her leaving when Miles put in her now well-rehearsed notice, so she had to try another tactic. She feigned an illness that needed a recovery longer than most would tolerate their maids having and was concerned how worried the Mistress looked. This Mistress was not one to discard an ill maid so easily, and she ordered Miles to go to the doctor.

In his private room, Miles tried to remain poker-faced as he poked and prodded and frowned at her good health. Finally, she couldn't stand it any longer and she confided to him her true problem: that she was really a lyrebird, with a gift of impersonation.

The doctor wondered if he should examine her head. Perhaps the girl was delusional—a maid thinking she was an author. She claimed to be Miles Franklin, working undercover to research the servant question.

He surveyed her for the signs of mental illness. Was she gripping her chair too tightly? He could ask her to draw a circle; a recent study had found that drawing a circle from right to left was a matter of concern. A 'person with a well-balanced brain, such as a mathematician' commenced the circle from left towards the right. Other signs to watch for were a 'habitual contraction of the forehead, resulting from the skin forming eccentric lines'; placing one boot on top of the other when standing or sitting; tapping posts as the person walked; or twisting their moustache.

He studied her. Her forehead was young, smooth and unwrinkled. She did not have a moustache to twist, and she did not play excessively with her hair. Her feet were poised together on the floor. She did seem anxious, but not hysterical. She had an educated voice. And she was a change from the roll call of complaints of rheumatism, cataracts, painful corns, swollen tonsils and 'woes of the flesh' that waited outside his rooms.

Finally, the doctor laughed and made her promise to include him in her book, and he lent her some books. His report to the Mistress did not divulge her secret.

The year she had set aside for her research was nearly up. As a break from washing up, Miles accepted a position as a nanny to a doctor's young children. She only had to keep them fed or asleep and take them out to play, rather than attempt to educate them, as she had during her disastrous stay with her cousins.

When the children were ready for bed, Miles watched the elderly cook prepare the dinner. The cook's head shook with the tremors and she kept dabbing kerosene oil on her forehead, hoping it would stop her trembling.

Miles edged away from the lit stove as the cook bent dangerously near the flames with her kerosene perfume. She had at last recovered from her burns; she had not been left with any permanent scars, and her eyebrows and lashes had regrown lush and dark. She did not want to risk another injury, particularly this close to finishing the year. She felt the now-familiar rush of guilt that this life would not be the rest of her life, and instead be preserved as pages, while the servants she had known in Sydney, and now Melbourne, grew older and weaker.

She knew that Vida Goldstein and her sisters were waiting for her with an open invitation to stay with them in Melbourne for as long as she wished.

Her cap was fraying. Her diary was nearly full.

It was time to write the book; she would dedicate it to all the Alices.

~

Stella, Sybylla, *dear little girl*, Sarah. Around Miles flutter her real names, the affectionate names she inspires, and her impersonated names.

Sarah has served her well. She needs another name now. The critic has heard that she has a new book coming out; he has written to her, commanding she supply more information so he can include this news in his upcoming column.

Miles considers what to do. She needs to distance herself from 'Sarah', as the name would too readily identify her to her employers. She must call herself something else. It will be the name of her book.

When domestic service is discussed, the generic nicknames given to domestic servants are collected together in a named yet nameless group. They are 'Jemimas', 'Mary Anns', 'Lizzies' and 'Janes'.

A newspaper had published a poem by 'The Butterfly' lamenting that the 'Mary Anns' have gone: 'like wings of the morning/They have gone like the last broken glass'.

Miles decides.

Like a butterfly, Mary Ann will emerge from Sarah, just as Sarah transformed Miles, who created Sybylla from Stella.

Stella. Sybylla. Sarah. Mary Anne.

They are all Miles.

33

Easter 1904 was fast approaching. A letter to *The Sunday Times* despaired that a 'holy day had been corrupted into a holiday' and called for 'triumph over temptation'. In Sydney, the Man from Snowy River and his wife sat in the members' stand at the Easter Racing Carnival, away from the revelry of the 'horsey section of the public' that read his books of poetry. He would write another book; this time, he had decided, it would be a novel and it would include horses, races, the outback and a romance.

Damn the critics. As he had once told Miles, give the public the thrills they want.

In Melbourne, the weather was celebrated as being the finest in years. Vida Goldstein, her sisters, Aileen and Elsie, plus their mother, attended their weekly Christian Science testimony meeting at the Athenaeum. They nodded along with the tales of the triumph shared on stage of a faith that had healed injuries, ailments and illnesses. They did not discuss Mark Twain's satirising of their religion: 'I tried Christian Science for a cold. I had a savage cold, too. The test was a good one. I went to a Christian Scientist, and we prayed together for some time. He told me to think I didn't have a headache . . . his directions gave me another headache.' Twain would later profile the church's American leader, Mary Baker Eddy, and observed: 'It is odd and strange to see educated and intelligent people among us worshipping this self-seeking and remorseless tyrant.'

Educated and intelligent, the Goldsteins had invited Miles to their meetings, given her *The Christian Science Journal* to read, and reassured her that Christian Science was not a 'cult', nor an 'aristocratic craze', nor would it give her a headache. Miles had politely listened, for she was their guest and she enjoyed a good story. And to join Christian Science was just one invitation among many to reach her in Melbourne ever since word had spread about that Miles Franklin was in town.

'The most exclusive people want to meet me,' she wrote to Mrs O'Sullivan. She only had her servant clothes, so Vida and her sisters loaned her dresses, skirts and blouses made of silk, organza, muslin, wool and lace, and delicate petticoats that felt soft against her skin.

For a photograph that framed them in an oval border, like a looking glass, Vida and Miles posed with their coiffured hair piled into modest pompadour styles on top of their heads, and signed their names across the frame of their photograph.

But to feel triumphant she did not need a mirror, or a new hairstyle and clothes, or a religion. Her diary was her testimony; time, not faith, had healed her burns. Having completed her year as 'Sarah Frankling', everyone was now talking about 'Miles Franklin' again after *The Bulletin* had revealed her undercover investigation in its Easter edition. As an excited afterthought, she sent him a full-length photo of her dressed as a maid.

'Most seductive,' Stephens replied. But, 'my dear inconsistent girl', he added, the story and headshot had already gone to the printers. She was disconcerted by his response, because to be seductive or inconsistent was not the image she thought she portrayed.

When the story appeared in Stephens' weekly 'Red Page' column, the readers saw her as the 'dashing housemaid' who 'flitted about Sydney and Melbourne's best homes' and was now 'busily writing up her diary'. His column reminded readers that Miles Franklin was 'the girl who wrote *My Brilliant Career*'. His description of her unsettled her as much as him calling her seductive. It reminded her that two years had passed since that success, and they were still calling her a 'girl'.

She was 24 now. They could at least call her a woman.

In Toorak, Miles' former Mistress, who had entertained the English cricket captain and the governor-general, read the *Bulletin* article too. She went into the city and stopped her carriage outside a sandstone building on Melbourne's most exclusive city street, where a discreet sign marked the entrance to the Alexandra Club.

Inside, she listened as the women-only members gasped, speculated and squirmed as they wondered and worried which of their maids might have looked like Miles, spying on them all while she peeled potatoes. They fretted and argued over whether to invite Miles to their club to talk about life 'downstairs', or to send her letters from their lawyers over these shocking 'Maryantics', the quip a woman columnist at *The Bulletin* coined for Miles' undercover life as a maid. They were particularly concerned about any of the maids they had employed recently, who had left within weeks or months.

The Toorak Mistress remembered a small, well-spoken kitchen maid called Sarah. She had peeled potatoes and washed up after dinner parties, but then she'd suddenly resigned with a mystery illness, even after 'Sarah' had been sent to her own personal doctor. She decided that she must speak to that doctor, but she already knew: it was obvious. She was the society dame who was under the observation of 'Mary Anne'.

In the days after the story appeared, an invitation penned on monogrammed paper arrived for Miles, signed with a name that sent her memory shuddering back into her servant clothes. She had flashbacks of guests with soft, stuffed stomachs, and her arms deep in a sink of their dirty dinner dishes. She wrote, excited and anxious, to Mrs O'Sullivan: 'One of my Mistresses over here wants to entertain me and wants me to stay with her.' The invitation, she explained, was from the 'Mistress' of the 'great big house in Toorak', who had sent her new maid to the doctor when she tried to resign because of illness. Now she wanted Miles to meet her for a cup of tea and cake, or to stay in a guest room she had once cleaned.

'I think this speaks well for both of us,' Miles told Mrs O'Sullivan. 'She is simply lovely . . . I hope you will excuse a chaotic scrawl, as I am awfully rushed and engaged for each meal every day . . . Thanking you, dear, dear self for the generous way you have helped me.'

Miles signed the letter, put it in an envelope and rushed out the door. She was going to be late for her next appointment. She was about to meet a celebrated novelist.

On that finer-than-usual Easter day, the novelist Tom Collins waited on the steps of Melbourne's General Post Office. He did not think of himself as bold but he'd recently enjoyed success with his novel about a philosophical drover with two horses, Fancy and Bunyip. If he wasn't bold, he decided to be brave, and wrote to Miles from his country home in Victoria, on the banks of a river where he wrote under a lamp whose glare he softened with his hat. His letter had been forwarded to her and he was thrilled that she was so close; he had plans to be in the city over Easter.

He felt they had much in common, being debut authors from the bush. Except that Miles had been 21 when her book debuted, and his debut had appeared when he was in his sixties. That his success came so late, and hers so early, he could attribute to the saying 'Such is life', which was the title he had given to his novel. These evoked Ned Kelly's last words, before the noose took away the bushranger's ability to speak.

He saw someone wave, and then someone else, as finely boned hands fluttered in his direction. The hands belonged to his friend Kate Baker, a schoolteacher, and her friends, who had conjured up excuses to be on the steps of the General Post Office at the time when he was due to meet Miles.

He was pleased to have on hand his entourage, but he was also irritated, because he wanted to meet Miles alone. She had already captivated him, and he hadn't yet met her in person. He had read *My Brilliant Career* with admiration and now he held the photograph that she'd sent him in response to his letter, in which she was dressed in her servant attire for her new book. She was calling herself Mary Anne.

He'd used a pseudonym too, Tom Collins, but he wrote to her using his real name, Joseph Furphy. And he would call her Miles.

He checked the time on his watch against the clock hour.

She would be here soon.

~

Miles had been flattered but embarrassed by the novelist's letter arranging their meeting, to which she was now hurrying to make on time. It had reminded her of the letters from young women she had received after publication of *My Brilliant Career*, which she had later bundled up for safekeeping.

He described her portrait as having a revealing 'frankness' (her mother would agree with that) and 'courage' (Granny called that *froward*). He said the portrait possessed 'generosity', 'sweetness of disposition' and a 'mental capacity of the highest order'. 'You are an exceptional girl,' he enthused.

His enthusiasm made her nervous. Reality was always such a reminder of the truth. She was yet to publish another book, even though her 'Maryantics' were creating an expectation that one was imminent. She needed to go home, finish writing the new manuscript and see it in print; then the novelist could say she was exceptional.

She had agreed to meet the novelist, but rebuked him: 'I haven't got a tack of brains.'

Miles was relieved to see he wasn't alone. From the General Post Office, the group walked to the gallery in the State Library and Miles relaxed because, while the novelist was fawning, the women who accompanied him were light and lovely. She especially liked the schoolteacher Kate Baker and her friend Molly. Kate celebrated meeting her in 'flesh and blood'.

'I conceived you as another Jane Eyre,' Kate wrote later, 'but you are just yourself, with the daring that can only go with virtue and goodness that is never fearful . . . your book is an almost startling revelation of a woman's heart.'

They sat in a circle under a painting by John Longstaff called *Sirens*. The canvas was a mist of green oil, in which nymphs were singing silently to drowning sailors; the sailors' arms reached out to them as a last gasp of desire before death. Miles' laugh bounced around the gallery.

Furphy observed Miles in the same way he had once watched the drovers who had become characters in his book. The other women in his eyes were like blurred paint. Later he told a friend that Miles was soulful. She was poetic, but slangy. He described her voice as a contralto, higher than a male tenor but not piercing like a soprano. A siren's song.

He was lost.

Miles had more appointments; this time with journalists. Every interviewer wanted to ask her about *My Brilliant Career* and acted like her first book had just come out. 'Please, don't ask me any thing more about it. Be a nice interviewer and not talk about *My Brilliant Career*,' she implored the reporter from the Melbourne *Herald*.

Granny's local paper picked up another interview from *The Book Lover*, which reported that 'no-one dares to mention the title *My Brilliant Career* before her' and that the mystery of her last year's whereabouts was solved, as she'd been working as a maid to research her new book.

The articles appeared after she had packed her small bag and said goodbye to the Goldsteins, then ridden to the port in a carriage decorated with flowers. One of her last Melbourne invitations had been the offer of a guest cabin from the management of a shipping company. She was travelling home on the SS *Peregrine* like a lady, rather than as a maid in steerage as she had been when she arrived.

A steward shows her to her cabin. Sometimes it feels like she could live on *My Brilliant Career*'s fame for more than a hundred years. If only it had brought her money to live on; this new book will bring her better fortune.

There is a knock on her cabin door and the steward hands her a spray of roses. She opens the card and reads: 'I hope that little Miles remains unbroken.'

It is unsigned, and she wonders if it is from the novelist. She puts the flowers in a vase in her cabin and unpacks her travelling bag, which is heavy with gifts of books from the Goldsteins.

As the *Peregrine* steams towards Sydney, Miles reads a novel, *The Roadmender*, set in rural England. The book is written by Margaret Barber who, like Miles, had shielded herself behind a male name, Michael Fairless, lest anyone think of her as a little rural girl.

It has a snake in it: it reminds Miles of her own childhood serpent, which still accompanies her in her waking dreams.

The roses begin to shrivel from the salt air. Somewhere on the steamer, the snake sleeps as she leans over the rails and feels the spray from the sea.

34

It was the last days of autumn. The *Bulletin* articles about Miles were now lying about in drawing rooms, on breakfast tables, libraries and in waiting rooms across the country. At Elsiemere in Kirribilli, at feeding time the zoo gossiped about which Sydney 'superior boarding house' the famous author had secretly worked in as a maid. Alice burst into more uncharacteristic tears, as something about Miles made her cry.

At her weekly salons at Lynton, Rose could say that she had been among the first to know about Miles' secret life as a servant. She had been buoyed by Miles' last reply to her, from Melbourne in March, when Miles teased: 'Dearest, it was good to get a note from you. I had nearly given you up as unfaithful and contemplated finding another sweetheart . . .'

That was cheeky, because Rose had been the last person to know Miles was even in Melbourne at all. And now she had discovered that Miles had slipped back into Sydney Harbour, sailing right past the shore near Lynton, and then disappeared west. Her sources told her that Miles was now a guest of one of the prominent feminists, Cara David, in the Blue Mountains. This was yet another disappearing act and, like Miles' Granny, it was time she gave Miles a scolding.

'This is only a line to welcome you home again though *it was naughty of you* to pass through and never come to see me. It would have been delightful,' she wrote. '*The Bulletin* gave you away . . . everyone knows you are home writing the book.'

Rose could not understand this push–pull relationship. Miles was at times like a child. Her spirit child.

She would not dwell on Miles being so mercurial, and spending time with people other than her. It made her feel ungracious. Instead, Rose turned to work, for that was her solace and it sustained her through disappointment.

There was her usual volume of correspondence. After more than six months' investigation, the findings of the NSW Royal Commission into the Decline of the Birth-Rate and on the Mortality of Infants had been released, and the statistics told a story. Since the turn of the century, births had declined.

Women were selfish, the royal commission decreed; this was the reason for the decline. It blamed 'deliberate interference with reproduction', the unwillingness of women to 'submit to the worry and strain of children', a 'desire to avoid the discomfort of pregnancy, birth and breastfeeding', and a 'love of luxury and social pleasures'. The commissioners recommended that the Poisons Act be tightened and, as a concession to comfort and safety, that maternity wards and private hospitals be expanded, and female toilets provided where women worked.

Rose would have something to say about all of that. First, though, she must complete a lecture tour in the regions, as she was mindful of country women feeling shut out by the city. By the end of the month, she was miles away from Sydney in the Northern Rivers beef town of Casino, where, in a small wooden hall crowded with farmers' wives, she assured one and all that she was not a man-hater but a lover of humanity. She called for the cause of women's equality to continue, for the age of consent to be raised from fourteen to sixteen, and for children to be protected from 'the brutal outrages of ruffians', as that was a crime worse than murder.

She graciously accepted the applause.

As Rose had heard via her sources, Miles had briefly gone home; she had then taken the train that zigzagged slowly from Penrith up the mountains to the village of Woodford, where her friends, the Davids, spent their weekends.

From the train, Miles saw eucalypts clinging to rock, and the blue mist meeting the sky. It was Ngurra Country, and for Miles a sanctuary away from frustrating interruptions by her mother, repeatedly reminding her to finish her chores, or asking her thoughts about housework, dresses or dinner things that Miles did not care about. She tried to be as sweet as little Laurel would have been, or Linda. But after a year of working as a servant, Miles did not want to see another pot, mop or scrubbing brush; she only wanted to hold a pen and disappear so she could write.

At Woodford, Cara's cult was not Christian Science but the cult of vegetarianism, which was reported to be 'making progress' as a fad among the upper classes as well as the middle classes. It was for her migraines, Cara explained, and Miles marvelled at her home gym, with its dumbbells and chest expanders that were meant for training boxers and athletes. Miles listened, fascinated, to Cara's stories of living in Tuvalu, where she had swum nude in the lagoon, traced the islanders' tattoos and learned Samoan while her husband, the famous geology professor Edgeworth David, researched the coral reefs. The professor periodically appeared with papers for marking under his arm, muttering about his students.

There were coral specimens in their house, bleached white from a lack of sea; and pictures of a young Fijian princess, whose royal parents had asked Cara, a former teacher, to educate her in Australia. Like Miles' younger sister, this princess was now only a picture, for she had died from the colonial spread of the flu when she returned to Fiji on holiday. Miles shared Cara's sadness, for Laurel had been her and Linda's little princess too.

On walks, Miles heard the beats of the bush again, and the rushing of waterfalls after rain. She absorbed the stillness. Despite the bracing mountains, she felt an unending flatness. Her pen lay unused on the desk.

~

Linda did not seem herself. Her latest letter showed her to be in an uncharacteristic mood that surprised Miles. Linda was always so stoic and, if you believed facial reading, which was currently in vogue, a refined nose like Linda's suggested harmony, while Miles' snub button-nose revealed that she was vivacious, talkative and petulant.

For once, though, Linda's harmonious nose was failing her. 'I have been worried lately,' she told Miles. 'I don't know what to do about getting married. I am often of a good mind to throw the whole business over. Life isn't worth living with one worry over another. I hope if I do happen to get married you haven't forgotten your promise of years ago to be bridesmaid.'

Linda restlessly asked questions: 'Does Mrs David eat butter or eggs?' 'Do you ever hear from The Banjo?'

Linda listed all their relatives and neighbours having children. The Lordly Phillip—who still thought he was the model for Miles' hero, Harold Beecham—and his wife had had a baby, and Linda knew that she was expected to be the next person to have children if her current unharmonious feelings passed.

'You can be their old cranky maiden aunt.'

The mountain air is making her nose cold but Miles feels the mist of her mood lifting. Perhaps it is the vegetarian food, or Cara's daring stories, or Cara's 'anti-hell' attitude after Miles' diet of Christian Science in Melbourne, or Miles' decision to ignore Granny's advice. She looks through her diary and begins to write.

She pastes extracts from the diary into her manuscript. She writes about waiting for hours at the first employment agency, about Mr Finlayson's aggressive baldness and small feet, and Mrs Finlayson's rolled-up sleeves even though the maid did all the work. She winces as she remembers the stove exploding in her face and becomes wistful about her 'brown-eyed milkman'. She wonders if he has met another girl, and that he only thinks of her now as spilled milk.

She reveals her nose of petulance when she writes that her Jewish mistress at the villa, with her chicken of a husband, was lazy because of her siestas, and that she was a 'bully' and a 'shrew'. But she is affectionate when she writes about the boy.

She remembers feeding the boarding house's 'zoo', and the waltz with Lieutenant Bedford, the officer in the hall. Alice's tears when they shared their goodbye kiss.

Outside, the mountain mists settle, the woods whistle and the birds call for the night. Miles continues to write.

35

In Melbourne, Vida Goldstein stared at the figures for her journal, *The Australian Woman's Sphere*. They were showing a loss like her campaign for a Senate seat had been, in the December election last year when she was the first woman to stand for parliament. It had been exhausting.

Vida wrote to her remaining readers of the *Sphere*: 'I had against me the combined power of the morning and Labor papers, deliberate misrepresentation by two of them . . . As soon as my candidature was announced the enemy prophesised a physical breakdown, and [I suffered] humiliating insults from men at all meetings. From all accounts I stood the racket of the campaign better than most of the candidates.'

If the papers weren't picking apart her policies, they dwelled on her dress. She appreciated the opinion piece that observed: 'No-one thinks of a male politician's dress—unless he should appear in moleskins and a billy can.'

She had hoped the sisterhood would send her to the Senate and into history. But the prediction of a more cynical feminist, Helen Spence, that 'women do not always support other women', had been proven by her loss at the election. Now Vida feared for the *Sphere* as well. She wrote to Miles: 'I am passing through deep waters with the *Sphere*, but I hope to come out alright. Though at this precise moment things don't look at all promising.'

In June, Miles had zigzagged down the mountain again with her manuscript in her lap, then tried to settle into the routine of the Franklin home with those who remained.

It was quieter without Laurel and her two brothers. Norman was settled at a property neighbouring their cousins' the Bridles' sheep property. Her other younger brother, Tal, had left school and was seeking a life at sea, like Paterson's brother who perished on the ship of gold. Her father was still pursuing his own dreams of business that Miles and her mother could see pitching her family back into poverty. Linda had returned to Granny's side, waiting for her wedding day to Charles.

Each day Miles waited for the quiet darkness to write in peace, if she hadn't been able to find time during the day because of interruptions of chores. To escape, and to assuage Rose's feelings, in July she made an effort and met Rose in the city. They had tea with the critic, Stephens, who had a new office in the same laneway as his apartment; he hosted soirees there that rivalled Rose's except that women weren't invited. From what Miles had heard, his salons were heavy with cigars, whisky and ego, a rattier version of the Man from Snowy River's elite Australian Club. It grated that she and Rose were of the wrong literary sex to be invited.

Rose asked her to come to her salons. *Come and stay, little girl*, she invited, as her warmth had returned to Miles. She was always her spirit child.

Back in Penrith, when Miles couldn't concentrate or was worried, she wrote letters, for there was a new sisterhood: the three Goldstein sisters—Vida, Aileen and Elsie—as well as Linda. Of the Goldsteins, Miles felt closest to Vida, who she considered the gentlest and very loveable. Best of all, Vida preferred to talk of politics, literature and America rather than marriage.

But in her latest letter, Vida confided that she was struggling. In the spirit of their sisterhood, Miles offered to write a gratis series for the *Sphere*, because her time in Melbourne had reminded her that her name still carried weight.

'You are a real brick,' Vida replied gratefully. 'I feel torn in two, with the desire to have a story of yours in my paper and a great unwillingness to take advantage of your generosity but I have an inward conviction that I will.'

Vida's mother, Isabella, also wrote regularly to Miles from Melbourne, for she could always find time 'to help a little sister': 'I am glad to hear you have cast the devil behind you (discouragement being the very devil!), that you were pressing ahead,' Isabella congratulated. 'I feel you have been working efficiently, it must have been a help to have Mrs David to chat with you . . . I find Miss R Scott a help too . . . it is curious how that little lady suffers so . . . she is so jealous of other women . . . but what business is that of mine? How horribly human we are.'

Isabella posted to Miles a *Christian Science Journal* article titled 'Christian Science in Relation to Christian Character'. She added as a postscript: 'Many of us have a conceit of artistic or sensitive temperament.'

The article promised that 'We glean spiritual harvests from our own material losses.' Miles dutifully read it, and then returned to her manuscript. Writing was her spiritual harvest.

She could not bear to think about material losses. She couldn't afford it.

~

At Granny's station in Talbingo, rain streamed over paddocks and thunder echoed down the gullies. In the gloom of the storm, Linda had returned to her natural harmonious state and was looking forward to other material things on the horizon, such as a wedding date set for November.

Miles was relieved Linda and Charles were marrying, for their future as well as her own, as it would divert Granny from trying to marry Miles to the nearest bachelor with a horse and some social standing, like one of the Baxter sons from the Stillwater district. The lull in Granny's badgering would be like a honeymoon, until the gloss of Linda's wedding wore off and Granny homed in again on Miles' unwed status.

Linda told Miles to expect a roll of plain pale-green silk to arrive soon in Penrith for the bridesmaids' dresses. The silk was in vogue, as *Weigel's Journal of Fashion*, her mother's faithful fashion guide, had declared mignonette to be 'the most charming of all the pale green shades' for the spring season. Linda explained that she had strict instructions from Granny regarding the fabric's arrival, and to send the bill back to Granny as a roll of silk was expensive luxury.

Linda explained in her letter that Granny had said, 'Tell your sister not to delay about this' and, Linda added, 'Be sure you answer this. If you haven't time, get Mother or someone else to write.' The implication was stay focused on the wedding; Linda and the rest of the family knew what she was like when she was writing a book.

'I will be your bridesmaid,' Miles promised.

When the green silk arrived, her mother pinned the pattern around her like leaves of a lettuce. She knew she must be patient. It would be finished soon—the dress, and the book.

It was a green spring, as *Weigel's* had promised. Paterson's *Evening News* celebrated that this season, the first spring since the drought broke, was a wonder of green.

In its annual spring exhibition, the Royal Art Society of NSW hung Norman Lindsay's pen-and-ink drawing *Pollice Verso (Thumbs Down)* sky high on the wall so as to avoid close scrutiny of its central figure, a group of nudes and creatures pointing at Christ on the cross. This was art so the critics still craned their necks.

Norman Lindsay paced around his studio, alert with fury. He read aloud the critics' reviews to his art model, Rose Soady. He began with *The Daily Telegraph*, which declared that *Pollice Verso* had been painted by an artist with 'an imagination in an advanced stage of decomposition'. He vented to his brother Lionel, who helped him write a letter in his defence to *The Bulletin*.

Across the state, a harvest of rich crops was anticipated. In Penrith, amid orchards crowded with bats feasting off new fruit, Miles received a letter from Rose Scott, inviting her to stay at Lynton. Vida Goldstein was visiting Sydney for a lecture tour that Vida hoped would turn her finances from red to green.

This time, it was Miles' turn to be torn. She should see Rose again, especially with dear Vida there too. The garden at Lynton would be at its spring peak, and the warm coastal breeze would be spreading the scents of jasmine, gardenias and roses. But she felt limp because of a lack of funds, which now kept her awake at night more than her midnight writing. And she had a toothache.

She held a hot water bag against her cheek and rubbed oil of cloves over the source of her pain.

Miles' tooth throbbed. Like the silk, dentistry was an expensive luxury.

'I am grieved to hear you are so down about things,' Vida wrote to Miles after she had arrived at Lynton. She dearly wished to see her friend, and Penrith was much closer than Melbourne.

Miles was so close and Vida's lectures had now finished. If Miles could not come to Lynton, she would try to see Miles en route if she took the train up to the Blue Mountains to see Cara David and eat vegetarian food in the mist.

'I think I know something of what you are going through, because I have the same problem to work out—a financial problem, and I too seem the plaything of circumstances . . . My lectures were the most ghastly failure.'

She had talked about politics; not horses and war, like Paterson had with his successful lecture tours. She confided to Miles that she was frustrated. Vida knew there was a world of interested readers, if only she could manage to get the *Sphere* into their hands in any decent quantity.

She had shared stories with her readers, and with Miles, about her successful American tour in 1902. In San Francisco she had met the organiser of the international women's suffrage conference, Carrie Chapman Catt, and visited Chicago, where the snow turned black as it fell through the polluted air. She'd viewed Utah mountains that made the Snowy Mountains look like hills, ridden dizzying roller-coasters at a giant amusement park, taken train trips across deserts, and met president Theodore Roosevelt, who she thought looked like an owl until he shook her hand with military force in his Oval Office.

She was less than impressed with Congress. It was empty for important debates, and visitors shouted at Congress members from the balcony. Politics in the United States, Vida opined, 'was in the hands of unscrupulous men, who have risen from the ranks and made money'.

Vida did not blame the failure of her recent Sydney lecture tour on Australian women's provincialism, or their fatigue about the vote for women. According to her Christian Science faith, she had failed because of her lack of preparation. Prayer could shape destiny, just as it could heal illness.

Miles only agreed on one thing: failure was ghastly.

Miles put thoughts of failure out of her mind while her mother made her stand still for another fitting of the bridesmaid's dress.

'Stop fidgeting,' her mother snapped.

Miles tried to channel stillness, as if she was one of Lindsay's art models. But she was feeling unsettled, and that made her fidgety. Alice at the boarding house had called her a box of jumping fleas.

She had finished writing her new book and had called it 'When I Was Mary Anne, a Slavey'. She was pleased with the title, and had decided she would try Mr Robertson first, as he'd been so kind with his last rejection, or at least as kind as rejections could be. At the post office, the postmaster weighed the manuscript, and she worried what it would cost to send. The last pathetic royalty cheque from her London agent, Pinker, for *My Brilliant Career* was two pounds.

Miles was fretful without a new writing project. The limbo of waiting, while her manuscript was being read by a publisher in a city office, made her anxious, and the fittings irritated her.

She tried to share the excitement of her mother, her sister and Granny as the wedding day approached.

In her letters, she was polite and reserved but she snapped when Joseph Furphy, the fawning novelist, suggested in one of his regular letters that Australian girls had moustaches. In her reply, she listed a hopeful string of 'some dire mishaps that may befall you'; then she marched to the post office and sent it off.

'I fear I may have offended him,' she told her mother, regretting her letter, which was already en route somewhere between Sydney and Victoria.

'Nonsense. No one ever pays any heed of you.'

Miles was grateful for her mother's matter of factness. It grounded her, as much as she resisted and railed like Sybylla in *My Brilliant Career.* And her mother now understood her as being different to other girls or at least accepted the fact.

Furphy was not put off by her fantasies of his death and sent an earthy reply.

'Well, I never. He's not in the least crushed,' she said to her mother, amazed, as she waved the latest letter from the novelist.

Her mother laughed and, for a moment, her frown lines lifted.

Miles tried to stay 'merrily Miles', as the novelist's friend Kate had dubbed her. He deserved more than fiction, if only because she had been so rude to him with her fantasies of death.

Dear Mr Furphy,

I can't tell what frame of mind I am in at present—one without a rudder somewhat. I don't know if I will bolt off course, or sulk at the post, but don't be alarmed if I do come a cropper in the near future, as I have time to fail to all appearances, and then succeed again before I am thirty; and a phrenologist gave an opinion that I couldn't be crushed,

> because I could never be brought to accept defeat as final. One thing is, I will fight to the finish, even if I marry . . . and he gives me a death in life existence, such you have warned me of.

The novelist had sent Miles the *Discourses of Epictetus* by the Greek philosopher Epictetus, who valued stoicism, integrity and asserted, 'He is free who lives as he wishes to live'. The first page of the book was a reproduction of a painting of the Moirai, the three sisters who determined destiny on their spindle.

Miles was determined to assert her free will, like Epictetus, because her life was not a thread to be spun by fate.

As Linda's wedding day neared, and each new dawn in Penrith brought ever more chatter of domesticity and dresses, of rings and rituals, Miles' mind wandered the earth for inspiration, only to return close to home, as it always seemed to do. She was the lyrebird, who mimicked life around her.

The chatter became an idea. She listened more closely.

Yes.

Her heroine will be a young local woman, Dawn, who is resisting pressure from her grandmother to marry the first local bachelor who proposes, because she is in love with a local athlete and wants to be an actress. As a tribute to Vida and Rose, she will set it against the background of the election in which women were able to vote for the first time.

The story formed in her head. She would create a town like Penrith, with a meltingly hot asphalt road next to the railway station, a pub with three kangaroo weathervanes, and carts full of pumpkins and melons. Linda would be her blueprint for Dawn, for she is so pretty. She imagined herself as an interloper who becomes friends with Dawn and her grandmother—an actress with white-streaked hair, who stays in the boarding house owned by Dawn's grandmother.

With each new dawn, Miles wrote.

It is November, 1904, in the last days of spring. The dress and the book are finished. Wearing her mignonette pale-green silk dress, Miles waits at the entrance of St Stephen the Martyr, Penrith's historic Anglican church, named after the saint who was stoned to death for blasphemy. Outside, its exterior is crumbling from the sun and a rainbow of light filters through the stained-glass window.

She hears the organist, a miniature figure against the soaring gold pipes, play the first notes of the Bridal Chorus, and she begins to walk. She smiles at her parents, Granny, relatives and family friends. She feels slightly out of her body. A ray of light.

Behind her, Linda radiates. At last she is a bride, dressed in a white silk gown and train to meet Charles, who waits with his best man at the altar. Miles hopes that under his vest and jacket Charles isn't wearing the hair-guard made from Miles' hair.

From the side of the altar, Miles watches Linda recite her wedding vows underneath her veil decorated with orange blossoms.

Wilt thou have this man to thy wedded husband, to live together after God's ordinance in the holy estate of Matrimony? Wilt thou obey him, and serve him, love, honour, and keep him, in sickness and in health; and, forsaking all other, keep thee only unto him, so long as ye both shall live?

Charles slides the ring onto her wedding finger, and Granny raises her eyes to the heavens in relief.

After the ceremony, the bridal party is photographed at a Penrith studio in front of velvet curtains. Linda is harmonious and Charles expressionless under his frowning moustache. Looking at the camera under her enormous frilled hat, Miles rests her fingers on her face. She is playing her part as the poised bridesmaid, just as she promised Linda she would, and she tries not to blink as the photographer pulls the cord and the flash pops.

That night is cool, as the *Evening News* had predicted. Miles takes off the dress and folds it carefully away in tissue. She will write to her brother Norman and describe the ceremony for him so he doesn't feel too far away.

In their room, Linda lies in bed, watching Charles move towards her. She has vowed to obey. She knows the Bible, Ephesians 5:21–24: 'Submit to one another out of reverence for Christ. Wives, submit yourselves to your own husbands as you do to the Lord . . . Now, as the church submits to Christ, so also wives should submit to their husbands in everything.' She is shocked at feeling a naked man.

In her room, Miles falls asleep alone on the sheets, obeying her own dreams.

36

Tracts of eucalypts twisted the bush after a summer of bushfires had set the state aflame. It had been a 'tornado of fierce fire and withering heat', and a 'demon of destruction' that mocked too soon the hope for a plentiful season the green spring had promised. In the towns and farms, 'martyrs fell from neighbourly duty', rather than blasphemy, as they tried to save homes and livestock that had only just recovered from the drought. Those who survived cursed nature and, in private moments, God.

In Penrith, the smell of burnt bush clung to the breeze. Miles was now used to the rattling train, the slouching men outside the pub with the weathervanes, and walking on the dusty, hot road and feeling the heat warm her shoes. Rather than provoking irritation, as these familiar scenes had once done, now they provided inspiration for her new book about 'the marriage question'.

In the weeks after the wedding, Linda had written to her from Montrose, the Graham property near Stillwater, where she was now ensconced as the Mistress with her own servants. This letter was Linda's attempt at being happy; she knew that being married was supposed to make one so.

'I have everything I can possibly ever want,' she told herself, as much as she told Miles. 'I am quite happy so far. But at times the most awful homesickness comes on . . .'

She was suddenly cryptic: 'I never want to go through the same week as I had at first. I really wished I could die.'

Miles was curious. Had Linda wished she would die because of the homesickness? Or was it that mysterious part of the wedding night, which was, Linda implied, a nightly death in the darkness?

In her new book, Miles wrote a scene in which the young Dawn confides in the older narrator in her room and parades around in her kimono.

> 'Well, it's this way,' said Dawn, pulling my kimono close about her beautifully rounded throat and curling her pink feet on a wallaby-skin at the bedside as she sat down upon them. 'I heard grandma telling you something about me this afternoon, and I suppose you think I'm a terrible girl.'
>
> 'A beautiful one,' I said, revelling in the curling lips and rounded cheek and chin . . .
>
> 'I want to tell you why I want to be on the stage . . . It's all very well for grandma to settle down now and want me to be the same but . . . just fancy marrying some galoot about here and settling down to wash pots and pack tomatoes and live in the dust among the mosquitoes, always!
>
> 'I'd rather die.'

Miles continued writing throughout the summer in her own smoky land of melons.

~

While Miles wrote her new book, George Robertson considered her earlier manuscript, 'When I Was Mary Anne, a Slavey'.

Stella 'Miles' Franklin, aged 18, in 1898. She began writing *My Brilliant Career* that same year, and it was published in 1901. 'Please on no account allow "Miss" to prefix my name,' Miles instructed her publisher. SLNSW

Miles was compared to Charlotte Brontë, and *My Brilliant Career* to Parisian Marie Bashkirtseff's memoir, *The Journal of Marie Bashkirtseff*, which had a cult following after Marie's death, aged 25, in 1884. 'I am my own heroine': Marie Bashkirtseff. Musée d'Orsay

Talbingo homestead, her maternal grandmother's home, which Miles referred to as her 'Eden'. SLNSW

Miles' youngest sister, Laurel Franklin. SLNSW

Linda Franklin, Miles' younger sister. Miles admired Linda's classic looks and aristocratic nose. SLNSW

Sarah 'Granny' Lampe, matriarch of the Franklin family. Granny was both proud of Miles and frustrated she would not settle down. 'You have a froward heart!': Sarah Lampe. SLNSW

Feminist Rose Scott, c. 1900, who campaigned for suffrage and women's rights. '[I want] men's respect, not their love': Rose Scott. SLNSW

A.B. 'Banjo' Paterson, who saw Miles as a potential partner in work and romance. 'We can do our work all night': A.B. Paterson.
SLNSW

Norman Lindsay, 1904, provocateur, artist and illustrator, who delighted in Miles as 'another Marie' (Bashkirtseff).
ITBF/Wikimedia Commons

To prove her investigation occurred, and for her planned book, Miles arranged a portrait session at Cole's Studio Book Arcade, Melbourne, in her maid's uniform, likely the first 'maid' to pose for the photographer. SLNSW

'Keston', the Kirribilli home of Justice Richard O'Connor, his wife Sarah and their children, where Miles worked undercover as a maid. It is now apartments. 'It was imperative I get work to sustain myself': Miles Franklin, 1903, writing as a maid. City of Sydney Archives

Linda and Charles Graham on their wedding day, in 1904, after a long engagement. Miles honoured her promise to be a bridesmaid and is pictured far left. 'I hope if I do happen to get married you haven't forgotten your promise of years ago to be bridesmaid': Linda Graham. SLNSW

Miles' parents, Susannah Franklin and John Franklin, photographed in later life. Miles' mother had wanted to go to America as a young woman but married instead. SLNSW

Miles with her friend, feminist Vida Goldstein, who encouraged her American ambitions and was one of the first women to stand for the Australian Senate in 1903. SLVIC

The Skipper, "After Suva"

Author Jack London and wife Charmian sailed from San Francisco to Australia in 1907. 'Are you a socialist?': Jack London to Miles Franklin after Miles wrote to him asking for help placing the Mary Anne manuscript in America. C.bigorgne/Wikimedia Commons

San Francisco, April 1906, as fires destroyed the city after the earthquake. 'The whole city crashed and turned into ruin': Jack London.
Multichill/Wikimedia Commons

Alice 'Pops' Henry, Miles' dearest friend and mentor in Chicago. Together they edited *Life and Labor*, the magazine of the Women's Trade Union League. SLNSW

Jane Addams, social reformer and founder of Hull House, where Miles first stayed when she arrived in Chicago. Fae/Wikimedia Commons

William 'Bill' Bross Lloyd, known as the 'Millionaire Red' and his wife, Lola Maverick Lloyd, 1907, who cared for Miles at their home, Wayside, while she was convalescing. Winnetka Historical Society

No longer a 'bush girl', Miles was at ease with Chicago's rich and powerful, such as the Lloyds. SLNSW

Miles' friend and Gloves Union organiser, Agnes Nestor, who campaigned for shorter working hours for women; the ten-hour day was passed into state law in 1909. The eight-hour day would not be legislated until 1938 in the United States. 'To drown the monotony, we sang "Daisy Bell",' said Agnes Nestor of the 60-hour weeks she worked on the factory floor. Moheen/Wikimedia Commons

Miles' friend Zelie Emerson, co-founder of the journal *Worker's Dreadnought*, with Sylvia Pankhurst. Animalparty/Wikimedia Commons

Sylvia Pankhurst, who visited Chicago in 1911 and inspired heiress Zelie Emerson (above right) to join her in the fight for suffrage, and the improvement of women's working conditions in London. Library of Congress

Miles Franklin became secretary to Margaret Dreier Robins, president of the Women's Trade Union League, in 1908. She then went on to become the League's secretary and publicist, and assistant editor of their new journal *Life and Labor* with editor Alice Henry. SLNSW

Working for the Women's Trade Union League, Miles helped to support the gruelling garment workers' strike of 1910, during a bitter Chicago winter. LoomCreek/Wikimedia Commons

Sylvia Pankhurst visited Chicago's gaols in 1911, accompanied by Zelie Emerson and city officials, to check on the welfare of women arrested for picketing during the garment worker's strike. Chicago History Museum

Miles, c. 1910, relaxing on the rooftop of the hotel where she stayed in Indiana Street, Chicago, contemplating her next move. 'What the future holds, I know not': Miles Franklin. SLNSW

It was clear that they would have to cut the voluminous word count and insist on a consistent narrator, as it was too confusing in its present form. At first the narrator was Miles, the undercover author mimicking a maid; then abruptly Miles disappeared and was replaced by 'Mary Anne', the maid. Was she Miles, or Mary Anne? Perhaps, after a year as a servant, she wasn't sure herself.

In his last rejection letter to her, declining the sequel to *My Brilliant Career*, he had warned her that it was acceptable to write about country bumpkins but not the better class. Now, in this book, she had been even more reckless. She had satirised Sydney and Melbourne society by writing intimately about them from the viewpoint of a maid.

The Toorak Mistress who had employed Miles may have been graciously portrayed in the manuscript but she would be horrified to see elite guests parodied as fat social climbers. In Sydney, the row of villas with harbour views that were homes to families who were Jewish was so specific that she might as well have provided the address where she had worked. She'd called the hard-working merchant a contemptible 'cock', and his wife worse. The 'superior boarding house' on the harbour at Kirribilli could easily be identified from her description and she'd made fun of the guests there as inhabiting a zoo. It was alright to break a milkman's heart at the engineer's home, and flirting with a naval officer attached to the vice-admiral was charming; but implying that the other officers staying at the boarding house were cads to the women who called on them sank any chance of her book being published.

Most troubling of all, it was obvious to anyone who knew political and legal circles that the large, wealthy and influential Sydney family she worked for after the boarding house was that of Richard O'Connor, the High Court judge, and how could she call his wife an 'old demon'? The spheres of influence in

Sydney and Melbourne were simply too small and powerful to take such a risk. The servants' feelings didn't occur to the publisher as he read on, then stopped.

Robertson, anxious to get out of his office and go to the summer cricket test, was exasperated at Miles for once again putting him in this position. Despite the author's high-profile name and the conversation-provoking subject matter, it would be fruitless to do anything further with this book, even if he was prepared to tackle its narrative problems.

That fatal gift of impersonation. Miles had said it herself.

He sighed and began his rejection letter.

~

When George Robertson's letter arrived, explaining why 'Mary Anne' was unpublishable, Miles sulked and curled up, dejected, in her room just as she'd said she might in her letter to Joseph Furphy. She put the rejected manuscript in the suitcase with the sequel to *My Brilliant Career* that her mother had rescued from the back of the pigsty. It was filling up with thousands of words that she despaired of ever being read.

There was still one more book. Miles clung to hope for a new dawn of success with her current project about marriage and the women's vote. She reassured herself that this new manuscript she was working on did not insult the better class; the title she had chosen for it, *Some Everyday Folk and Dawn*, promised that, like *My Brilliant Career*, it was full of nonentities.

By March 1905, the new manuscript was finished. She did not have the money to luxuriate in rewrites—she had to get it published or she would perish in Penrith—but she realised that she needed to get a friendly eye on it.

Should she send it to Joseph Furphy? He was now preoccupied with his imminent move to Western Australia and his own writing. She was no longer in contact with the Man from Snowy River, apart from the occasional letter from his sister. Rose was overwhelmed by her own correspondence and lectures, and Vida was mired in financial stress with the *Sphere* in Melbourne.

She could trust one literary friend.

She dashed off a letter to the critic: 'Well, my old demon awoke, and scribbled again. If I send you the MS result, will you read [and] tell me if it will add to, detract from, or leave stationary my career.'

She was intending to wait for the critic's reply. Then she calculated the cost of her waiting time in shillings and pounds; soon after she posted her letter to Stephens, she posted him the manuscript anyway, 'so you won't be able to refuse', and also sent the manuscript to George Robertson's publishing firm, Angus & Robertson. It was her fourth attempt at a book, and another that she had painstakingly written in longhand.

She walked away from the post office. She was not yet 30; if the phrenologist was right, she could not be crushed.

~

The mail between Penrith, on the outskirts of Sydney, and the city centre, where A.G. Stephens lived and worked, only took a day by the rattling train. On 31 March, the news was dominated by a police court hearing that involved illegal gambling houses. A married woman, who had jumped into Sydney Harbour and been rescued by two labourers, was 'suffering the effects of immersion'. There was news about the upcoming annual Easter Show and increases in the price of fruit.

There was nothing so sensational or captivating that it diverted for long the attention of the critic in his office, so he soon turned to the pile of parcels and envelopes that awaited opening.

He recognised the handwriting on an envelope. Miles.

With his critical eye, which the artist Lindsay so loathed, he scanned her request for him to read her latest manuscript, about people who weren't 'swell'.

The Mary Anne servant manuscript had been dirty laundry because of the risks of being sued, and they were aware that Miles would take some convincing to change anything, because it was widely known that she was still angry about the 'toning' changes to *My Brilliant Career* and being called a 'girl'.

But she'd now written this new book, which she called *Some Everyday Folk and Dawn*. Whether there were 'swell' people or not in the pages, he worried that, only a few months after her last attempt at a book, it was too soon to have produced a novel that was ready for a publisher. She wrote so fast; driven by that fever, her ideas and words were thrown on the page. Then, when the fever abated, she did not seem to take time to rest, or to review what she had written.

The manuscript hadn't yet arrived, but he knew from the urgency of her letter it would be another rushed draft. He feared that, if she kept going at this frantic, feverish pace, without further publication and payment, she would not have a career at all.

My Brilliant Career was a tour de force and Henry Lawson, bless his alcoholic liver, had recognised its potential. She needed another mentor. He knew Paterson had tried, but he was too intent on his own glory and, from what Stephens had heard at his Friday-night literary soirees, too intent on Miles herself.

He did not have time to read 191 pages of a rough first draft.

He sighed. A deep low sigh, similar to George Robertson's when he appraised Miles' drafts. The sigh of an editor and publisher who held her hopes in his hands.

He would think of a solution. Some way of giving Miles hope.

'Do you think of me as a leisurely person gloating over 191 pages of MS? When I see 191 pages, I dodge,' the critic replied:

> Now, use this if you want to . . . I have an idea that the *S.M Herald* wd like to get hold of a young, attractive, stylish, good looking, intelligent, teasing kind of person . . . It would be an opening in journalism, would enable a country girl in Syd [Sydney] if she wanted & might be worth £3 or £4 a week.
>
> If you ever hear of such a yg [young] person, she might write to Mr. T.W. Heney, editor spontaneously, as if a great idea had struck her . . .

Newspaper journalism for women meant being the women's editor for a newspaper, endlessly describing fashion trends or offering housewifery tips. She wouldn't have minded editing the sassier column in *The Bulletin*, which had published a story about her upsetting the Alexandra Club in Melbourne, but, given the fears of publishers about her social satire, she'd probably end up being sacked or sued. Some of the magazines were becoming interesting, though; she was intrigued by the recently launched *New Idea*, which had published an undercover account of life in jam factories, as well as articles encouraging women to swim.

It took Miles less than a day to spontaneously act on the critic's solution to her financial and literary failures. She would see what the *Herald* offered, if anything, because everything she wrote now seemed to rot.

In autumn, a thunderstorm and rain sent the debris from the fires rolling into villages, burying the ashes deep into the soil on which the Marulan Tiger had once roared. And, in late May, Miles rushed to the newsstand and looked for an article by 'Vernacular'. The *Herald* editor had reluctantly agreed to Miles using this pseudonym for her articles; he preferred his celebrity authors to be named, as Paterson was before he became a rival editor at the *Evening News*. He missed Paterson.

Miles had been insistent. It was difficult to explain that the name Miles Franklin now only reminded her of her one-off success, and she wished to forget it ever existed. She wanted a new name, or an old one that felt safe, like her first name, Stella, which her mother, Linda and Granny still called her and had done so since she was born. They recognised that 'Miles' was a character she had created.

A year ago, she'd been in Melbourne with Vida, and the newspapers and magazines were writing about her. Now *she* was the journalist. She liked the anonymity of it and, under the cover of 'Vernacular', she relaxed. She still wrote fast, but the editor was used to journalists' hurried copy; he appreciated her style, and was prepared to clean it up.

Paterson noticed and tried to woo her to the *Evening News*. Instead, she later wrote for *New Idea* a memoir of working briefly as a student nurse, in the year before *My Brilliant Career* was published. One day she might utilise that nursing experience for more than an article; for now it served a printed purpose.

She mainly wrote travel pieces for the *Herald*, and its editor encouraged her social opinions, except for the Mary Anne stories because, like Robertson, he had an aversion to being sued. Her eye went deeper than pretty scenery, as much as she enjoyed writing pretty scenes. She wanted people to know the land, not just admire it or talk about its hardships. She arranged a meeting with a minister who had some influence and family connections, and watched as country boy after boy came in with hat in hand and asked for a job with a uniform in the city.

She wrote: 'They were typical country lads of the desirable type—comely, muscular, honest, and respectable to a degree.' Not all, though, were Harold Beechams: 'They were sons of settlers located on a belt of poorer ridges, surrounded by four magnificent estates of wealthy men, acquired in the days of the early grants.'

Having grown up seeing their parents suffer through the droughts, the bushfires, the floods, and the plagues of mice and rabbits, they thought that working as tram guards, policemen or hospital attendants promised an easier life. Of 23 sons who had recently come of age in one district's network of families, Miles reported that only seven had remained on the family property or started their own farm. The rest had swapped the farm for a city street, and their farmer's clothes for uniforms and caps.

Charles and the Baxters, who had loaned her horses in the hope she'd stay in their saddle, and her cousin Edwin Bridle at 'Wilga Vale', near Peak Hill, were lads from the land who had stayed, at least for now. She would be going west to visit the Bridles' sheep property and her brother, Norman, another lad from the land, who was still working nearby as a jackaroo. The Bridles' land was an 'exceedingly fertile holding', and 'timbered with pine, box, myall and oak'. She liked that their family name reminded her of a horse.

An early winter layered the surrounding goldfields when Miles visited Wilga Vale. Norman was now 19, and he looked more weathered. He and her cousin Edwin escorted her to the Peak Hill Show, and they watched the horse jumping and sheepdog competitions, then wandered through the amusements that covered the showground. She paused at a booth where a palm reader, who said she was from Bombay, examined Miles' hand. Edwin hovered, hoping to hear about Miles' heart line.

The egg-shaped scar on her palm, from her match burn accident while working at her second and brief employment in Sydney, had faded to a translucent pink blotch. Long lines crossed it and feathered the skin.

'You have a long life before you. Easily 102,' the Indian palmist predicted. 'But you have been nervous, and under strain.'

She looked more closely at the top of the palm of Miles' small hand.

'You will have great success,' she explained. While everyone wanted to hear that, the palm reader perceived that this young woman had a mystic cross on the mount of her finger. 'A lucky cross,' she declared.

Four manuscripts in three years were now in Miles' suitcase of rejections. The editor at Angus & Robertson had only read six chapters of *Some Everyday Folk and Dawn* before recommending it be declined. It was 'small beer,' he had told Robertson. It was weak. Inferior. And they both thought there'd been enough said already about women's voting.

Miles had already had her great success, that was her cross to bear. She wondered if her palm would allow her another success before she turned 102.

From her window seat, Miles watches children run up to wave at the train as it barrels south, travelling as fast as the sheep and rabbits that run from its track to safer ground. Late in the winter evening, she reaches Cooma, not far from Granny's Talbingo property.

'Have you found anyone you like better than yourself?' Granny had once asked her, and Miles felt the bite in her quip. She did not know if she liked or knew herself after the crushing years since *My Brilliant Career*.

If it wasn't for the *Herald* articles, she would have curled up like a snake inside the suitcase that contained her rejected manuscripts and asked her mother to lock her inside. Instead, always with a bag of travelling clothes in hand, she has been moving from story to story, just as the Man from Snowy River had done before he became an editor. She does not want to pause or think.

At Cooma, as she alights from the train, she can see ice on her breath. The next morning, she catches a horse-drawn coach and, wrapped in a horse rug, she persuades the driver to let her have the reins until the next town, where she picks up her horse for the final part of the journey to a snow race carnival in the Snowy Mountains that she will write about for the *Herald*.

Every time a new article is published, she feels a jolt of confidence, and her bank balance is jolted with a new cheque. Rather than move to the city or live with Rose, Miles stays living at home, saving what she can.

She is due to go on a cattle muster and then return to the goldmines of Peak Hill, where she had earlier in the year stayed with the Bridles. Edwin had been excited at the prospect of her return, but she did not agree to go back until she was commissioned to write about the 'woods of the west' and the life of a jackaroo.

As she rides along, she mulls over the rest of the year, which looks familiar. Another summer in Penrith, and some more articles for the *Herald*, with the occasional visit to Rose. She dreads the inevitable questions at Rose's Friday-night salons about her lack of further published books; she is glad she is not invited to Stephens' men-only literary nights. When she does appear at Rose's, she wears a merry smile, and teases questioners with: 'Have you seen the articles by Vernacular in *The Sydney Morning Herald*?'

She isn't rotting, but she knows she cannot be left in this situation for too long, or the rot will set in.

She cannot think of a subject for a new book. Perhaps the skull reader had been wrong about her head, while the palm reader seemed to talk only about the past.

The horse's hooves sink into the soft track, and its mane is fringed with ice. It is restless and eager to reach their destination.

She urges the horse on. She must push forward too.

Miles canters deeper into the snow.

PART THREE

Stella

37

It was April 1906. In Sydney, there was anxiety about a sailing ship that was overdue in port, and last seen at sea in a heavy storm. In Melbourne, a miner from Cape Town, South Africa, was found hiding aboard the ship *Salamis* and was charged with being a stowaway, unable to pay his ten-pound fare. In the Pacific, Miles Franklin, aboard the steamer RMS *Ventura*, introduced herself to other passengers as Stella; she did not promote her book, *My Brilliant Career*. And on 18 April at 5.13 a.m., at his property near San Francisco, the author Jack London felt the earth split. When the shaking stopped, he rode his horse to the nearest mountain; from its peak, he watched a distant tower of fire erupt in the city centre, and then he galloped on.

A fortnight after the earthquake, the *Ventura* anchored under a new moon in San Francisco Bay. As the sun rose and the fog lifted, Miles rushed to the deck to see the city. She scanned the still-smouldering ash, the tangle of hoses on the shore, and the clock tower on the Ferry Building that had stopped at thirteen past five when the earthquake struck. It was quiet now. Everything had become eerily still: the screams; the crashes; the shaking pavement, which a survivor felt 'pulsated like a living thing'; the fires that had consumed buildings for three days.

Aboard the *Ventura*, the passengers could only see and smell the ruins. They had been told of the disaster when they docked in Hawaii; the news had been carried on board by locals who had family and property in San Francisco and were hurrying to join the ship. The *Ventura* took on extra coal to speed its carriage of supplies to the stricken city, and it listed under the new weight. Now in San Francisco, it was surrounded by boats and tugs heaving off the emergency supplies and frantic relatives.

Miles was fortunate. After her fare, the remains of the 60 pounds that she had saved from her more than 30 *Herald* articles was tucked away and stitched into her pockets, while those *Ventura* passengers who had bank drafts were left with useless pieces of paper until they could find another city that had not been torn apart. But she had no idea where her host, Vida's friend, Carrie Whelan, was or if she was even alive. She would have to try to find Carrie or hope that Carrie would be still able to find her, here on the *Ventura*; she had accepted, along with the other passengers, the captain's offer of staying aboard the ship for two dollars a day.

The moon rose once more over a shattered city on the shore.

Miles' voyage to the epicentre of an earthquake had started four years earlier, when Vida Goldstein stayed with Rose Scott in 1902, after returning from touring the United States. Miles had been in her own world then, after the abrupt end to her romance with the Man from Snowy River. In Melbourne in 1904, when she had packed her 'Mary Anne' servant clothes away and stayed with Vida and her sisters, Miles listened more closely to Vida's stories of meeting suffragettes fighting for the vote in America. Vida said that she had met Carrie and her fellow suffragettes in San Francisco, and then steamed across the mountains of Utah and Colorado, which made the Snowy Mountains look like hills.

She told Miles about the giant metropolis of Chicago, which she thought was the dirtiest and busiest city she'd ever experienced. People whirled about like tornadoes there! It had exhausted her just trying to keep up with them. Washington, Vida had thought, was more dignified.

As that year moved on, Miles had paused over small square advertisements in her newspapers, which made capitalised promises promoting the Oceanic Steamship Company's sister ships: the *SONOMA*, *VENTURA* and *SIERRA*, offering 'the shortest sea route to the United States, Canada and London' via SAN FRANCISCO, NIAGARA FALLS and the capitol (WASHINGTON)'.

Vida's sister Aileen, planning her own trip to London, sensed America was the land of opportunity to bring Miles back to Christian Science: 'I can only hope that if you do go away to America, you may meet some of the Scientists there, then you will be able to see what a great power it is there & perhaps meet people who have been Scientists for years & years & have passed through such trying experiences as you are in.'

Vida's mother, Isabella, wrote to Miles after Aileen had gone to London, where she said that she was 'having a happy time among the Scientists'. But, to Miles' relief, Isabella preached only that Miles should join the exodus of artists from Australia.

'Well, my dear, what plans have you for the future?' Isabella asked:

> Are you so fixed that you cannot make tracks for England, or America? In either place, you should get piles of work to do. There are more opportunities to develop Australian talent abroad than in our own country. There is an unwillingness to give a 'leg up' here, which is most distinctively Australian,—so it appears

> in my judgement. Jealousy, pettiness, and personal animus permeates our political, literary, social & religious . . . Nothing on this earth can soon alter, except a spiritual awakening.

Miles was awake to the possibilities abroad. England was the more obvious choice, and it was an author's rite of creative passage to go 'home' to the mother country. But her experience with the English agent Pinker—his disregard of her requests for retaining her original title of *My Brilliant Career*; the paltry royalties; the slow distribution to Australia, the country where it would sell most; his casual rejections—had made London pale as a destination to seriously consider. America seemed more a land of opportunity, if only she could afford the fare.

Miles had hoped her ship would come in with the advances for her new books. Then all seemed lost in a sea of rejection, until the critic suggested she write articles for *The Sydney Morning Herald*, and the pounds slowly built up in her bank account.

It was still stultifying living in Penrith, and the critic and Rose were puzzled as to why she stayed living at home on the outskirts of Sydney when she could now afford lodgings in the city. Outside the Goldsteins and Linda, who had warned before her wedding, 'Be sure you don't go to America before I am married. You are the only sister I have got—I would feel something was wrong if you wouldn't be there,' she did not freely share her thoughts that were forming into a plan. She learned to stay quiet when she confided in Joseph Furphy, who absurdly warned her that she would end up married to a colonel, and that Australia needed her talent. If only he was a publisher.

So, when she stayed with Rose, she deflected questions about her future. She knew Rose wanted her 'spirit child' to stay close rather than be a free spirit.

Instead, she quietly visited the Sydney agent for the Oceanic Steamship Company to discuss the fare and departure dates, and asked Vida to introduce her to a feminist, rather than a spiritual network, in the United States.

In the spring of 1905, Miles had returned to Wilga Vale and her cousin, Edwin Bridle, had taken her for a picnic by a creek surrounded by sheep. The day ended with a sudden hailstorm. As they ran for shelter, with Miles' dress clinging to her, Edwin had thought that it was the 'happiest day of my present life'; Miles had only thought to find shelter from the pelting hail.

When she read his letters after that day, which began with 'Stella, my darling' and declared 'I am yours forever', her throat closed at his cloying words. His letters did not speak of America or England, like the Goldsteins' did, but of finding his 'Guiding Star'.

He had not listened to her gentle rebuffs to his declarations of love in the hail; he was coming to Penrith soon to see her, if he could wait that long.

'I was all the time thinking of the little pet expressions you use to me such as, "You're Mad", "You're Silly", "Silly Billy", and I was beginning to think that you were not far wrong after all,' Edwin wrote. 'But Stella My Sweetheart, I would like to be with you again to hear your voice, even though you were using the terms I have just quoted. Your voice is sweeter on my ear than anything I have ever heard in life . . . I love you all the more when you are testing me to see what stuff I am made of.'

She would have to be clearer with him. It was hard enough, now that Rose knew her plans and had sent her an anguished letter, asking, 'I know nothing of your plans . . . why this long journey? Why, why, why?' She couldn't disappear on Edwin, like she had done with the milkman, and he would not be sadly satisfied with a casual flirtatious goodbye by the harbour, like the young handsome officer at the boarding house.

Then a paragraph from him made her stop: 'I have been getting a fair amount of teasing since you left . . . that I was going to get married when I went to Sydney. Of course, I stoutly denied it, but I was wishing in my heart all the time that it was a fact.'

Granny had heard rumours, and she wanted facts, for she has lived long enough to want to know the truth about rumours: 'Is it true you are going to marry Edwin Bridle?'

Miles looked into the future of a life with Edwin on his sheep farm. Of days helping with the sheep, scanning the horizon for looming bushfires and floods, and long days of housework and cooking. At night stealing away from their bed and its duties, which Linda had warned her about, to write while he snored and sweated.

She would be like a lyrebird, mimicking her mother and sister, but in a cage. Her mother was sewing maternity dresses for Linda, who was now pregnant from those nights she implied were ones of horror.

Edwin had written: 'I can hardly bear to be away from you for any length of time.'

She wrote in *My Brilliant Career* that 'It was only men who could take the world by its ears and conquer their fate, while women, metaphorically speaking, were forced to sit with tied hands and patiently suffer as the waves of fate tossed them hither and thither, battering and bruising without mercy'.

The fortune teller at Peak Hill had pored over the mystic cross on the palm of her hand. Her fate was in her hands. The fortune teller was at least right about that. She would write, then, and grasp a lifeline. It led to an ocean liner steaming through the Sydney Heads, with black clouds from its funnels drifting back towards a man left behind on the shore.

In the months, then weeks, leading up to her departure, during their brief reunions, Edwin did not—would not—listen when she told him that his letters 'weighed too heavily on her feelings' and 'interfered with her work'.

When he finally understood her plans and that she was going away, he was determined to wait, even after she wrote to him that he should consider meeting someone else he could love. 'It is only a few short days since I was with you and you certainly have not forgotten the promises you have made to me then (although you may have made them possibly against your real feelings) . . . But whatever you may do or say to me now, my love for you is too deeply rooted now . . . if you had put your foot down on it at the start it may have had some effect, but not now.'

He assured her, 'I will only have one love in this life, and that it will last until the end,' and promised not to write so often. 'I will wait on you patiently until your mind is calmer than it is at present.'

That was annoying. She *was* calm. Her mind was clear. It had been clear since she confirmed her ticket, and her mother, dear mother, had given her approval for her to travel alone to America, where she would be hosted by Vida's contact, Carrie Whelan, in San Francisco. Then she planned to meet another Carrie in Vida's network in New York, Carrie Chapman Catt, who led the suffragist movement in the United States.

To Miles' surprise, her mother had looked more wistful than worried, although Miles knew her anxiety would well up later.

'I had longed to go to America,' her mother confided to her. 'But instead, I married.'

38

In Sydney it was the last day of the Easter Show, and the papers carried news of the San Francisco earthquake. Those in the bush read about a natural disaster that for once was not theirs to endure. In Penrith, Miles' mother calculated with relief that her daughter would still be en route, and so would be safe on a ship at sea.

In New York, Mark Twain, who had once lived in San Francisco, dwelled on *The Spirit of Humanity*, a painting inspired by the earthquake. It depicted a woman cradling a child and comforting another woman at her knee, and would be sold for relief money. 'I keep thinking about that picture,' Twain wrote to the artist Robert Reid. 'I cannot get it out of my mind. I think—no, I know—that it is the most moving, the most eloquent, the most profoundly pathetic picture I have ever seen. It wrings the heart to look at it, it is so desolate, so grieved. It realizes San Francisco to us as words have not done & cannot do.'

In San Francisco, a man preached on the street: 'You have had your time, and now God is going to have his time.' He was shouted at by the desolate and grieved survivors, who told the patrolling military to order him to stop.

Jack London walked among the hordes of the homeless, who huddled in parks and cradled their children in the spirit of their humanity. He watched as they ran from a new fire that took their refuge away. Men were dynamiting buildings to reduce the fire fuel but, as the hours passed, London heard these constant explosions quieten and realised that the desperation had been abandoned because there was no more dynamite. He saw burst water mains, and realised there was no more water to fill the firemen's hoses. He saw the streets 'humped into ridges'; the architectural marvels and the twisted steel rails of the trams were mangled into ruins. He wrote that 'all the shrewd contrivances and safeguards of man had been thrown out of gear by thirty seconds' twitching of the earth-crust'.

Still marooned aboard the *Ventura* moored in the bay, Miles had not heard yet from Carrie Whelan. It was likely Carrie's house had been destroyed, for she lived in the city centre, at the epicentre of the earthquake. At best, perhaps she was now wrapped in a blanket to protect against the ash and fog. At worst . . . the reality was that it was possible, if not likely, that she had died.

'Do not worry,' her new friend from the ship, Edith Jones, told Miles. Being a good soul, 'Jonesie'—as Miles had playfully dubbed her weeks before, as they steamed towards disaster—suggested Miles come with her to the Seventh-day Adventist Sanatorium, Loma Linda in southern California.

She did not trust in God, like Edith did, but Loma Linda sounded like heaven compared to San Francisco, and it shared its name with Miles' sister. The alternative was to join a ship that was preparing to go on to Canada and London, and then back to the United States and across the Pacific to Australia, where Edwin waited.

Her mother would have heard about the earthquake by now, from telegraphed news bulletins. Miles resolved to find a working post office somewhere, in or outside the city, which had not been burned or destroyed, and to let her mother and Linda know that she was safe. In the meantime, there was no point watching a city suffer, like a ghoulish tourist, so she and Jonesie volunteered at a Seventh-day Adventist relief camp in the city.

She took notes for an article for *The Sydney Morning Herald*. She was unnerved by the smell of decay mixed with the smell of the sewage that spilled into the streets and water mains. She feared another fire or disease, or buildings falling so completely into their basements that, as she wrote later, 'there is not more than a teacup of ashes' to show they were there. She watched groups of soldiers maintaining martial law; but survivors looked too exhausted, hot and dusty to riot, or to break into saloons that had already been looted if they had not been destroyed in the earthquake or fire.

Horses dragged a cart piled with food and supplies; they panted as they trotted by, and she wanted to reach out to them and soothe their hanging heads. With the electricity and trams suspended, horses were again the only mode of transport, if they could be found. She made notes for her article about the shouts from desperate survivors, how the horses were 'pathetically overworked' and 'some of the gaunt and sweated creatures ran for 48 hours without rest'.

She noticed with grim amusement that some creatures of leisure and pleasure were dragged into service by orders of martial law. A bridegroom, trying to leave the city with his bride, was detained to carry blackened planks; a wealthy factory owner was made to carry bricks. Both men were smeared with dust. She thought that there was a 'little malicious satisfaction' in watching the turmoil of the earthquake level class distinctions as well as buildings, and shake society to its core.

Back on the safety of the *Ventura*, Jonesie and Miles were finalising joining the Seventh-day Adventist community in Oakland across the bay, until they could arrange a ticket to Loma Linda when their plans suddenly changed.

'There is word from Carrie!' Miles told Jonesie.

Carrie Whelan's building had been badly damaged but not destroyed. At her refuge in Oakland, she had heard the *Ventura* was in port, with supplies and Australians aboard. Miles' ship had come in but under terrible circumstances; Carrie now felt even more responsible for a lone young woman from the Southern Hemisphere who had arrived in the city of disaster.

Carrie's sister began arranging a boat to fetch Miles to Oakland, and Miles immediately asked if there was room for Jonesie on the boat too. They could all squeeze in—just two small, adventurous women from Australia. On the tugboat Carrie's sister chartered, Miles and Jonesie felt the fog on their faces as they sailed to the other side of the bay.

Oakland had been damaged by the earthquake, especially its chimneys, but—unlike San Francisco—it hadn't had 24-hour factories running or early-morning restaurant kitchens fired up, ready to tip their flames into the city after the earthquake. Most of the fires in Oakland's houses and businesses had long cooled by the time the earthquake hit at dawn, and the few fires that broke out were quickly smothered. Within four hours the water mains had been repaired, so water flowed and the city now functioned as best it could after taking in thousands of refugees from the city across the bay. Every house in Oakland was sheltering someone if it had room, as were the nearby residents of Berkeley, where the university's arches and pillars spread their arms of comfort over the traumatised escapees sheltered within its still-standing walls.

In the safety of Oakland, Miles read Jack London's *Story of an Eyewitness*, which he had telegraphed to *Collier's* in New York from the first working telegraph station he could find, and it had been rushed to print in a special edition. Now it was on sale at newsstands among the other headlines, standing out with a bright-orange cover dedicated to San Francisco.

As soon as she got to Oakland, Miles had sent her own eyewitness article to *The Sydney Morning Herald*, which published it as 'San Francisco. A fortnight after'. Now, after reading London's article, she reasoned, on impulse, that he and she had an earthquake in common. A disaster has brought them into each other's writing spheres. So she would take a chance and write to him, asking him for publishing advice in her new land of chances.

She was realistic. He was the celebrity author of *The Call of the Wild* and she doubted he knew about her, or the Man from Snowy River, because Australian fame rarely travelled further than England. She reasoned, if he saw her as another writer, she might get a reply, as she had with the poet Henry Lawson. She asked Carrie for a directory, or if she knew London's address.

~

At his Sonoma Mountain ranch, in the Valley of the Moon, London was restless after the intensity of the earthquake. There was correspondence to be answered. Letters had come in their hundreds ever since he'd published *The Call of the Wild* three years before, and then *The Sea Wolf*, and *The Game*. Now readers were awaiting his next novel, *White Fang*.

He wrote so often about canines that his friend George Sterling had nicknamed him 'Wolf', but he did not howl in his Valley of the Moon. He would instead be a sea wolf. He was building his ketch, the *Snark*, to sail to the South Pacific as far as Australia, where this writer, Stella Franklin, said she was from in her letter; then he would sail it to Africa.

This Australian writer was interesting for her being Australian, and she had written about the earthquake too. She wanted—as all writers who sought him out seemed to want—his advice on publishers who might be interested in her manuscript about working as a servant. Out of respect for a fellow writer and her sense of adventure, and because he saw it as a mark of his writing discipline that, no matter how many letters he received, he answered them, he typed his reply:

> Dear Miss Franklin,
>
> After having some irritable and exasperating experiences, I finally, some years ago, resolved that I would never again recommend either a writer or a book to a publisher or editor. And ever since, I have resolutely kept this vow, in spite of the fact that some of my nearest and dearest friends have approached me on such matters. So, you will see how impossible it would be to do this for you . . .
>
> You have certainly cut out a big chunk of interesting adventure for yourself in playing Mary Ann in the United States. Are you a Socialist? And if not, why not?
>
> Wishing you all the success in the world, and regretting I am unable to lend you a hand in this particular matter, believe me, sincerely yours,
>
> *Jack London.*

He left it with the others to send, then thought no more about the author from Australia.

Miles is grateful for a roof over her head in a damaged city. The *Ventura* is preparing to leave and will soon steam beyond the bay to Canada. Instead of supplies, it is now heavy with refugees who can afford to escape the chaos for relatives and opportunities in other cities and countries.

Jonesie prays by her bed. Miles unpacks her nightgown from her trunk of clothes and manuscripts. She will send the rest on to New York, but nightgowns and manuscripts need to be kept close.

As she pulls out her nightgown, she disturbs her papers, which are heavier than shoes. She had packed 'When I Was Mary Anne, a Slavey' and *Some Everyday Folk and Dawn*. She'd packed the failed, rejected sequel to *My Brilliant Career*.

Jonesie climbs into bed after her prayers.

'Goodnight, dear Stella,' she murmurs.

'Goodnight, dear Jonesie.'

Miles listens to the city breathe outside her window.

39

It was June 1906. In Sydney, feeling the chill of a southerly come in from the sea, readers of the *Herald* were engrossed in Miles' article about the earthquake. Australia was not ready to forget her yet.

Across the Pacific, in San Francisco, a woman complained that relief workers had not provided her with a skirt, or her husband underwear, despite trainloads of supplies arriving. In southern California, trains arrived full of patients with tuberculosis, who sought sun, croquet and a cure that could not yet be found. On board one train were Jonesie and Miles, bound for Loma Linda in Redlands, California, where, as Jonesie had promised, the air smelled of oranges, apricots, sweet peas and pepper, rather than disaster like in San Francisco.

Tired from the journey, they joined the prayers at their first dinner. It was like Miles' retreat in the Blue Mountains with her vegetarian host, Cara David, as the sanatorium's kitchen only served vegetarian food. They ate breakfasts of honey, milk and strawberries, and oranges that tasted as sweet as their scent. As they strolled about Miles admired the cleanliness of the white, unscarred buildings among the groves, the serenity of patients playing croquet and sunning in the solarium, and that the director's wife, Sister Burden, seemed burdened only by her name.

Miles had reached into her savings to pay the extravagant twenty dollars for the month to be here, but consoled herself that it was a discounted rate. She and Jonesie luxuriated in baths of salt and carbonated bubbles, and had massages and gym classes. They were relieved that the sanatorium did not admit patients with tuberculosis, whose influx to California from other states so alarmed the locals they had nicknamed the hordes 'lungers'. Miles and Jonesie did not want to be lungers, with lungs of blood and an early death like Marie Bashkirtseff, the Parisian memoirist, whom Miles had been compared to in the first heady days after *My Brilliant Career* was published.

Miles sent a brochure to Linda to show her namesake sanatorium, which advertised that it catered to nervous women and enabled them to find rest. Loma Linda meant 'beautiful hill'; her sister was her own beautiful hill of content. The brochure invited the weary, the distressed and the ill; although Miles did not really have money for such a luxury, she did have a nervous disposition, so she felt at home.

~

At her home in faraway Montrose, Charles's property by the disappearing lake, Linda sat covered by a blanket she had wrapped over her womb because it was so cold. She could feel the baby pushing against her pelvis as she read the letter from her sister, postmarked from California.

Linda was enjoying having their mother visiting while her mother-in-law, Mrs Graham, was in Sydney for the winter as the frost got into her elderly bones. It was in Linda's bones too. Her sister was warm among the orange trees, rather than surrounded by frost-covered eucalypts. But Linda was not keen on vegetarian food; her mother would make rabbit stew or lamb for tea, to keep up her strength for the baby.

The baby was restless, her mother said. The birth will be soon, and her mother knew, because she had endured the results of the marital bed six times, yet only seen four of her children live to adulthood. Laurel's headstone in Penrith was already bleached and mottled by time, their brother Mervyn was at peace in Tumut, and Una, the wee one, had been buried soon after birth in the cemetery near Stillwater. But she was here, safe with Charles, her surviving brothers away working, and Miles was in California.

She snuggled further down into the blanket to write her letter. 'Dearest Sister, could never tell you how delighted I was to get yr nice little note & hear all about you. Mrs Graham did cry about you the poor old thing. Because like all old people she was sure you were in the middle of the earthquake.'

Mother was here, she told Miles, and such a comfort. 'Everyone thinks of her as so young, yet she will be a grandmother. It is a pity to make a grandmother of her.'

The baby kicked again.

Linda's life had played out exactly as she and Miles had predicted in their letters when she had told Miles, in that wobbling upset moment, that she was unsure about whether to marry Charles. She had gone ahead with the wedding, with her sister beside her; and now she was having the baby, and Miles would be the cranky maiden aunt as they'd laughed about.

The birth was approaching any day now. The family were already calling the baby 'little Charlie' as if, she told Miles, 'he had anything to do with it'.

'I have the worst of it.' She checked herself and became harmonious again. 'But perhaps I will have the best of it in the end'.

Linda wished Miles was closer. What was Miles doing at that present moment? Was it the moon or the sun in the sky, were days lost or gained over the ocean?

And she felt sorry that her sister had left their poor cousin Edwin waiting. She decided to give Miles a scolding, like Granny would: 'You bad girl to leave such a lot of broken hearts behind. To be hoped you won't break so many in America, if so, stay with one of them or console the poor thing.

'Heaps of loves and kisses, Yr Loving Sister, Linda.'

She hoped her letters would catch up with Miles when she returned to Oakland from the sanatorium, where Miles had directed Linda, Edwin, her mother, friends and Jack London to reply.

Linda felt heavy. Yes, the baby would come soon.

~

In California, Jonesie and Miles were making more plans. Jonesie was staying in her heaven of apricot and orange groves to join Loma Linda's nursing school. Miles could not afford to stay, and she had once tried nursing as a teenager. Like governessing, it did not suit her temperament. She was certain New York would.

The month of rest and the California sunshine had given the pair of them a glow that lungers could never achieve. They embraced goodbye, with genuine promises of writing, because they had travelled across an ocean, witnessed disaster in San Francisco, and experienced the dreamy atmosphere of Loma Linda in just a few months of friendship.

Arriving back in Oakland, Miles was grateful for a roof again, as its parks were still populated by tents, and she heard stories of long queues for food in San Francisco. She would need to move on soon, to New York; but Carrie Whelan, who welcomed her back, explained that she had heard Carrie Catt had gone to Europe for an extended stay, so she would no longer be able to host Miles in New York as Vida had suggested when she was planning her American trip.

'You can stay here,' Carrie Whelan reassured her, like it was a normal visit, instead of a refuge from an earthquake and inferno.

That was very kind, Miles said, but she did not want to be a burden on a burdened city and would make another plan.

'Chicago?' Carrie asked.

Carrie offered to write to Jane Addams to see if she could stay at her house of activists, Hull House. From the Australian newspapers that carried 'woman's world' columns, Miles knew of Miss Addams, who wrote of child-labour reforms rather than fashion: 'The greatest charge I have to bring against child labour is that it pauperises the consumers. If I wear a garment which has been made in a sweatshop or a garment for which the maker has not [been] paid a living wage . . . then I am in debt.'

Vida had warned her Chicago was a tornado. Its snow fell as soot.

'Yes,' Miles said.

A snowy, sooty tornado sounded exciting.

Carrie gave her a batch of letters that had arrived for her while she was at Loma Linda for the earthquake had not stopped the post.

News tumbled into her hands. Linda had given birth to a son, Edward, and Miles felt the ocean between her and her sister in Australia, who cradled a newborn in a house surrounded by paddocks and bush.

'Just this inst. received your letter. A doz. congratulations. It was such a relief I have been so anxious,' Miles scribbled, and enclosed a strip photo of herself wearing a sombrero. She told her sister that she and Carrie were going for a swim in the late-summer evening, rather than how much she missed her.

She sifted through the rest of the mail and was thrilled to see a typed reply from Sonoma, with Jack London's stamped address at an angle at the top. She must learn to type. She noted that London had done a quick edit on the letter, inserting words in pen above the type—the familiar mark of a writer who always wanted to make a last-minute change before they sent it as the final word.

It was disappointing that London would not help, but she was consoled to know that it was a rule that he didn't help anyone. She laughed about his socialist question; Granny would be horrified to hear the word. She must write to Granny in her next batch of letters, as Granny would want news. Most of all, the news Miles refused to tell: if she was returning home to marry Edwin.

Linda had told her not to break any more hearts, Edwin was holding his heart from breaking in letters like the one that had also been waiting for her.

She was still his 'darling Stella', she read.

'I am just as much as in love with you now, although the broad Pacific is rolling between us at present, but be sure a love such as ours will overcome all obstacles . . .'

'Are you ready?' Carrie asked, and Miles put Edwin's letter away.

She would reply later. Carefully. Edwin's couldn't be a spontaneous postcard, like she was able to write to Linda. He interpreted every word as hope.

'My love for you is more powerful than ever if that could be,' he declared.

In the bay with Carrie, the cold water lapped her skin. Jack

London was right; she was carving out a new adventure. She swam, and Edwin once more washed far away.

After Carrie confirmed Jane Addams was expecting her, Miles mapped out the same route that Vida had taken in 1902. She would take her time, like Vida did; but she would not be visiting President Roosevelt.

She boarded the Overland Express and gazed at Sacramento Valley, then felt the strain of the train as it climbed into the snow-capped Sierras. She dozed across the desert and stirred with alarm when she heard the train's loud bell ringing a mile from the station, until she realised it rang loudly every time it approached a new stop.

At Salt Lake City, she left the train and visited the Kenyon Hotel. Its grand exterior revealed its tariff, but she did not pay that because, in return for a room, she wore the Kenyon Hotel staff uniform, briefly working again as a maid.

Then, in the spring, she took the Overland train, this time to Colorado, where she donned a high-neck blouse and skirt at the Hotel Colorado and served champagne, wine and whiskey, which to her was all the same vile stuff in any country.

'I received yr welcome letter . . . I am sorry you are working as a barmaid,' wrote Granny, who was running out of room to write all the addresses for her granddaughter in her address book as her letters followed her to Sydney, then Melbourne, and now America. This wandering the earth—arriving in the aftermath of an earthquake, and now a barmaid in a city full of Mormons—was quite enough adventure for one unmarried woman. Especially with the worry of Linda who, she told Miles, was home again but could not breastfeed, so the 'baby is to be reared by hand', as though she was describing an orphaned lamb.

Now Miles will be a mother next, if only she would return. 'Tell me it is true you are going to be Married to Edwin Bridle, it is reported as such about Tumut,' she ordered.

The stress that her grandmother put on marriage only emphasised to Miles what marriage really meant.

~

The Roaring Fork Valley is scented with pine trees instead of eucalypts. Miles has a day off and is touring with some guests in a group, riding a red roan pony she has borrowed from one of the rich people at the rich hotel. On their way up to Hanging Lake, she hangs onto the tail of her pony as it clambers up the steep paths, just as she learned to do riding up gullies in the Snowy Mountains.

'Shoot something,' one guest urges her as they ride up by the rapids. Because, if she can ride like she was part of a horse, surely she can shoot as well.

'Oh, I can't,' Miles demurs.

He insists, and she flinches at the feeling of the cold metal as he presses it into her hands. Cocking it, she aims at the nearest log, which shatters as the bullet hits it.

'You have fired a gun before!' he reprimands.

'Oh, half a dozen times,' she deflects as she recoils at triggering death.

A horse sags under the weight of another guest, who announces he is the strongman of the touring circus. Miles and her pony look like a doll and a miniature horse beside him.

'Join us,' the man invites, and Miles laughs. Her Granny is aghast at her being a barmaid, but what would she think if she ran away with the circus?

The strongman rides closer. 'Marry me,' he urges.

Such a nuisance, she thinks. For once, she is grateful for Edwin's proposal, so she is not lying to the strongman when she tells him she has a sweetheart at home who wants her hand in marriage too.

Back at the hotel she returns the pony, and to her place at the bar. The guests are amused and curious when they hear her stories, her Australian accent; they ask her questions, and her name. She does not camouflage her identity with another name, like Sarah Frankling did, because Miles Franklin, the author who promised so much and delivered so little, is unknown in California, Colorado and her new destination, Chicago. She tells them to call her Stella.

She can be Stella Franklin, barmaid, circus performer, traveller. She can wander the earth.

40

It was October 1906. In San Francisco, the early winter wind from the bay blew across the tents still clustered in the city's parks. A squatter, Mary Kelly, refused to leave a cottage in which she and others, still homeless, had found refuge. Authorities demolished it around her; Mrs Kelly stood defiant while the last floorboard was taken from under her feet.

The city now demanded that rates be paid for each tent, and there was outrage when those who could not pay were threatened with removal. The tent dwellers warned they 'would shoot to kill' anyone who tried to forcibly remove them.

In San Francisco Bay, Jack London, awash with royalties, continued building his boat, the *Snark*, for its South Pacific voyage. But he did not have a wolf on board to guard it, or the funds to pay for it

'We expect lots of action,' he told an editor, for more royalties and serial payments would be needed to complete the boat. 'And I am a writer of action.'

Half a continent away, Miles Franklin's overland train pulled into Chicago and as she alighted she felt the city's grimy grandeur that made Sydney seem so small and clean.

There was an unseasonal spring snow. Flurries of grey snowflakes fluttered on her nose, and pooled into ice on the pavements. The chill wind snuck under her jacket and clung to her stockings, and she shivered. She was careful not to slip as she tried to keep up with the crowds accustomed to the ice under their feet. Her neck arched as she looked up at soaring buildings that created wind tunnels like canyons.

As her streetcar rattled away from the city centre, the sky became darker with smoke. Buildings became smaller, dirtier, poorer. The faces more tired and worn, from the lives that ground them down, rather than lifting them to heights that they might only access if they worked as cleaners in the city's buildings. Around her, she heard a clash of accents and languages, and felt the world had collapsed into her carriage.

She had been given instructions on how to get to the address; now, alighting from the streetcar, she hoped that she had arrived at the right stop for Hull House on South Halsted Street. Even in the cold air, it smelled like San Francisco, only there was no earthquake, just overcrowding. The branch of the river bubbled with refuse from the meatworks. Garbage overflowed from boxes of waste bolted to the pavement, on which toddlers learned to climb. Lovers wiped them down and sat together on them.

She had entered the jungle; it was wilder and more dangerous than any zoo. The giant chimneys of the factories cast shadows over the slums and their plumes of black clouds coated the snow as it fell. From the slaughterhouses, there was the distant lowing of a cow, or the final, frightened squeal of a pig.

Everyone knew about the meatpacking industry and its stockyards, ever since the previous year's serialisation of Upton Sinclair's *The Jungle* in 1905, and now the book. Jack London, in his review of his bestseller, declared it 'the anti-wage slavery book they had been waiting for'. It had caused a decline in meat sales, with its accounts of pork contaminated with tuberculosis and workers' flesh being ground with the meat.

'It is alive and warm. It is brutal with life. It is written of sweat and blood, and groans and tears. It depicts, not what man ought to be, but what man is compelled to be in this, our world, in the Twentieth Century,' London wrote in admiration. President Roosevelt was alarmed rather than admiring, and ordered an inquiry into food and drug safety. Upton Sinclair was frustrated rather than triumphant, because he had wanted to hit the heart about working conditions and animal cruelty at the stockyards; instead, he said, he had hit the stomach. Especially the president's.

As Miles walked towards Hull House, children played with tomato cans and dodged the traffic of carts, loaded precariously with wood and goods, as they moved along the slushy street. In the reception area, a Hull House regular visitor, Hilda Polacheck, acted as interpreter for weeping women who were worried because their sons had been taken by the police for stealing milk or coal from trains.

The House's permanent residents were live-in volunteers. They all had left wealthier lives to live with Jane Addams here at Hull House, because Jane—'Miss Addams', as she preferred, did not believe in drop-in charity but in settling among those you offered to help. Put your mink where your mouth is, and share the fur with those who are cold, she advocated. Miss Addams was like an American Rose Scott. But Rose had not turned Lynton into a decaying mansion in the middle of the poorest areas of the city and opened its doors to whoever needed or wanted to come inside. Jane had expanded into neighbouring buildings, which were once a saloon and a morgue, and were now filled with classrooms and meeting places, rather than drink and dead bodies.

Hull House and its adjoining buildings now occupied the entire block. Miles was astonished at the size and the scale of its operations; the House's yearbook recorded that it educated, entertained or advised 9000 locals a week. They were, she learned, mainly European migrant families, who had come to America on the promise of an industrial revolution—which, they had discovered, in fact rewarded few.

They came through the front door to attend a class or meeting, or to hand their children over to a creche because, when the mothers were asked if they wanted art and music, they said they only wanted childcare so they didn't have to tie their children to the furniture to keep them safe while they worked. But they did also come to hear and learn music, to see art, to practise traditional crafts and to find romance at dances, because that meant feeling human when they felt there was so little time, energy or money for humanity in their lives.

The Hull House theatre staged plays; but sometimes 'going to the theatre' meant being in the audience for a union meeting with activists rather than actors on the stage, and the theatre's curtain provided cover if their employers discovered they had been socialising for reform rather than recreation. From theatre seats they watched and participated in the proceedings of the Laundry Union, the Garment Workers' Union and the Women's Trade Union League; and they heard women argue for equal suffrage.

In the kitchen, Italian immigrant women made vats of pasta and tomato sauce for dinner. In another room, women wove blankets and shawls, sharing stories of long days in factories, where they worked from 7 a.m. to 10 p.m. They no longer worried about their children working the same hours, after Jane Addams and one of her first volunteer residents, Florence Kelley, managed to get the law changed, but they knew that there was plenty of secret child labour going on, because this was the way of the jungle, and some parents needed their children's earnings.

In other Hull House rooms, men and women attended English lessons, and college education classes were taught with a slide machine called a stereopticon, which was marvelled at as a magic lantern. Some wrestled, boxed or played basketball in the gym; others learned the trumpet or piano in the music rooms, or had a bath in the public bathrooms, for often there was no running water at their homes. In the Mazzina Club, young Italian men read current affairs and studied Italian drama, rather than their own family dramas in their poor flats; some families went to the People's Friendly Club, where anyone over ten years old could vote on the club's decisions, their hands stretched high in a rare moment of choice.

Jane Addams had long ago given up telling her admirers that she was not an American heroine, and that people peering into her face for signs she was a saint would only find lines. She was 46, but the demands of Hull House and her campaigns—to protect children from factories; to agitate for garbage collection that was free of corruption; to demand an end to unsafe working conditions; to lobby for a condemned building to be turned into a playground—gave her a permanent air of energy that showed on her face, because how could it not? Her back was permanently crooked and it hurt, but she ignored the pain and got some relief from her medical kit, consisting of four glass vials and some custom-made pills compounded by her pharmacist. She was capable of compounding them herself, because of her medical school training, but, with the demands of Hull House, she did not have time for that. Photographs of her and her closest advisers often showed them sitting at a desk with their hair in uncoiffured buns, because they did not have time to tidy themselves up.

With her guide, Miles crossed into the next building, which housed the Jane Club, where she would be boarding for three dollars a week.

She was at the crossroads of a city that built and destroyed dreams.

~

In her Jane Club room, Alice Henry pulled her prematurely grey hair into a bun and went downstairs to the dining area, where she perused the upcoming lectures at the House. Among the talks scheduled were 'New Zealand: Where there are no strikes and old people have pensions', and 'Crowded houses', about the slums. Until coming to Hull House, Alice had found America smart but shallow. Hull House was the reassurance that she had been seeking: America really did have a soul.

Her back was still stiff from the all-night train from New York, where she'd been lecturing on Australian women's suffrage. She had come to the House at the invitation of Addams.

'Hello, Miss Addams,' Alice greeted her host, who told her that another Australian had just arrived from Sydney—a 'Miss Stella Franklin', who had written a book.

'Do you know her?' Miss Addams asked.

Like many Americans, Miss Addams thought Australia was so small that everyone must know each other; but no, Alice did not know Miss Stella Franklin.

She knew of a book, written five years ago, by a 21-year-old from the bush, which her friend, Catherine Spence, had called 'clever but unpleasant'. That book, however, was not by a Stella Franklin; there must be some confusion. Few Australian women travelled to America, and now Alice was intrigued.

At dinner, the two Australians sat together. Alice eyed the younger woman beside her, who was confidently light at the table, and whom everyone called Stella. She had sailed into the aftermath of the San Francisco earthquake.

'You have written a book?' Alice asked. 'And you know Vida Goldstein?'

'Yes,' Miles replied, and did not want to say more, because she enjoyed having a secret.

Alice, being a journalist, pressed on, and asked what the book was called.

Stella reluctantly shared the name of her book, *My Brilliant Career*, and that her pen name was Miles.

She watched as Alice connected Stella, the stranger, to Miles Franklin, the author, and saw Alice's reserved politeness become friendly. The book still had some value after all.

'Call me Stella,' she requested.

After both women left their rooms at the Jane Club, Miles briefly boarded with a dressmaker. Then she moved with Alice to rooms in the city's north, owned by a doctor named Josephine Young and her father, which were far better than the tenements around Hull House. Miles teased Alice with a nickname, 'Pops', because her new friend was older and serious.

Alice had stenography skills and a small inheritance. She had originally volunteered at the Suffrage Association of Chicago and become its West Branch chair, because they valued her seriousness; then she'd joined the Women's Trade Union League at the invitation of its president, Margaret Dreier Robins.

Miles was envious. She had no inheritance, and her savings were depleting with every dollar she spent. Without secretarial skills like Alice's, or a medical degree like Josephine Young's, or contacts in journalism and the book world like Jack London's, her options were once again limited to a lower rung of life.

There could be a new story, she decided. She would rejig her Mary Anne book. She told Alice that she would investigate department stores and domestic work, like Jane Addams and the fierce women at Hull House did; she would go undercover again. Why, here in America, women journalists had turned undercover reporting into a front-page art form, and, as for books, look at the success of the investigation-based novel *The Jungle*. She could turn her servant work here in the States into a novel, or a play. It could be washed and re-served.

'It will be an investigation,' she told Alice and her new friends at Hull House. They nodded their approval.

She wanted their respect, because they were the most interesting people in the world. But she desperately wanted a job where she did not have to scrub or serve, so she also resolved to do a secretarial course because that would help with her journalism. She would have a desk, as a New Woman should have. There was no dignity in domestic service.

In December the snow was falling again and piling up along the pavements. In the nearby stockyards, knives froze in blistered hands and slashed through icy carcasses to produce festive Christmas meals. All was bloody, rather than bright. Ice, like a broken jigsaw puzzle, floated down the river.

At Hull House, Jane Addams, along with the House's co-founder Ellen Starr and their residents, decorated a fresh, giant Christmas tree lit with hundreds of tiny candles, and arranged crates of presents for the community's children. There would be songs in German, Italian, Polish and Irish Gaelic.

Miles and Alice were excited by their first Christmas in Chicago, amid snow rather than summer's heat. They jostled among the Christmas shopping mobs to buy presents for Jane

Addams and their friends at Hull House. The crowds were overwhelming, and a policeman saved an elderly woman laden with parcels from stepping into the path of a fast-moving wagon. At the Children's Memorial Hospital, a homeless four-month-old was named 'Christmas Baby'.

Miles pulled her coat tighter, for she was not yet used to winters that plunged so dramatically below freezing, and darkness that descended so early. She thought in wistful moments of Charles and Linda, who were having their first Christmas with their son, her baby nephew. She hoped that one day she could show him the wondrous window displays of Marshall Field's department store, adorned with toy rajahs atop mechanical elephants.

~

In Australia, there were toys in the shops, but the crowds were sweating rather than shivering. Edwin hoped this would be the last Christmas that he and Miles would spend apart, and that she would soon be Mrs Edwin Bridle. At his property, he was tired after fighting a bushfire for two days. To pull burning logs away, he had used terrified draught horses, who could smell the smoke on their tails as they dragged their loads through the dark.

The bushfire had now been extinguished, and the burning wood he'd hauled away at midnight was harmless, blackened stumps. At the post office he sent a gold half-sovereign coin—like Miles had earned as a servant, imprinted with King Edward and St George slaying the dragon—to Miles in the next mail as he had promised her; but he wished there were presents under the tree for her instead, adorned with ribbons and her name.

He looked out the window at the paddocks. Miles understood the land's harshness and loneliness. He had been so lonely until their romance.

'You came into my life at a critical time,' he wrote at the start of summer. 'A very lonely time. After living a strictly moral life, it was just beginning to enter my mind if life was really worth it, when I looked round & saw other men who lived the life of a libertine, and then settled down . . . and then I found that you care for me.'

She was special, he knew that: 'How much you are ahead of me in brilliancy, and genius.'

He would need to give her more freedom. He could do that. He would permit her to travel as often as she pleased. And he was prepared to live a life of celibacy. She had warned him that she was 'not strong enough to bear all the trials of maternity' and so he had suggested: 'We could live together in a way that you suggested at one time—for that would be infinitely preferable to me than marry some other woman.'

Yes, she would come home to him, 'and I would not give a hang what the world might think of us'.

He could not stop writing to her, and sent another letter on the federal election day. He was worried about socialists. They were a danger. He knew she would understand his concern, because she was his 'Only Love'. 'I would not like to see the Socialists get elected as I've made my living all my life off the land, but if they have their way with all their schemes for land taxation, it will be hardly worth our while to remain on the land, and I will go to Sydney, and join the unemployed.' But he didn't want to bore her with political arguments, and he knew that she would be trying to keep up with election news, despite being so far away.

He was in a hopeful mood amid his worries because of her previous letter, he wrote: 'It made me feel very near to you indeed, and I feel more hopeful about our future happiness; and that it will come to something more than a dream. I have always lived a life of self-denial, but I feel sure that there would be no happiness for me if I was to lose my only, only love.'

He had promised to try and find her some emu feathers for Christmas, but he reminded her that emus were protected birds and feathers were scarce. In the meantime, he would send a gold half-sovereign in his next mail. He was in a 'sound financial position', he promised, as long as the socialists didn't prevail.

At Wilga Vale, Edwin and his family decorated the tree. His mother boiled Christmas puddings, and the steam spiced the hot afternoon. He missed Miles.

I will wait for you, he promised.

After a day among the crowds, Miles and Alice return to Hull House to listen to Anna Strunsky and her husband William Walling give a lecture on the uprisings in Russia.

Walling declares, 'The people are autocracy's last hope.'

It was *speechifying*, Miles thinks afterwards. She had been impressed by William Walling referring to Anna as 'Miss Strunsky', not 'Mrs Walling' or his wife, and so honouring her choice to eschew 'Mrs'.

Anna had told the *Tribune* on the eve of their lecture: 'I believe in the freedom and ideality of love, in its expression of an ideal equality, and cannot allow my ideals of the marriage relation to be cheapened and misconstrued for me by meaningless convention.'

The thought of 'Mrs' always raises Miles' spirit of protest, and here was Anna protesting against marriage conventions as much as capitalism. Anna has given her a precedent to retain her name and change it at will. She can be Miles, or Stella, or Miss Franklin or Frankling, or whatever fancy name she invents, and it will be hers alone.

Yes. She will strike against ever being a 'Mrs', like Anna has done.

After the talk, there is a dinner for the comrades, and Alice Henry sits next to William Walling, while Miles sits beside William Bross 'Bill' Lloyd, the son of the newspaper publisher Henry Demarest Lloyd. Like Walling, he is a member of the Socialist Party, which is at odds with the millions in his family's bank account and properties. She is told his nickname is the 'Millionaire Red', although the Chicago *Tribune* is careful as he sits on their board.

Such men are *petted lions*, Miles decides. Golden with power and privilege, they stalk with the pride of their family and education, and their dens are mansions with yachts; but they roar in support of workers and women's rights. She finds them fascinating, as much for their contradictions as their conversations.

Bill Lloyd leans flirtatiously close and tells her he visited Australia with his father as a boy. 'I wish more Australians were present,' he says loudly.

The table turns to her and Alice for, when he roars, everyone listens. Miles blushes; she would love more Australians here too.

She looks around the table. There is wine and scotch flowing; but she smiles and takes her lemonade or water. She listens to the conversational debating and jostling around her. An elixir to her ears. She doesn't need tonics in brown bottles, or harsh whiskey or bubbling champagne. Just this.

41

It was April 1907. In San Francisco, the earthquake anniversary was marked as a 'resurrection', but in the city's courts, 1700 civil suits and class actions against insurance companies were still waiting to be heard.

After the winter, and a frustrating wait for repairs, Jack London and his wife, Charmian, finally sailed the *Snark* out of San Francisco Bay, past the Golden Gates and into the Pacific Ocean. He was disappointed it was deserted. There were no schools of flying fish, no dolphins, and no sharks hunting for prey until their sole crew member, bored and hot, jumped in for a swim. A fin appeared and he thrashed to the safety of the boat.

In Chicago, as the city warmed, so did the unrest. Chicago police chief George Shippy banned the colour red from a demonstration; it was not allowed on the little girls, or on a fluttering necktie or ribbon, because Shippy declared it was an anarchist tint. The mayor sacked Margaret Dreier Robins' husband, Raymond, and his supporters from the Chicago School Board in a purge of radicals.

On a Sunday in April, Miles seized a copy of the *Chicago Tribune*. If rolled, it was the size of a club and its ink smudged her fingers as she thumbed through its pages until she spied a small column on page 57: 'No Dignity in Domestic Service'. It only appeared as a letter to the editor but, she consoled herself, it was a start.

As well as the *Chicago Tribune* letter, she'd also published a longer article about domestic service in *The Sydney Morning Herald* the same month, seizing on the debate to encourage servants from poorer countries to immigrate to Australia so as to fill the demand that she'd read about in a months-old Australian paper that was sent to Alice and her. She finally had two published pieces out in the world at once, and in two different countries. If only they were books. That would come.

Over the winter, Miles had learned to walk on black ice. She was no longer surprised by grey snow, or the bursts of a freezing breeze that she called dragon's breath, which hissed under her skirts as she left the department store after a day working there in the stifling warmth. She perfected her dragon glare to men who admired her legs when the gale blew her skirts up over her ankles.

When she finally reached the warmth of her apartment rooms, she would wash the snow and frost off her face, put her gloves and hat and coat near the radiator to dry, pull the pins out of her hair, and snuggle into a bathrobe and slippers. Sleep was still interrupted by attacks of insomnia and homesickness that sometimes left her weeping with tiredness and sadness, rather than the sirens that wailed from fire wagons that galloped down the streets and the light that washed through the windows from the lamps lining the sidewalks. It was often late by the time she arrived home at night, after a dinner of bread, soup and codfish at a cafeteria, or evenings at the theatre, or talks at Hull House, which shone brightly in the darkness of the unlit surrounding streets, because the city did not light up its poor areas.

She had also started a secretarial course. She found the thunk of a typewriter as satisfying as using a pen. She reminded herself, yet again, to remember American spelling, and that the 'z' was sitting under the 'a' among her typewriter keys and she had to slip her little finger down to tap it. The strongest feelings of being in a foreign country sometimes arose from the smallest things.

For a moment, she would gasp from homesickness rather than the cold. Alice was lucky: she spent her day debating and preparing policy papers at Hull House with Margaret Dreier Robins and Miss Addams, rather than bending over a stranger's stocking in the shoe department, or standing behind the counter as a sales clerk in a tower of glamour and goods. This was not the brutality of the stockyards, or the dirty drudgery of domestic-service work; but the department-store pay was still so little and the hours still so long that she did not have the time or the money to browse among the wares that she sold. She worried too about what she knew from Alice's work with the Women's Trade Union League. Workers were paid in cents for the clothes and shoes and accessories that were stitched and beaded in rundown rooms and factories around Hull House, then wrapped in branded gift boxes and sold by her for dollars.

~

On Edwin's sheep farm Wilga Vale, the red haze of bushfires had faded with the end of summer, and Edwin marked the days. It had now been eighteen months since that day he and Miles had run together in the hail, and nearly a year since she sailed for America, vaguely promising to return.

He would write again, because the American mail had been disrupted by striking crews. The latest was the *Ventura*'s sister ship, the *Sonoma*, whose crew had been jailed for a month and a new crew had to be found. It had caused chaos with the shipping news, and the last scribbles from Stella had made him worried.

As he read her descriptions of long days and busy nights in Chicago, he thought that her life seemed too frenetic. He fretted about her health, and her safety. He preferred the rural life to the cities with their poverty and vice, which unsettled him. Perhaps, if he did well enough, he could live like a wealthy squatter and they could have a flat in the city to occasionally visit and see a show, or find somewhere like Penrith, which was closer to the city life.

She had told him she wanted to try out her 'literary wings', but she was grounded in a Chicago department store to pay her rent, like any girl in Sydney or Melbourne, and she had not mentioned any new books to him. Both Sydney and Melbourne were a continent closer to him than Chicago. She did not need a city; she could write here at his property—their home—as no wife of his would be a shopgirl.

He felt the awful longing to be with her overcome him again.

She would be Mrs Edwin Bridle.

'If I was doing the thing I most wanted in the world, Sweetheart, it would be going full speed across the Ocean to America to make you my wife . . . I have had a fearful longing the last couple of days to have you with me again. I am continually thinking of you but at the times the longing to be with you is awful.'

It was time.

His only love.

'Will you come back to Aus. with me if I go over about the end of the year.'

The warmth of summer is beckoning. On the ride home from work in the city's streetcars she squeezes among burly men and tired women. She wrinkles her nose at their tobacco breath. The days are longer now, her chest does not hurt from her seasonal flu, and she can walk along the lake without shivering.

Some days the wind tunnels through the buildings almost lift her off her feet. How silly she was to think of Sydney as a big city, in which she needed a chaperone like Rose Scott. Compared to Chicago, Sydney was like Goulburn.

She feels a little gasp of homesickness again. She writes to Rose Scott, to ensure she does not feel forgotten. She tells Rose that Australia is 'still the greatest and grandest place on the globe' and, if Rose visits her in America, 'she would be given a royal time'. She and Alice Henry would introduce her to Miss Jane Addams.

She walks faster, as fast as the Chicagoans.

She is thinking of a short story idea, about a homesick Australian in Chicago. She can scribble it on the blank side of her typewriting papers. She can write through her homesickness.

She thinks of Edwin, and his last letter. Her reply was now en route.

He wrote, 'I know too well the lonely sort of life I am leading.'

She thinks of him, a solitary man surrounded by the stillness of his sheep farm, then disappears into the crowd.

42

It was summer 1907. In Honolulu, the *Snark* was docked for repairs, and Jack London was happy that he'd seen the dolphins and shoals of flying fish he'd been looking for as they sailed closer to the Hawaiian islands. The locals taught him how to surf, and he felt the force of a wave behind his board was 'like being thrown by Titan's hand'. In Chicago, a heatwave rippled throughout city and coated the nights. The streets around Hull House were deserted because it was too hot for the kids to kick a can. Their parents smoked by their windows, hoping for a passing breeze. Instead, there was thunder.

At Hull House's annual magic 'May' party children who lacked household water were given ice cream that was like white snow instead of grey, and Miss Addams officially opened the House's 'five-cent' moving picture show that premiered *Cinderella*, accompanied by a piano. Miss Addams had declared that 'nothing of a character calculated to injure the juvenile mind will be tolerated', unlike other five-cent shows, where criminals were held up as heroes; so Chicago police chief Shippy had approved of the new Nickelodeon, as the five-cent theatre shows were known. He was glad it was in Hull House and not in a saloon, or part of 'amateur night evil'.

Ice cream seemed to be offered everywhere Miles went, and it dripped around her fingers or melted from the spoon. It was served at parties, at dinners, at luncheons and in delicatessens and parlours, and she wondered if the American summer ran on ice cream, like the winter relied on coal. It was creamier than last year's, and did not drip with bacteria because the new pure food laws had cleaned up the ice-cream industry, just as they had cleared up the meat.

The sugar laced her tongue. She would need to watch how much ice cream she ate. Her grandmother had told her 'by your photo I would think you are getting very stout' and Miles did not want to be fat, like the idle rich she had seen while a servant.

It was humid, and sometimes she wished for a southerly that would break the heat, like in Sydney. At night she threw open the windows to bring in any air. The department store was stuffy, so she wore a lighter skirt in regulation black. It was close to a parlourmaid outfit, only she was serving merchandise instead of tea. Rather than gloves, furs and boots, she was now selling three-piece bathing suits in silk, sailor collars for the children and hats for their summer vacations.

In Penrith, the Southern Hemisphere winter cooled the house and Linda wished her sister was closer than Chicago. Linda was used to her being distant; first, when Miles was in Stillwater while Linda was Granny's companion in Talbingo; then in Penrith and Sydney; then, briefly, Melbourne. But America was another foreign world. She wondered what Miles was doing, whether she was awake or asleep. Linda wanted to sleep.

In between his naps, the baby played on his grandmother's floor and warily eyed the dog that tried to steal his food.

As he played, and the dog sulked, Linda helped her mother pack up the house they could no longer afford to live in. Her mother looked desperate, she thought. Her father—and his mad schemes.

He was avoiding Linda's quiet fury. She was only quiet because good women did not show their anger, or their vices. Miles would have, though.

'Have you heard from Stella?' Linda asked her mother.

Linda tried to distract her mother from the grim situation, and her own longing for her sister, by talking about the past few months, which she had spent with Granny in Talbingo, and about her and Charles moving to south-east Queensland. It would be hot, she prattled, even in winter. Warm rain will fall in buckets.

Charles had sold their Lake George property for their move to Queensland, where he declared there was more profit and promise. He'd sailed on ahead, to get the new house ready for the family and stock the property. It had once been rented by the Queensland governor for his summer residence, she said. There was plenty of room for her and Father. It would be alright.

The baby cried.

She was annoyed at her sister. She had written to her twice. Had she moved again, and the mail not caught up with her? Well, Linda was moving too.

Still, Miles was her 'very dear' sister, she could not be annoyed at her for long:

> My very dear sister,
>
> I don't think you got my last two letters or you would have sent me a line. I wrote thanking you for the pretty cup you sent baby and for all the postcards . . . We are going to settle

> down in Queensland. Charlie has bought a place at 'Warwick'. A house of 17 rooms—the Governor's summer residence. So we will have plenty of room.
>
> A great many motor cars passing through here now on the way to the mountains. I suppose you often have a ride in them. You always have such grand friends.
>
> I often think what a grand time you are having. Look after your health. That is the chief thing in life. Look after yourself as no-one can do it for you.

She went on to make rapid comments for her sister, which read more like a laundry list of life:

> Penrith is the same dirty town.
>
> Mother has no friends now she has no home.
>
> Baby is a grand little chap. Everyone is in love with him. He gets a spoiling.
>
> I went to the spring show, I was feeling sick. I was with Phillip.
>
> It is cold up here, I thought it would be warm.
>
> I must close as it is getting late.
>
> Goodnight dear sister.
>
> Heaps of love and kisses.
>
> From Linda.

She added a postscript: 'Baby sends Aunt Stella kisses with a slobbery mouth and dirty face.'

She wiped the baby's face clean. He would be a year old soon, but he was yet to meet his wandering aunt. How old will he be when she holds him for the first time, or would he be too tall and strong to be held? He would grow to be like Harold Beecham, Miles' hero, who Cousin Phillip still believed was him.

She gave the baby some paper; he clutched a pencil and she clasped his hand in hers to steady it on the page. The circles of his pencil marks looked like kisses, and she enclosed it with the letter for Miles. She added a note: 'Scribbles on the page on pencil. This is from baby. Answer it.'

She would send the letter before they sailed for Brisbane.

When Linda's letter arrived, Miles hugged it close. Dear sister. Dear little nephew, with his O's that looked like kisses. She worried about her mother with no home and no friends, because debt was socially contagious. She was glad she was being looked after by Linda, who balanced the family, and who gave her mother joy with a grandson. Although they both agreed their mother looked too young to be a grandmother. Miles did not know what she gave her mother other than more worry.

She went through the rest of her mail. There was no letter from Edwin. She was surprised, and a little hurt. Had he jilted her? She had asked him to wait She liked that he was at a distance, but that he was still there.

It was Fourth of July, and Chicago's police chief Shippy told the *Tribune* that he wanted the celebrations to be safe and sane. He had a leader's face, as hard as his baton, and his police hat framed his bushy moustache and his eyebrows that frowned with official neatness. In his picture, he crossed his arms over his double-breasted, brass-buttoned police jacket that was brocaded with stars.

He declared that he had banned the carrying of firearms and the placing of explosives on streetcar tracks: 'I am determined that Chicago will enjoy a "safe" Fourth. As for the sanity of it, I have no control over that.'

Miles could feel the mood in the streets even without Shippy's warnings and declarations. It was a party that promoted only patriotic hysteria, she decided, and there was enough of that already in the world.

As night fell, the first fireworks shot up into the smoggy night, and rained orange and yellow sparks. Next door to their apartment she could see a man sitting on his side doorstep, throwing crackers onto the street. She cowered in her room, covering her ears against the whizzing and the banging and the sudden bursts of shooting, the drunken singing and the police whistles. Her nerves jangled with the sounds of the stars and stripes until only acrid smoke hung in the dawn sky.

This is not a celebration, she thought. *This is insanity.*

August brought the hottest day of the year and a furnace breeze came from the south-west, melting ice creams. There were storm clouds in the distance and a faint roll of thunder, but no rain. Only a strike of lightning anger from Chicago's telegraphers, who had been picketing for weeks outside the headquarters of Western Union on La Salle Street. The *Tribune* feared they 'had cut the city off from the world'. The Women's Trade Union League was giving 25 dollars a week to the telegrapher strikers' fund to support the female groups among the picketers.

One of the striking women stood in front of the Western Union building's doors, spreading her parasol and daring the police and strike breakers to push past her to enter. Other women spread their picket signs like angel's wings.

Since the fourth of July, Miles had been on edge. Her nerves had barely recovered from the chaos. She had the cross thought that Americans had far worse things to free themselves from than England. The heat of the city, at first so welcome after the freezing winter, had created exhaustion. She sweated in the city's surprising humidity.

'Look after your health', Linda had urged. She knew how her sister struggled with sleep, and with her nerves. Linda must be in Queensland by now, in her governor's mansion. Lady Linda.

The Australian journal *The Book Lover* had asked Miles for an update on her life in Chicago. She penned a letter of sunshine, carefully constructing a story of her glamorous life abroad. She described meeting the socialist William Walling, and Anna Strunsky, who inspired her to always keep her name; America's obsession with ice cream; and surviving the fourth of July. She assured readers that she kept up with the news through the Australian newspapers and journals her friends sent her, and via Alice Henry. She did not mention she was working in a department store, only that she was doing a sociological investigation of America's 'dens', because that sounded like the work of a New Woman, in a new country.

She did not mention, either, being tired and frazzled. Nor the claustrophobia of the streetcar, the monotony of the store, the stodge sold by cheap cafes. Sometimes she felt like she was a machine, only existing to provide herself with food, shelter and the clothes she could afford. Artistic dreams seemed to come only when, or if, she could sleep.

She tried to sleep. The city did not.

~

The heat continued. In her department store, as well as bathers, there are new season silk petticoats and tailored hats, evening wraps, plaid and tweed for city dressing, and motoring coats for 'automobiling'. Miles thinks that the fashions in Australia are a year ahead of Chicago, although she wouldn't mind a motoring coat.

Arriving at her apartment, squashed and tired after the streetcar, she looks out for her mail. The telegraph operators are still on strike, and Alice comes home with stories from the picket line; the regular postal service is still being delivered.

She sees the familiar emerald penny stamps on an envelope, and for a moment the day lifts, because it is postmarked from Queensland.

She opens the letter.

Dearest Stella,

I got your letter as I was leaving Q'land yesterday.

I have very sad news for you my dear . . .

Our dear little Linda . . .

Miles reads on. The words, and her world, break.

43

It was September 1907. In Australia, *Book Lover* readers were pleased that, despite the rumours that Miles Franklin was lost in the 'wilds of America', she was actually in Chicago. 'We fancy that many will be glad to hear such late news of the doings of the best of writers that Australia has produced during the last five years. Miss Franklin slipped off very quietly . . .' Readers were assured that everything was utterly delightful and jolly for Miss Miles Franklin, and she was 'having a very good time', and 'in perfect health'. She was enjoying luncheons and dinners, and indoor picnics, where she ate with her silver plate on her lap in sitting rooms with 'delightful' friends and 'delightful' music, and 'it was so sociable and informal, you wouldn't believe!'

The article warned that Miss Franklin 'shows no intention as yet of her return'.

Back in Penrith to clear out the rest of their lives Miles' mother watched her grandson Edward play on the floor, and cough, for the cold was still heavy on his chest. She turned and scooped him close to her, wiping his nose and then her own tears. Her only surviving daughter, Stella Miles, should have received her letter by now.

A telegram would have been too brutally brief for such grief, so a letter was a gentler way to give Miles such sad news. And Mrs Franklin could not have sent a telegram, because of the Chicago telegraphers' strike.

'Charlie, poor boy whose love, hopes & ambitions were dashed at a stroke,' she had written in her letter to Miles.

'Poor motherless baby!'

She did not ask her only surviving daughter to come home and be a mother.

~

Away from the front lines of the strike, the Women's Trade Union League secretary, Miss Alice Henry, talked to Miss Addams about Miles, for whom she had grave concerns. In the days after receiving a tragic letter from her mother, Miles' health had declined to the extent that Alice had taken her to the Passavant Memorial Hospital.

Alice told Addams that, nine days after Miles' sister had arrived in Queensland at their grand new home, she had passed away very quickly from pneumonia. The husband, Charles, after giving their baby to Miles' mother, had shut up the new house and gone to be with his brother.

Miles' parents had been intending to move to Queensland. Now they would soon be homeless, with a wee one, and were deciding what to do.

~

The Passavant Memorial Hospital offered free hospital beds to a city in which very little was free. Around Miles in the small ward, other women stared at the ceiling, or moaned in pain, or whispered softly to visitors. In her assigned bed, she lay in a state that she later came to call her *dungeon of despair.*

She would tell Alice one day about her dungeon, and how she had grieved so deeply that she felt she had died too: 'I resent death . . . Each bereavement kills me, really. Each loss of a friend stabs me nearly to death.' But she did not tell Alice this for decades.

Now, in 1907, there had been so many deaths to endure since *My Brilliant Career* had changed her life. The books she'd written in bursts of fever afterwards had died from rejection, one after the other. The unpublished manuscripts were still in the suitcase she'd brought to Chicago, which was their cemetery. Each had been a little death. She had not written another.

Edwin's last letter had questioned why she was working so hard and producing so little, so far away. 'What progress have you made so far?' he had asked, and it read like an accusation, although it was from concern: 'I don't want my love to work the life and soul out of herself and then be unable to accomplish anything.'

Edwin had not written letters of love and longing over the summer, and it was clear that their engagement had died in the mail. His abrupt ending of their relationship had hurt her more than she'd expected.

She had carried inside her the death of her little sister Laurel since that night in Penrith, when she had watched her slip to the moon.

Then Linda had warned her not to break more hearts in America. Her sister never hinted that she'd be the one to break Miles' heart.

Linda had never told her how ill she'd been since the baby's birth, and how she was already very weak when the pneumonia came. Granny had said it was a terrible time, and that 'her milk left her', but Miles had assumed Linda had recovered, as mothers do. Linda had said she'd been ill when she'd gone to the spring fair with their cousin Phillip, but it seemed to be a passing comment, tossed off in her characteristically harmonious way. She had begged Miles to write soon, and then gone off to Queensland, where she was supposed to live a long life in harmony with her family.

Her mother had told her that Linda had gone where she can 'cease from troubling and where the weary are at rest'.

The baby's grandmother was now his mother, and his father, Charles, was a lost soul, still grieving at his brother's home in the north of New South Wales, far from his child.

Her mother now held the 'dear little babe'.

'It was very sad, in a strange land.'

As the Passavant pastor did his rounds, he would pause by the Australian woman's bed. She listened politely or shook her head at his offer of solace and prayers for her sister. He would then move on.

She would not worship God and be servile to him. Women suffered the pangs of child-bearing but they got nothing in return, except the hope that things would be better in the next world.

No, God was unreasonable. It would be best if she struggled on without him and told no one.

The doctor observed his patient. Miles exhibited the hallmark traits of 'neurasthenia', which the *Tribune* described as a 'fashionable disease among women, nevertheless, one of the most dangerous that has ever threatened a complete breakdown of the body and mind'. It wove together insomnia, depression and irritability. It afflicted those with finer nervous systems, so it was usually finely tuned women who collapsed on their chaises longues. But Jane Addams knew all humans were finely tuned, because she had seen factory workers collapse into Hull House in a tangle of nervous wires. And young women who were sad in a strange land.

Passavant Hospital did not offer treatment for neurasthenia, and Miles could not afford a clinic that did. There were spa treatments that prescribed salt water and massage, or warm carbonated baths, for water soothed the soul, if you could afford treatment for the soul.

Miles was too unwell and too poor to travel to an expensive spa back west or to the oranges at Loma Linda, where Jonesie was still studying nursing. Her friends would not subject her to the local Cook County Insane Asylum and Infirmary that locals in hushed voices called 'Dunning'. It was a 'tomb for the living', near a cemetery for the unclaimed and forgotten. Dunning would be a living death, next to the abandoned dead.

Jane Addams knew what the Passavant doctor would suggest—a quiet room and a prescription of Mitchell's Rest Cure, which she herself had endured under Dr Weir Mitchell's hand when she was Miles' age, after one year in medical school. First, it had been her back pain, and then her nerves. She did not want Miles to be subjected to others' decisions about what she could and could not do.

Dr Mitchell prescribed that the woman suffering neurasthenia needed to be kept still, and fattened with pints of milk, to restore their blood and nerves. If she was already fat, the milk should be skimmed. He thought it was best for the woman to be taken from her home environment to rest—away from children, husband, social demands, and worst of all, too much intellectual activity. He prescribed no books, no art. No debates or conversations that might stir the soul. Instead, rest. A ceiling to stare at, and walls.

Charlotte Perkins Gilman had written a widely read account of being subjected to the cure; she had stared at swirling yellow wallpaper and feared that, if she got worse, she would be sent to Mitchell for immobility and milk. This was not Dunning, but it was still a living death for anyone with an intellectual mind. Given her own experience, Jane Addams cautioned against Mitchell's Rest Cure for Miles, because 'To be put to bed and fed on milk is not what a [young woman] requires.' She and Alice agreed on another plan.

~

In Passavant Hospital, in the dim light of her room, Miles was visited by the intern, Dr Allen Johnson, on his daily rounds. He monitored her heart with a stethoscope and she felt its coldness touch her skin. He had heard she was in a death-like state, from her grief at her sister's death, but her breath still flowed steadily. The intern went regularly out of his way on his rounds to hear her breathe.

To try and interest her in something other than bed—and, if he was honest with himself, because he liked her to be near him—he took her to his operating theatre and asked her to sit like an audience member on a stage.

A girl was wheeled in on a porcelain table. Her scalp and eyebrow had been torn away by the belt of a factory machine, and they hung off her head like half-peeled orange skin, exposing a juice of blood and flesh. As the intern stitched and dressed the scalp, he glanced at Miles. He checked her for signs of life as frequently as he checked the girl under his hands.

~

In her ward, the days pass. Alice visits. Dr Johnson lingers by her bed. A cold rain falls outside; an autumn wind turns into a gale. The sun, weaker than in summer, rises and lights the curtains hanging on the window of the ward. Every day and night, the chaos of the street below carries on.

She will remember this time at the hospital. She will create a character who has a 'psychic rebellion', whom she will name Constance. She is a young woman working in Chicago who collapses in her rented room from pneumonia complicated by nervous exhaustion.

She is found and hospitalised at a public hospital that is very like Passavant. The female doctor inspired by Miles' friend and landlady, Dr Josephine Young consults with an alienist, as psychiatrists were called, for the mind was an alien thing. He takes Constance on as his pro-bono patient.

She will tell the alienist that she is 'cursed by feeling' that she is a 'terror to herself'.

She is not cursed, he assures her, but has 'divine sensitiveness'.

'Rubbish. Other people have delusions and illusions. I have too much common sense, I know my own length too well.'

Constance resents the specialist. *What could he know of weakness?* she thinks. What could he know of the devitalising sense of failure that was always with her?

'Why,' she asks, 'should I continue living?'

He suggests that love is around the corner, and she feels her curse, or her divineness, rise up: 'There is a theory that any woman can be rescued from the shoals of failure and despair by finding some man to ask her in marriage, but before I could be happy in love I should at least need to realise myself.'

For now, Miles lies in bed, and doctors and nurses pass around her. The windows are closed against the cold, and the curtains droop in stillness.

44

The autumn of 1907 deepened. Outside Chicago, in the town of Winnetka on the lake, William Bross Lloyd's wife, Lola, tried not to think about where her husband was, or with whom, as their three children played on the lawn. It wasn't cold enough yet for the sealskin jackets that their father had made for them, although they would need them soon.

In the neighbouring mansions that graced the lake, the curtains were closed. The wealthy had drifted back to the city after their summer by the water, but the Lloyds were always in residence. Wayside was their family home, and also home for those who had fallen by the wayside, continuing the tradition of William's parents, Henry Demarest Lloyd and Jessie Bross Lloyd. Family friend Jane Addams, had dubbed Wayside an annexe of Hull House

Sitting close to Alice, Miles looked out the window of the train. She could see leaves the colours of bushfires falling from the trees. The sky looked clearer, and there were clouds, rather than smog. The train pulled into a small station with a sign, 'Winnetka', and Alice guided her outside. The air was cold and clean. It soothed her lungs, rather than stung them as the dirty and bitter-cold air of Chicago did.

A car waited for them at the station and carried them to a large wooden and red-brick house with a blue roof, surrounded by elm trees and bordered by the beach on the lake. There was a ramshackle welcomeness about it. Instead of sterile lawns, there were shrubs and some simple lattice fencing around the house, shrouding the wealth inside.

Lola greeted them with the soft Texan accent that she had brought to Chicago from her years growing up on her family's ranch. She was the granddaughter of Samuel Maverick, a lawyer and politician who refused to brand his cattle, and so bequeathed to the American language his family name to describe others of a similarly unconventional turn of mind.

A fire was alight in the giant arched brick fireplace, one of six fireplaces throughout the house. The original house had been an inn, called the Wayside, where, according to local legend, the best whisky between Chicago and Milwaukee had been served. But the name fitted the Lloyds' open-house philosophy. Wayside meant 'neglected'. Marked by neglect or disuse. Adjacent to a road, or path.

As Miles looked around the house with Alice, she didn't know which path in life she was on anymore.

~

Miles was given a bedroom. She would be well looked after with the Lloyds, Alice reassured her before returning to Chicago and her work. Alice and Jane Addams had arranged with Lola and Bill Lloyd that Miles could stay as long as she needed to recover.

Miles nodded, trusting in Alice—dearest Pops—and Miss Addams' decisions. And where else could she go? She was not well enough to be alone in their flat. Hull House was full of residents, who paid board as well as contributing to its organisation and events, and a bed at the Jane Club was not permanent.

Australia was a transcontinental train ride back to San Francisco, followed by a long sea voyage. And what train or boat would she take after that? To where? Stillwater had been sold, and now Penrith too.

A surge of sadness, and the rising up of failure.

Alice kissed her goodbye.

'Thank you, Pops,' she said.

~

There was an engraved Weber piano in the house. Miles sat down on the piano stool and felt the ivory keys touch her fingers. Perhaps when she was better, she would start music lessons again, and rent a piano.

She could drink milk, as little or as much as she wanted. She was encouraged to eat what she could stomach. She played with the children, but only if she felt like feeling the life of their little hands in hers.

In defiance of the rest cure she exercised her brain in the Lloyds' library, as she had done when she had been a servant in the wealthy houses in Sydney and Melbourne, except Lola was not her Mistress and would not order her to clean the floor or cook the dinner.

Lola took Miles into town to go shopping and she bought a Winnetka postcard for her mother. She put a cross on the postcard where Wayside was, and where the Lloyds' automobile shed was tucked among the woods, so her mother could see where she was staying, and that their land rolled down to the lake.

'Miss H brought me out here last Saturday,' she wrote. 'There is no talk of me being fit for work for months yet. I'm getting jolly sick of it.'

She was feeling fragile. Homesick: 'I wrote to you last mail but did not get any mail from home this time.'

She addressed the postcard to Queensland, where her mother had returned to look after her grandson for Charlie now that he had also returned to their house of grief. Miles' father was a day labourer in the state somewhere. Was Queensland the family's home state now, where Linda had died? Where, if Miles joined them there, dear Charles might look to her for what she could not give?

She could return to Talbingo, and finally make her Granny happy by finding a Harold Beecham. Or by being the dutiful granddaughter, as Linda had been, caring for Granny in her old age. Granny would be relieved she'd stopped wandering the earth.

Could Melbourne become her home? Alice had done well as a journalist in Melbourne before she moved to the United States, and Vida Goldstein, her mother and her sisters kept in touch. Vida was still campaigning and thinking beyond Australia. She wrote to Miles that she was 'dreadfully disappointed for all the American suffragists at the "failure" of Oregon', where the amendment to the state's constitution, to grant women the vote, had yet again failed to gain a popular majority. Vida had described their flat as being in a 'dreadful muddle', yet she hoped it would be ready for visitors soon.

Miles was not ready to return to Melbourne, where she was still known only as the author of *My Brilliant Career.*

There was always Rose at Lynton, who would be thrilled to have her spirit child so close again. She could write stories for the *Herald*, and avoid questions about her next book at Rose's Friday-night salons.

She knew that Rose and Vida would not judge her for returning with nothing but stories to tell of the people she'd met. She would judge herself. She always did.

It was Lola's 32nd birthday, and William Lloyd gave her an alligator-skin bag. *My heart*, he called her, and she wanted to forgive what she didn't want to know. Throughout the day, Lola noticed that their guest—Miss Franklin, or Stella, as she liked to be called—was nervous. Despite the birthday festivities, she was sort of cross. She was on edge, and Lola was annoyed. It was her birthday after all. She regarded Stella's moods as being so 'unevenly' exasperating.

Lola reminded herself that Miles was still recovering, and her moods were changeable. Lola was used to moodiness among the guests who came to stay, because they were all on the wayside, really. Miss Henry would be here this afternoon, and her steadiness would steady Stella.

Lola did not know that birthdays reminded Miles of her age. In October, in hospital, she had turned 28, and her aunt Helena, who lived with Granny, had sent her an annual belated birthday note, containing an unwelcome reminder. Time was passing in the Windy City, but the wind did not age. She could not stop the wind, only brace herself for its force.

Before Lola's birthday, another automobile had turned up in the Wayside drive with Demarest 'Demy' Lloyd at the wheel. He was tow-haired, with a boyish smile and status as a 'Harvard man'.

Another *petted lion*, like his older brother.

At Lola's birthday and again at Thanksgiving, he flirted with Miles at the table, as William Lloyd had done when she sat next to him at the dinner after Miss Strunsky and William Walling had called for a revolution. Demy's talk was of Boston, yacht racing and automobiles, and she suspected he was a king of indoor games. She noticed that he did not have a moustache, which was good, as she disliked the moustache fashion. She thought it was like a 'furry toothbrush' above a lip, and any man with a moustache who tried to kiss her was distasteful.

Demy was married, but he did not act as if he was married. He was a 'dude'. She did love American slang. Did he have a brain buried under his silly 'ass' behaviour? She once wouldn't have dared to use such language. Instead, she would have said 'silly billy', as she had called Edwin. She was getting sassier now, using language her grandmother would be horrified by, like *hell* and *damn*, like a man. Chicago was a sassy place.

Edwin, the *silly billy.* Why did she care so much? She could write about it and toss her feelings away. She could invent another character: Sybyl Penelo, a stenographer who lived in Chicago. It would be as though she was Sybylla Penelope Melvyn's American cousin. And Sybyl would share the same feelings as Sybylla.

She would be full of sass, and say things like: 'When a man becomes too vigorously engaged to me, I change my geographical location and then he jilts me. I just love to be jilted. It relieves me of all the responsibility.'

It was a relief to be here at Wayside. In future, her only responsibility would be to herself, and her books—if she could write again. She was not well enough yet.

~

The lake has become colder, and the breeze is wet when she goes for a walk. She walks along the woodland paths thick with fallen leaves. Her boots squashing them, rather than making footprints in dust.

The woods have a different beat to the bush. There are no sharp cracks, or a kookaburra's laugh or a lyrebird's mimic. Here the songbirds have flown south for the winter, in flocks so big they formed their own clouds. A few birds remain and shelter in the trees. There are snakes hiding in the woodland's wet undergrowth; perhaps they sense her snake, which is always with her.

She will be leaving Wayside soon. That decision she has now made, so she wants to absorb these final moments.

As she walks, she breathes and feels. She feels a little more alive.

PART FOUR

The Survivor

45

It was early 1908. In the South Pacific, Jack London had reached Samoa; he wrote to his agent in London, anxious to know what price his novel, *White Fang*, would have in New Zealand and Australia. He and Charmian posed in the rigging for a photo, and the ropes looked like nerves.

At Loma Linda in California, Jonesie was disappointed that Miles was no longer coming west for the rest of the winter, so she would not be caring for her friend among the orange groves.

Back in Chicago, Miles laced up her ice skates. A grey sky sifted the light. Grimy alleyways were filled with steam from boilers generating heat. The city's ponds had frozen over; she would write to her mother on the postcard she'd bought, which showed people swimming in the pond she was now skating on. The pond was just two blocks from the apartment she shared with Alice and Josephine, her in-house doctor, flatmate and landlady.

She had promised to write to Granny too. She feared being like Granny, with her mind and face atrophying. The curse of life's final years was such a weariness. If she was cursed with old age, she decided, then *God forbid that anyone would entertain her out of pity.*

In Ohio Street, not far from Hull House, ice hung on the windows of an upstairs apartment in a building surrounded by rickety houses, flats and sweatshops. Inside, Margaret Dreier Robins wrote another cheque to keep the Women's Trade Union League, solvent. She did not want for heat or hot water as money flowed from her inheritance, and from Raymond's self-made wealth from a gold strike. They could afford much more luxury than they allowed themselves. Instead, they followed the example of Jane Addams and, upon moving to Chicago from New York, had resolved to do more than talk to the poor and live rich. Like Jane Addams said, 'the existence of charity denies us the consolation and freedom which democracy at last will give'.

But the Robins' support for a high-profile mining union organiser, William 'Big Bill' Hayward, who was acquitted of ordering the assassination of a former Idaho Governor, attracted hostility and suspicion that even their money could not protect them from. Her sister, Mary in New York, was outraged, while Margaret was both amused and indignant. Later, Mary publicly refuted the vicious rumours: 'The feeling against Margaret among the middle-class women ran so high that she was blackballed by the Chicago Women's City Club . . . the rumor would not be silenced, and the tale spread in all seriousness that she was so busy organizing girls into trade unions that she even neglected her baby; who froze to death on the fire escape; she who, to her unending sorrow, never had a baby.'

Margaret was strong, like the WTUL's emblem of two women in Grecian dress, one holding a baby and the other a shield, against a rising sun in the background. Their hands were clasped above a placard that read 'The Eight-Hour Day. A Living Wage. To Guard the Home'. The average working week was 56 hours, a living wage was unliveable, and guarding the home provided a frail barrier to the hardship outside. There had been progress, and Margaret was planning campaigns to take the League to a truly national level, coordinating more closely with the branches in Boston and New York run by her sister, Mary. Margaret regretted the telegraphers' strike had been so local; Chicago was not enough.

Sometimes it seemed her main value to the League was the flow of funds from her and Raymond's fortune. She was now also paying her personal secretary twelve dollars per week from her own pocket, because the League's funds did not stretch that far.

She had written to the lovely young friend of Alice and the Glove Union organiser Agnes Nestor, Miss Franklin, last fall, when Miles was still at Wayside, and offered her the position.

> My dear Miss Franklin,
>
> The more I work the more I seem to have to do, which is not at all the old adage that 'when you begin to knit a stocking you surely will get to the end sometime'. Perhaps I am trying to knit too many stockings at once but whatever the cause, I am wondering if you will be able to help me . . . I am very anxious to have someone to take care of what I term my correspondence and work as national president of the Women's Trade Union League . . .

Miles had been anxious about the offer. She had completed her stenography course, and she could answer the telephone with the aplomb of a 'Hello Girl', as receptionists were called in Chicago. Mrs Robins implied that there would be more than that to do as well. The offer, when she was still so fragile, was overwhelming; she did not know if she was capable of knitting one stocking, let alone as many important stockings as those of the president of the WTUL.

Margaret assured Miles that she was prepared to wait for Miles until the new year. 'Knowing that you are not strong, I ventured to consult Dr Young,' she assured Miles. 'Like a wise physician. She made many inquiries but when I explained to her that it was a work which meant going slow in the beginning, she felt that you were able to undertake it should you care to do so.'

Miles talked about it with Alice—her darling, wise Pops, who was moving on from the League to edit a union journal, but would still be in the same office.

Mrs Robins could be temperamental, but she was generous, Alice advised.

Miles could take one stocking at a time.

~

Miles returned to Winnetka for a weekend, to see Lola and the children, for she was not yet confident that she wouldn't wake up one morning feeling like she was in her dungeon of despair.

'Fine to see Miss Franklin,' Lola wrote in her diary, and Miles was grateful for her open invitation to stay with the Lloyds, and take refuge in their library and the lake and the woods. Other sanatoriums were too expensive—like the Winnetka spa that, in its advertisements, offered sanctuary during and after the convalescence, when the nerves and heart needed special care. Wayside in Winnetka gave her all that, and intellectual salve, too, with Lola.

Jonesie was too far away. Perhaps Miles could go back to Loma Linda later in the year, if things didn't work out, when she had saved some money.

~

Loma Linda, and Jonesie, remained postcards and letters as Miles soon became adept at managing Margaret Dreier Robins' bulging bag of stockings. Her regular pay was now double that of a department-store clerk, so her purse contained enough dollars to buy the five-cent special lunch or dinner at the Hearth, where she balanced a buffet tray after a day working at the Robins' apartment, or at the League's new official headquarters at the Board of Trade building, which was topped with a clock.

The head of the Chicago Federation Labor Board had given the League corner offices that were more like holes in the wall, given the size of the building. Agnes Nestor had voted for the move from Hull House to the city, as she detested the streetcar ride, drenched in sweat and smoke and the lingering stench from the stockyard, canneries and tanneries, down Halsted Street. It was a small comfort to avoid the streetcar, and Agnes put up her hand in favour. All her life, Agnes had fought for small comforts, and this was one of them.

In the new office, they felt the burly suspicion of the male unionists, who muttered among themselves. Were these League women using unions to get the vote? Would they stir up trouble the men didn't need? They had to admit that they got their gloves dirty with picketing, fundraising and running relief kitchens.

There was Elizabeth Maloney from the Waitress Union, Agnes Nestor, and the German-born 'Sister Emma', who had all experienced the hardship and exploitation of the factory floor. The rest were ladies with a college education; except for a dark-haired firecracker, plus a sterner, older woman who, like the German, had a withering stare. The two of them had accents they couldn't quite place, until they were told they were Australians.

The Federation president, the Irishman John Fitzpatrick, who had begun his working life in the 'killing pens' of the stockyards and who Raymond Robins described as a man 'built for war', wanted the women as allies on the floor. So that was that, then. And the younger Australian had such a lovely and cheeky smile.

With Alice, Agnes, Elizabeth and Mrs R's other lieutenants, Miles mapped out a code of behaviour to manage their new shared space. They would remain in their designated office area, rather than try to encroach into the smoke that hung like a border between them and the men. They would pay careful attention to their dress to be feminine and demure, but not so alluring as to look available. They would speak softly and sweetly, which belied the hard facts moving through their minds.

The unionists' confusion and attraction, as they loitered and sauntered past the League's little corner, were amusing.

Keep them at a distance. Keep them guessing.

Margaret was thrilled with her new lieutenant. She was worth the twelve-dollar-a-week salary, she decided. Miles now came so often to the Robins' apartment that Raymond had named her 'Lieutenant Franklin', and she would give him a salute. Cheeky girl.

Miles was a younger and more lively version of wise and intimidating Alice; Margaret found Miles effusive and inviting. She was her 'dearest little Stella-girl', she wrote on a card, who was most 'imperial and efficient'. She was so smart, witty and clever. The daughter she had always wanted . . . she pushed the pain of her childlessness away.

Still, Margaret thought that Miles clung too much to Alice, understandably, because Alice was so steady, stoic and straightforward. Miles, for all her effervescent efficiency, was flighty and anxious, especially about her health.

Alice and Miles lived and worked together, and she could tell that Alice felt responsible for the younger Australian, who had suffered so, although she now did her best to hide it. They were both 'women adrift', as the newspapers insisted on calling single women living out of home, as if they had no anchor. Alice and Miles showed that friendship was as strong as the bonds of family. Margaret did not want them to drift apart, but she encouraged Miles to branch out more on her own so the two of them could have a less intense friendship. They needed separate lives, so they could come together more.

This was not an order, but both Alice and Miles listened to her attentively. Margaret feared that Miles' depression and health fears were too draining for Alice and perhaps even Dr Josephine.

Margaret confided to Alice: 'all last winter your very natural worry and anxiety was a drain on your own physical strength . . . is it not time to think of yourself a little?'

'You have the right to friends your own age,' Margaret more diplomatically advised Miles. 'You are with too many serious, older people.'

That wasn't quite true, Miles thought. She had Agnes Nestor, who told Miles that she had begun her working life making gloves on a factory floor, tending to machines at long tables in 60-hour weeks, seated among rows of women. Until she had led a revolt.

'I was so tired, I could hardly work,' Agnes said. 'To drown the monotony, we sang "Daisy Bell".' It was a popular song:

Daisy, Daisy,
Give me your answer, do!

I'm half crazy,
All for the love of you!
It won't be a stylish marriage,
I can't afford a carriage,
But you'll look sweet upon the seat
Of a bicycle built for two!

The foreman had allowed it because the rhythm of their singing matched the movement of the machines, which was all that mattered. Agnes and the other women bent over their gloves, singing until they screamed.

As well as Agnes, she'd met Emma Pischel, from the Clerk's Union, whose brother Fred would call and ask her to restaurants she could not afford so she often suggested a cheaper cafe, and would pay her own way, as she preferred. He was charming but irritating—another *silly billy*. She and the woodchip heiress Zelie Emerson had bonded over their shared experience investigating department stores and scrubbing floors. And their love of hats, for Zelie's hats were, Miles exulted, 'an ecstasy of expense and beauty'. Miles tried some of them on, posing while Zelie nodded approvingly and adjusted the angles, feathers and fur.

Margaret had recently introduced Miles to a young professor of mathematics, Arnold Dresden, and his wife, Louise, who worked with the League. Miles regularly had dinner with the other stenographers, and occasionally they treated themselves to the fancier restaurant, King's.

The intern from Passavant Hospital, Dr Allen Johnson, escorted her to the theatre and to the vaudeville show where they watched an Australian whip-cracking carnival star. Miles had been taught to crack the whip and she now longed to do it, to feel the force of the whip's crack against hardened ground. She was irritated by the antics of the showman's girl assistant.

She could do so much better, she told the whip-cracker when she met him afterwards; naturally, he asked her to join his act.

'My Granny wouldn't approve,' she said in her now well-rehearsed line whenever she was invited to join the theatre, the circus or a whip-cracking celebrity.

Dr Johnson smiled at how happy she seemed. Miles wasn't sure if he was a doctor anymore, as he'd confessed to her that he'd been dismissed from Passavant Hospital.

'Whatever for?' Miles asked, astonished. He had seemed such a capable doctor and surgeon.

He blushed, embarrassed. 'I proposed to a patient and, when I told my superior, he dismissed me.'

'I would never have said anything,' she protested. She remembered the moment, in her dungeon of despair that had been Passavant before she went to the Lloyds', when her doctor spontaneously took her hand to do more than to check her pulse. She had not been in a fit state to consider any proposal when she was at Passavant, much less one of a marriage. Now, months later, it was still an irrational idea, and she was shocked that he had been so reckless as to risk his career over a few words he had shared with her. They had meant so much to him, and so little to her.

~

In the spring, Miles felt strong enough to move from the rooms she shared with Alice and Josephine. Margaret Dreier Robins jokingly warned that it was time. 'If you do not move, I will bodily carry you out,' she said and they laughed, imagining Margaret cradling her down the stairs of their apartment and on to her new accommodation.

When Miles had begun looking for rooms that suited a New Woman like herself, with a New Woman position in an office, she had recalled being told at the boarding house in Sydney, when she was caught dancing with the young officer, that a girl in her position could not be too careful. Her position had now changed, but she still was cautious.

There were few places for single women that were suitable in a city like Chicago. She did not want to live with a widow who was renting out a room to pay for a house she could not afford, because lack of privacy was the cost of a cheaper rent. She was too tired after work to make small talk with a stranger, or to clean up their kitchen to meet their fastidious standards.

Instead, Miles had taken her photos, her rented typewriter and her trunk of manuscripts still dormant among her clothes, to rooms in the Harvard Hotel, a four-storey stone building with large windows that looked out at a line of trees, that offered a housekeeper who changed the linen. There was a cafe downstairs, where she could eat, like at the Kirribilli boarding house, but this time she would be a guest in the zoo, rather than serving in it. She is now friends with petted lions, and with Lola, the lioness.

Her position has changed.

In the Harvard Hotel, she arranges her typewriter, and her family photos so they are always on display. It has been a year since Linda died, and the mourning is now a quiet murmur in her heart. She has joined the League's chorus to bring music into her life again, following Jane Addams' advice that the arts are a necessity for healing. The body needs clean water, nutrition and a day of rest, Miss Addams said, and the soul needs theatre, art, music and poetry. So Miles goes often to the theatre, because Miss Addams spoke of theatre as 'the house of dreams'.

As she sings, other voices chorus inside her. She is imagining characters and their lives, inspired by the stories she is absorbing in her work in the office corner. It will be a play, and she will call it 'The Survivors'.

She opens her suitcase too and sees the wads of pages of words, and feels the paper. It is her own Potter's Field, where Chicago buries its unclaimed and unwanted. The servant manuscript, 'When I Was Mary Anne, a Slavey'. Other novels—Sybylla's sequel, and *Some Everyday Folk and Dawn*. Short stories and fragments of ideas. She selects one of these forgotten paupers.

She does not speak of the play or new drafts. When she is asked about working at the League's office among the men, she tells them she is as 'quiet as a mouse'. She is also keeping her writing mouse quiet, and in the streetlamp-lit long hours of the night, she blocks out the world. The typewriter is the only sound in her hotel room of dreams.

46

It was January 1909. The Man from Snowy River had left his position as editor of *The Evening News* after deciding that the only seat he liked was a saddle. He would write, and ride. If a war came, he would become a correspondent again. He would be like Jack London, who had reached Australia, and was now in Tasmania.

At his retreat on a Tasmanian beach, London replied to his correspondence, and assured friends and family the *Snark* hadn't sunk in the South Pacific, as had been reported. He was the wreck, not the boat; with 'deep sorrow' he was abandoning the *Snark* voyage, and would sell the vessel in Australia once it was sailed over from the Solomon Islands.

'I am at times practically helpless, unable to cut a piece of cold meat with a knife and fork,' he wrote. 'I have been suffering from an obscure nervous affliction which defies all the doctors in Australia . . . I am compelled to abandon the voyage.' He now planned to 'go back to California to the climate where I have always succeeded in maintaining a stable, nervous equilibrium in the hope that my equilibrium will be restored.'

In Sydney, the artist Norman Lindsay, approaching his thirtieth birthday, had decided he would not spend another decade in puritanical Australia, though he was gratified that the National Gallery of Victoria had shocked the public by buying his sensational painting *Pollice Verso*.

Further north, in Queensland, Charlie Graham and his new fiancée, Edith, planned their wedding for March in a Brisbane church; Edith had fittings for her gown, which was netted in green lace. She would be adorned with orange blossoms, just as Linda had been.

And at Wilga Vale, Edwin Bridle faced another bushfire season while his new wife, Traillie—her name shortened in that Australian way from her patriotic birth name of Australia—scanned the skies. Soon she would have the first of their five children; to his relief, and just as her first name promised, she had no interest in spreading literary or any other wings beyond Australia.

The previous year, *The Sydney Morning Herald*'s women's pages had hailed his former dearest love's success in the United States, and reported her new job working for a 'woman of great wealth whose sociological and philanthropic work gives the young Australian writer an opportunity of seeing a side of American life which is not usually seen by the stranger'. In his life of wool prices, weather and now his wife, it did not matter. Miles was forgotten.

~

At the League chorus rehearsal, Miles' voice was strong in the Chicago cold that froze your throat. In the new year, she recorded her participation in the rehearsal in the diary she had begun, inspired by her friend Lola Lloyd, who was now nursing her new baby. Lola and the children had gone to her family in

San Antonio, Texas, for the winter, where Lola had found time to write to her friend Miss Franklin from the ranch.

Miles had bought a diary of a similar size to Lola's—small, with a speckled-rust cloth cover that opened to the yearly calendar and provided the current postage rates per ounce for packages. It wasn't as elaborate as Lola's; hers had the astrological signs on its cover, and listed eclipses and antidotes for poisons. The space in Miles' diary did not allow for reflections beyond a few words on each day. She liked the economy of it: a haiku of daily life.

She recorded that she spent new year's night with Alice, and they marvelled that this was their third year in Chicago. On 2 January, she and Alice went to the Robins' flat for belated season's greetings. The Robins had just returned from warmer Florida, where they had spent Christmas, and where they allowed themselves, for a short time, to relax and be rich. Margaret read to them like children, because she loved to see her 'girls' scattered around the apartment on the sofa and on the floor. As if she was the favourite, Miles blew out the candles on the Christmas tree.

January 3rd was a Sunday, and it was supposed to be her day of rest. Granny had once warned Miles that she would invite God's wrath if she worked on the Sabbath. Six days were enough, she had warned, sounding like a union organiser. Miles dined again with Margaret; she recorded that afterwards she attended a protest meeting, which she preferred to prayer.

Her diary pages filled up with weather reports that charted the skies, and her daytime activities. In March, the month of Charlie's wedding, it was unseasonably mild; Miles' mood was not. She wrote that she ate dinner in bed in her room, which now felt very lonely. Sensing her mood, Alice, like a mother, rushed over to check on her.

Her diary entries became flat. Listless. She wrote weather notes: *53–33 F (11.6–0). Came back to Harvard. Very depressed.*

Louise Dresden knew the best rest cure for Miles; she coaxed her from her bed and couch with tickets to see Ludwig Wüllner, the touring German operatic tenor and dramatic narrator, at the Fine Arts Building. She guided her fragile friend through the entrance of the theatre, and Miles took comfort in the healing sign etched above the building's doors: *All Passes—Art Alone Endures.*

In the weeks after the concert, Miles returned to her routine of late evenings out with Agnes and Alice, and her chorus practice of 'Garden of Flowers'. The sheet music was entwined with roses and thorns as she sang: 'Youth in spring, and a world in bloom / Garden of flowers with its sweet perfume'. In the early hours, when the restlessness came on, she took a sleeping tonic of barbiturate veronal and aspirin. It quietened the sparrows in her brain. When she was desperate, she added a shuddering sip of brandy to the mix.

There was another tonic, which sometimes still created its own fevers. She studied the pages of her smaller novel, set in Penrith, that land of melons and memories. She had selected this manuscript to rework, now that all that remained of her old life there with her family was little Laurel's grave, and this book.

She had decided to tweak it for an English and American audience. But she would keep the setting, as there are towns with orchards and rivers on the edge of many cities. She kept the main character, Dawn, and the narrator, who was somewhat like Alice. She kept the references to the kookaburra and the story of the first election in which women could vote.

In Australia, the critic had told her that people had tired of reading about women and politics. How provincial of him; how parochial to only think of their small country. Look what was going on in England. Led by the Pankhursts, women were storming parliament and bursting into cabinet meetings and being arrested and imprisoned.

Chicago had taught her the world was bigger than a critic's.

The fading of winter always helped her seasonal blues, although in Chicago the blues were more like a fog of sooty frost. She was saddened that Dr Allen Johnson, her romantically reckless intern, had died from pneumonia. Music and medicine could only heal so much.

In June, she took off her wool underjacket for the first time since last year and enjoyed the airiness of lighter fabric against her skin. After supper, she went for a walk alone up the hill and contemplated her new surroundings, in Madison, Wisconsin.

Margaret had given her leave for the summer, anxious that her lieutenant did not burn out and leave her with a workload that she could not manage without her. Miles had chosen the luxury of study, enrolling in summer classes at the University of Wisconsin. She welcomed the peace of the campus after the demands of Margaret, whom she found mercurial—as Alice had warned her—but also generous and kind.

The Dresdens were close by, as Arnold was now a professor at the university here. She dined with them regularly and played tennis, hitting the ball with the confidence she had shown Charlie on the drought-cracked courts near their farms. She could not dwell on his remarriage, but she knew he needed a mother for his son, and he deserved the happiness she had hoped for him and Linda. She would try to be happy for him, and for her nephew who had a new mother.

Her summer room at Kappa Kappa Gamma House was compact, airy and light, with a large bay window looking onto green lawn. It was furnished with a bed, wardrobe and desk. That was all she needed: a space to think, write and, hopefully, sleep. She had checked the room for cleanliness, a habit left over from her servant accommodation days; here her room would be cleaned by someone else other than her, for the girls who went to Kappa to study were used to studying and socialising, not scrubbing bedroom floors.

This summer, she would be like her new sorority sisters. Although most of them had vacated their rooms for summer, she could still smell the faint scents of their wealth and perfumes. She realised that she had not studied since she was a teenager at school, when her teacher had read her stories, about princes and castles, and encouraged her to write imaginatively about the realities of life instead. Princes and castles were not what girls were meant to imagine. Then she had had to leave school, to help pull starving cows from dust, and she had turned that dust into a book.

She sat down on the single bed and smoothed the quilt.

~

On the first morning, Miles registered for French classes, and a class in Tennyson's poetry, and throughout the summer attended lectures in philosophy and history. She joined the summer Glee Club so she could continue singing. With the other summer students, she sat on wooden benches with names engraved into the desks, and after class she walked at the pace of a carefree stroll, carrying books. She exercised in the red-bricked Armory gymnasium and read Tennyson on the grass.

She practised her conjugation of French verbs with her new friends, among whom were two she called 'Miss L' and 'Van'. She squeezed into her diary the paragraph of her day: *routine morning. Lecture in afternoon. Students' entertainment: Alice in Wonderland.* Then she added, crossing a red line of her diary into the next space: *Van brought his chair over to my seat.*

The weeks lulled. Miles, Van, and Miss L and her date went for a picnic on the beach, ate watermelon by the lake and cantered during riding parties. After morning classes, Miles would return to Kappa Gamma House and, as the afternoon sunshine warmed the room, she would sleep.

The quartet went paddling in canoes on the lake.

They were like the lotus eaters in Tennyson's poem:

> To dream and dream, like yonder amber light,
> Which will not leave the myrrh-bush on the height;
> To hear each other's whisper'd speech;
> Eating the Lotos, day by day,
> To watch the crisping ripples on the beach,
> And tender curving lines of creamy spray.

They watched the ripples on the lake in the amber afternoon, and dreamed and whispered.

In the last days of lotus eating, a letter arrived, forwarded from Chicago, with the return address: Blackwoods, Edinburgh—the publishers of *My Brilliant Career.* She had gone direct this time, with no poet or agent to distort her wishes, and the letter was promisingly thick, rather than a depressingly scrappy document, which she knew meant rejection.

She sliced it open, and read, and held the letter. When Van and their friends arrived, she told them her news.

'Do you like the title?' she asked.

They nodded, enthusiastic. *Some Everyday Folk and Dawn* was 'right cute'. Like her.

She wrote in her diary: *Happy days.*

There were lessons she'd learned from her publishing experience with *My Brilliant Career*, fortified by the poetry and philosophy seminars here on campus: don't trust that your words will remain the same, or that your requests will be honoured. She clutched the typeset proofs that the publisher had sent, which had arrived in a gloriously thick bundle, along with the publishing agreement. This time there would be no surprises about the title, or omissions for sense and sensibilities, or outings of her gender. She would check every word herself.

In her reply, she wrote:

> Dear Sirs,
>
> I am in receipt of your letter under date July 19th, and happy to note its contents. The agreement is also to hand. I have signed it and herewith return your copy . . .
>
> I am pleased you have retained the title. In one way I don't like it, but in another I think it will stick . . . I will write to you about the possibility of an American edition as soon as there is one.

She posted the agreement on the Monday, and then she and Van strolled across campus to the final Glee Club session of the summer season. She laughed when he serenaded her. On their last picnic, on the Wednesday, they posed while Miss L 'kodaked' their pictures—the Kodak company's Brownie camera had become so popular it had now become a verb. On the Thursday, their final twilight in the long summer evenings, Van paddled their canoe one more time around the lake.

On Friday, he came to the reception rooms of Kappa Kappa Gamma. She made a little note in her diary: *Van gave me his handkerchief to mop up my tears.* He soothed her, she confided.

Her diary had become her refuge, for feelings she did not always want to share.

Van thought her burst of summertime sadness was because their summer romance was ending. The handkerchief was indeed wet, and, when she woke the following morning, she was no longer so sure it would be another happy day. But she could take comfort in Tennyson's 'Ulysses': 'Made weak by time and fate, but strong in will / To strive, to seek, to find, and not to yield.'

The day after Van's departure, Miles went to the library and walked unyieldingly on the hill. And, on 16 August, she sent the final proofs of *Some Everyday Folk and Dawn* to Blackwood satisfied with what would be printed. On the agreement, and on the title page, she had claimed her name again: Miles Franklin. There was no foreword from a poet telling the world, however admiringly, that she was just a girl from the bush.

It would be wrong now, anyway. She was nearly 30, and a woman from Chicago.

On the train back to Chicago, she glanced out the window at the telegraph poles strung across the prairie, and the looming factory towers leaving clouds of soot that looked like a train against the sky. There had been rain, and it made her lower in spirits.

Once she had longed to see rain. Now she sighed at the sight of a grey cloud, a drizzle or a cold day. Tomorrow, she would be back in the League's office, and running until she dropped like the coming autumn leaves.

She would not yield.

The train pulled into the terminating station in Chicago. This time, she confidently got off and joined the crowd.

It is 14 October, her 30th birthday. Her mother will send her only remaining daughter a card. In her diary, Miles writes down the temperature in her diary that was below freezing.

She goes to the Robins' apartment in the morning, and comes home via the office. She does not mention the significance of the date. She does not make a fuss with a special dinner or cake at King's or the Annex or the Automobile Club with the Lloyds.

She waits for the hours to clock past midnight, so she can forget about her birthday for another year. Outside, the light clashes with the night, and the traffic of carriages, automobiles and streetcars does not seem to cease with the dark.

She does not want another sleeping tonic, because its grogginess stays with her during the day, however blissful it is to sleep. Instead, she sits at her typewriter, and the lamp casts shadows on the words.

47

It was early 1910. In Australia, the Man from Snowy River, his wife and her brother, on a holiday, attempted to cross a flooding river in their carriage but were swept downstream. While Mrs Paterson and her brother clung to trees, Paterson, in a move that would have impressed Jack London, seized hold of the flailing horses and cut them loose so they wouldn't drown. They and their horses all made it to the riverbank where they watched, wet and gasping, as their carriage swirled and sank.

In Chicago, a swirling snowstorm 'overwhelmed' the city. Fur was on sale and its advertising warned that there were still three months more of winter. The wealthy chose furs that were nearly the price of Miles' weekly salary: $8.50 for blue wolf throws, black wolf neck pieces and mink storm collars to protect against the dragon's breath. For a flamboyant mink coat, Miles would have needed to save for three months. That was not her style, nor her financial priority.

It was Miles' fourth winter in Chicago. Tonight, instead of wolf and mink, she braved the dragon's breath in wool and hoods to see a lecture by the 'Red Queen', Emma Goldman. Afterwards, she browsed copies of Goldman's journal,

Mother Earth, which opened with a poem called 'The Angel of Discontent'.

After her summer away, Miles had not returned to the Harvard Hotel, preferring to move to a smaller, cheaper hotel to save money. She had first tried the Eleanor Club, a charitable lodging run for the 'self-respecting, self-supporting girl', which was like the lodging she had briefly stayed in after Laurel's death, and the bad potato mash and fish still turned her stomach. The noisy clanging, the banging of doors and the baths drove her to new accommodation at a cheaper but more private and self-respecting hotel in Indiana Street. There, she discovered she could take refuge on the rooftop, from where she could see the city's jumbled skyline. It was too windy, wet, snowy or icy to go to the rooftop yet, but she could envision doing that in the future and taking in the view. She could hang high in the sky.

In May, Halley's Comet was visible in the sky above Chicago. Spectators trained their opera glasses at the stars. A cosmic watcher fell off their slippery roof. In the streets below Miles' hotel room and around Hull House, children in blankets searched the night sky for a bonfire of light. Miles did not look for the comet, beyond a glance at the sky on a walk after dinner, but in Winnetka, Lola scanned the stars.

Miles still felt homesick. The waves always happened more in winter, when she longed more intensely for the warm, jasmine-scented air, the salted breezes from the harbour, and the cracks and calls of the bush.

She missed her mother and Rose and Vida. And letters from Linda. She wished she was not such an angel of discontent.

The reviews of *Some Everyday Folk and Dawn* had not been hurtful as much as they suggested the book was forgettable—which was, in a way, worse. But she'd finally published a second novel and broken the literary drought, which had lasted longer than the seven-year dry that had once shrivelled the ponds of Stillwater and driven her family to Penrith. She must appreciate rain again.

She wondered how long she could last. She couldn't endure another Chicago winter. When summer came, she would go to Wayside and feel better. She would see Lola.

At Wayside, Lola was in her own winter of discontent. She suffered recurring, 'beastly' headaches; but when she was feeling clear, she took her children for long walks in the woods. They scampered ahead, looking for eggs and fairies that had fallen by the wayside while she stopped and paused and studied what she could not readily name. She collected fungi and recorded their Latin names in her diary: *Cyathus stercoreus.* Lola sketched their shapes. She noted *Hypholoma* growing on clusters of wood, and mould, *Stemonitis fusca* fruiting over bark in slim, phallus-like tubes.

As the months of her discontent continued, Lola upgraded her diary to one that had more space to write in, because she had so many more feelings to write down: 'tired and cross'. 'W. [William] never forgives me for being cross, even if I'm tired', and 'I escaped to cry alone'. William would come to comfort her, as she was his dear heart, but 'I am always the one who is humbled first.'

Her husband routinely disappeared down the drive in his automobile, with the red flag off the fender and an American one at the back flying in the wind, wearing his winter wind-protection motoring gear. He delighted in stripping off these outer layers in theatre foyers and skyscraper lobbies, to shock the gaping patrons who had thought he wore nothing underneath.

Lola knew there were others with whom he would undress during his visits to the city. But one of the few women she could trust was Miss Franklin. She could see how her husband admired Miss Franklin, who, when she visited, would flutter among them with her wit and intellect, like a wood fairy. She could see his veiled annoyance when his brother, Demy, captured the young woman's attention. But, with the intuition of a wife, she understood that Miss Franklin had a moral fibre that William could not break or burn.

Miles understood that Lola trusted her, so made sure to keep her aware of their movements. Bill, as Miles called him now, increasingly came to her office and asked her, rather than his wife, to be his escort to the theatre, the opera and concerts.

When Miles took some dancing lessons at a studio, he volunteered to be her dancing partner. 'Your husband is a *gay dawg*,' Miles wrote to Lola, delighting in her casual use of American slang.

The three of them sometimes went to his Automobile Club, when Lola and the children came to the city to watch him and Miles take dancing lessons there. The children giggled when their father exaggerated his steps and waltzed with his hand around the waist of a lady who waved to them. The older children, Mary and Jessie, recognised their father's dancing partner as the nice lady with the funny accent who had stayed until Christmas, and sometimes came back for visits. She did not look so sad anymore.

Lola recorded in her diary that the *Stemonitis* sprouted fine, fluttering brown hair.

~

Demy came more often to Chicago now and took Miles 'automobiling', because, like 'kodaking', this was a verb of leisure. She hung on as Demy sped down roads to the city, and country lanes, with goggles to protect her eyes. She didn't mind the driving goggles as they were protective and suggested adventure, but she was beginning to squint. As well as her specialist in her alien mind, who helped her with her recurring bouts of sleeplessness and depression, she would soon, she feared, need an oculist for her eyes. It was a sign of ageing she did not want to see.

Demy sometimes leaned in too close, like his brother did. He was divorcing his wife in Boston, and Miles understood that neither he nor Bill Lloyd took their marriage vows beyond the church in which they had originally been made. She did not believe in God, but she believed in faithfulness, and holding to your promises. *Why*, she wondered, *were women such a sport to them?* She decided that a monogamous marriage was monogamous for women only.

Miss Scott. Miss Goldstein. Miss Addams. Miss Henry. Miss Nestor and Miss Maloney. They would tell her that 'Mrs' was a prefix that would limit their movements as much as it would change their name. Some, she knew, preferred the company of women and that deepened into love; Miss Addams had first lived with Ellen Gates Starr, and then with the kindergarten teacher at Hull House Mary Rozet Smith. A dear, deep love that was never spoken about. Miles and others did not have to keep such open secrets.

There was also Miss Strunsky, married but refusing to use the name of her husband. And Emma Goldman, the Red Queen, who had fled domestic violence in her first marriage and refused to marry her consort, Alexander Berkman, to whom she'd stayed loyal throughout his imprisonment.

They were all Queens, who had shown her ways down a different aisle than marriage.

This is what Margery Currey Dell told her too, as did her husband. Floyd Dell, the editor of a literary magazine, who accessorised himself with a walking stick, for its flourish rather than to stop him falling.

Margery told Miles it was about women's freedom to love whom they chose; to be promiscuous without judgement, like men. It was equality. Miles thought that Margery was proselytising, like an erotic version of a Christian Science missionary; Margery had clearly been appointed to convert her to the lifestyle of free love.

'We swap husbands,' she said. 'And we teach virgins to live.'

Margery watched Miles' face for shock or gasps.

Miles looked at her, expressionless.

'Ah,' Margery said. 'Perhaps next time'.

She listened with growing distaste as Floyd and Margery extolled, seemingly for her benefit, their 'experiments in living'. As if resisting marriage, as she was doing, was not an experiment in itself.

She confided about Floyd and Margery to Charlotte Perkins Gilman, who had written *The Yellow Wallpaper*, the celebrated short story about a woman subjected to Mitchell's Rest Cure, and whose writings were far more captivating than proclamations about free love and sex that were designed to shock.

'They are a thimbleful of maggots squirming in their own juice,' Charlotte pronounced. Miles laughed. Margery was not a maggot. Floyd perhaps was. She would add Charlotte to her list of Queens.

Margery was persistent and invited her to a weekend away. There was that excitement again. An anticipation in their voices that unnerved her.

The next time was an afternoon. That was safer than a weekend. And it was much easier to make an exit than in the early hours of the morning in the streets around an artists' colony. The writer in her, the observer who *wanted to dig into people's souls*, was tempted.

'Marvellous,' Margery clapped.

Arriving at the house, Miles recognised the hostess as the sister of a writer and literary critic she knew, and disliked, who would later claim the earth was hollow and Atlantis existed. The regulars began wrapping their arms around each other as the hostess described sexual freedom as being as ancient as Babylon, where sexuality and sexual rites were sacred. Instead, she said, modern morality had scarred the joy of sex.

Miles listened. She put her hands in her lap, and subconsciously crossed her legs.

'You are denying life,' Floyd Dell told her afterwards, with a wave of his walking stick. She was a puritan.

Miles was cold. 'What you offer here would be death to me.'

'You will become an old maid,' Floyd baited.

'I'd rather be an old maid than an old harridan.'

'What do you want, Miles?' Margery asked when they were alone.

'What I want is an income that would free me,' Miles said, passion of a different kind rising in her voice. She wanted to study music, and write. 'Death was preferable to living in sin.'

It was her 'code', Miles added. Her 'sensitiveness'.

Margery was silent.

Margery and Floyd, with their intimations of 'initiation' and claims she was 'denying life', made her hostile. She had written about sex before, in her own suggestive, subtle way. There had been the slap in the sequel to *My Brilliant Career*, the novel that the publisher thought had far too much 'suggestion' in it to be publishable, as well as too many recognisable celebrities.

On another restless night, buoyed by the publication of *Some Everyday Folk and Dawn*, she had looked through the suitcase for her famous character and decided to give Sybylla another chance. She wrote to Blackwood, the publisher of *My Brilliant Career* and now of *Some Everyday Folk*, and suggested the sequel's publication.

She would stop at a slap. If she was to include the way Margery and Floyd talked about free love and open marriage in a novel, any publisher would think it pornographic.

The publisher in England does not want a sequel. It is still too risky, the story too suggestive, the novel too unformed.

It has been nearly a decade since *My Brilliant Career* was released. Sadly, she puts the sequel manuscript back in her suitcase, as if Sybylla was a genie that had to be contained. Or perhaps she was a witch, or a troll. She had given her so much, but also so little. The proverbial blessing and curse.

Because of Sybylla, Miles had become fleetingly famous and told she had the promise of genius. Now she is worried she will fade into obscurity. The field of the forgotten.

She closes the suitcase.

She will write another letter to the publisher. It will be firm, and not friendly. It will request the end of *My Brilliant Career*: all copies to be withdrawn from sale.

She hopes that everyone will forget *My Brilliant Career*, and Sybylla.

She thinks of the motto on the Fine Arts Building: *Art Alone Endures*. She will make sure that her artistic creation, Sybylla Melvyn of Possum Gully, will not.

48

It was November 1910. In California, after the disappointment of abandoning the *Snark*, Jack London had a new project: building a house on his ranch that he will call 'Wolf House'. At Loma Linda, Jonesie made plans to return home, as five years away from Australia was enough. And in Chicago, Miles locked hands with a group of women, some of whom looked so young they should have been in school. They walked steadfastly towards the line of police, and she could see the men's revolvers and batons raised.

For once, she did not feel the cold.

~

At the Robins' apartment, near the picketing women from the nearby factories and sweatshops, Miles dabbed at her bruises. She had been grabbed and pushed.

'I don't care who you are or what you are, you have to get out of here,' the officer had shouted at her, Zelie Emerson and Ellen Gates Starr as they tried to escort the girls through the police lines.

She was lucky she hadn't been shot. The police had discharged their revolvers into the air to disperse and frighten them, she and Zelie told Margaret. The next day she read reports in which they were described as 'aristocratic picketers'. She was amused. She would not have used 'aristocratic' to describe herself, but when she had tipped off the *Tribune* that college girls were among those hurt, the paper had run a sympathetic article about the garment workers, who had not worked for six weeks now, since the clothing company first announced a cut in their wages of a quarter of a cent per garment.

The Friday after the riot, Miles recorded the freezing temperature in her diary. The babies' milk fund for the mothers in the garment workers' strike was filling with donations; but, with 40,000 on strike, Margaret, Miles and the rest of the 'strike cabinet' worried there were too many babies' mouths to fill. Then there were their fatigued and starving mothers, and the single girls who did not have a family to feed them.

The strikers needed coal and gas, and rent money; so the strike cabinet arranged wholesale prices for power and, after a visit from John Fitzpatrick's Federation men, landlords changed their mind about evicting striking women with babies from their homes.

The unionists no longer shared an office with the women, but they had come to a shared understanding with them. They especially liked the Australian, who seemed to be able to get a story out of anyone, no matter how shy or stuttering, embarrassed or uneducated they were. Day after freezing day, Miles talked to the girls shivering on the picket lines, or in the crowds outside the union office, waiting for money from the milk fund. Her stories were for the newspapers, because she was now the League's publicist as well as the official secretary rather than Mrs Robins. They were also for the League's new magazine, *Life and Labor.* Alice was editor, and Miles the assistant editor. It was planned to sell for ten cents, with proceeds going back to the League, and the first issue would be dedicated to the strike.

In the safety of the office or her rooms, Miles felt the letter keys hit the paper, one after the other. The noise she made was a miniscule tap compared to the brawls outside, but it had its own power. She felt she had to make every letter count. She knew that now. She heard the nine different languages of the women as she typed, and they had all told her the same story.

She typed: 'The workers in the garment trades are almost without exception recently arrived foreigners who have left their native land to escape oppression and seek in this new country, freedom and decent treatment.' Instead, they faced 'industrial slavery'.

In the days before Christmas, she and Alice proofed the first issue of *Life and Labor* at the printers.

On Christmas Day, Miles slept in. She woke for Christmas lunch, and then slept again.

Blissful, blessed sleep.

~

It was January 1911. There were posters advertising 'PANKHURST, leader of the English Suffragettes', with an illustration of the 28-year-old Sylvia Pankhurst wearing a hat like a musketeer's.

In Chicago, in her room with a rooftop, Miles had upgraded to a fancier diary this year. In it, the word 'Engagements' was in glamorous gold writing. On 21 January, she noted a very important engagement: 'Waited for Sylvia Pankhurst.'

~

Alice and Miles waited in the warmth of Sylvia's hotel foyer. Not even one of the most famous women in the world was worth standing outside in the cold for.

'Is she coming?' Alice asked, irritated, for she was impressed with neither celebrity nor lateness.

Finally, in the afternoon, Sylvia emerged from the lifts and Miles noticed how petite she was. Sylvia apologised. She had been writing and avoiding the press, who irritated her by keeping on asking her why she was not married. She was described by the press as 'slender, gentle and red cheeked as the mildest man who ever cut a throat'. In Chicago, they caricatured her as looking like a snake, because she refused to wear a corset to emphasise her figure.

As they walked along, Miles tried not to fawn. To be like Alice and remain calm.

Later, at Hull House, Miles sat with Zelie and Sylvia, who had bonded during their afternoon visit to Chicago's notorious Harrison Street prison. Sylvia made a point of prison visits whenever she was on tour because of her own experience of imprisonment; she pronounced Harrison Street the worst she had seen. The stench and the dankness were terrible—and she should know, she said.

'Come to London,' Sylvia invited the two of them before she left. 'Work with me.'

Miles walked home afterwards, energised by the cold winds and the power of Pankhurst.

~

In April, as the Pankhurst posters peeled from building walls, a partial eclipse was about to occur, and a Chicago prophet foresaw a 'dark and dreadful day', or an earthquake. The shadow fell over the sun, but the pavements did not pulsate and the people of the city rushed on, with Miles among them. She was bracing herself for an upcoming conference in Boston. Demy would want to see her; she would hold him at a distance until he had his divorce.

As the weather warmed towards summer, the Chicago smog settled about her office window, mixing with the heat. She looked out through the haze at the skyscrapers that every year were getting taller; once-impressive buildings were now sitting in their shadows.

She could look down on the crowds below because she was no bush girl now, with a kerosene tin for a postbox; she had her own private office in a skyscraper, with an assistant to help her with her publicity work and her editing role of *Life and Labor.*

She told her aunt, 'I have my own switch and all sorts of conveniences . . . We have a mail chute just outside our door in which we drop our letters and when we want a telegraph messenger to take things we touch a button in the wall.' The soaring skyscraper had 'a barber's shop and a restaurant' and 'thousands of people'.

Recognising the important contribution she was making, the League had doubled her salary. They now paid it themselves, instead of it coming from Margaret Dreier Robins' purse. She looked over at Alice. Could she do this until she was prematurely grey, like Alice? She did not have Alice's calmness and stoicism. Alice was a reformer, not an artist. Alice did not worry about whether she would endure.

Miles still wrote at night when she couldn't sleep, as well as taking the occasional brandy and barbiturate tonic. Sometimes it was the old fever, rather than insomnia, that consumed her. She took sabbatical leave from her union work on Sundays and wrote as the church bells rang out.

She'd begun thinking about a new book, *The Net of Circumstance*, about an exhausted young woman in Chicago, working and single, who inspires a playwright with her struggle and spirit, and is courted by a wealthy man. She had written a short story too, 'The Love Machine', about a machine that compels a woman to fall in love. Science fiction authors usually made good money.

Sylvia Pankhurst's offer beckoned. 'Come,' Zelie urged, because she had already decided that she would follow Sylvia anywhere. Perhaps Miles and Zelie could start a new journal, like *Life and Labor*, but with a fiercer title—something like *Dreadnought*.

Her Granny would be absolutely horrified by such a move, if she was still able to be shocked. She missed Granny's letters that had faded away with Granny's age. She was 79 now, and had warned Miles that she was becoming too old to write. She had already told the family she did not want a lavish funeral or extended mourning, 'because the expense wasn't justifiable'.

'Have you found anyone you like better than yourself?', she remembered Granny's quip once more.

No, Granny, Miles wanted to reply. No.

It was getting warmer. She had left her sky office and packed her bags for a London holiday. Margaret had given her two months' leave and, acknowledging her exhaustion, one month's paid holiday. In London, she expected to see Vida, who, through a happy holiday coincidence, was there on a speaking tour.

She still had one last responsibility before her holiday, as the key organiser of the annual WTUL convention in Boston. To save on rent, she would vacate her hotel room, and arrange new rooms on her return in the fall. For the week before she left, she had arranged to sleep on the floor in Ellen Gates Starr's rooms at Hull House. Zelie was packing for London too, and would sleep on the floor with her. Miles hoped Zelie would bring her most fabulous hats.

She climbs the stairs to her favourite refuge: the rooftop of her hotel. It does not soar like her office, but it still affords a view and space. In the warmth, there is a chance to sit for a moment, and rest between acts, like she did when she was a servant. Except this time she is not at the beck and call of a Mistress. She muses that Margaret is ever more demanding and mercurial, but she has learned to hold her own, with Alice as co-editor and mentor. This coming holiday is an acknowledgement of her work. There would be more work when she returned to Chicago in the fall, and she would write in her diary '*no rest or peace in the office*'.

On the rooftop, she closes her eyes and relaxes into the striped deckchair. She wears a light, white dress and her hair is bundled up on top of her head. The snow has melted, and the wind is finally warm enough for the first geraniums to blossom in the pots behind her chair without shrivelling back into their stems.

There is sun, without any shadow of an eclipse. She raises her face to meet it. Above her, sparrows and songbirds swoop in their annual spring migration, confused by the glass and steel buildings in their paths that years ago were clear. The city is a haze of roofs and smoke behind her.

For these moments, the rooftop is her refuge. From the League, from Margaret, from the chaos of the Chicago streets, from the strike and from the sparrows in her brain. A moment to close her eyes. A refuge in which to be herself. These are the moments she treasures now. She will write in her diary, *Oh for some refuge. For myself. To be myself.*

The motto of the Fine Arts Building is never far away: *All Passes—Art Alone Endures.*

She must remember to send a postcard to her mother when she arrives in New York, telling her of her next destination.

49

It was September 1915. In Europe, searchlights swept the sky, looking for German Albatros fighters whose double wings bore the distinctive Iron Cross. A wind drifted beneath them, heavy with chlorine gas. Under the waves, German U-boats hunted in the Atlantic, and in May, the torpedoed Cunard liner *Lusitania* had sunk in eighteen minutes off the coast of Ireland, drowning 1195 passengers, including 128 Americans. The attack sparked fears about transatlantic travel, but the United States was not yet in the war.

In Australia, the Man from Snowy River accepted a commission to join the remount unit in Egypt 'to take charge of the horses', serving on horseback as he had during the Boer War.

In a Queensland paper, the war appeal of King George V was headlined: 'More Men and Yet More Men Wanted', and printed beside the 97th casualty list that had been published since the war had begun. *Don't look at them too closely*, Paterson had warned in 1901. *They are dead men.*

In her harbourside mansion, Keston, in Kirribilli, the judge's widow Sarah O'Connor, who had once had little else on her mind than her maid's too-pretty hair, prayed for the safety of her three sons at the front and that she would never read their names on any list. And in Chicago, the O'Connors' former maid, once known as Sarah, was now 35. Her birthday would be soon.

At her rooms, Miles pinned her pretty curls into rolls on top of her head, knowing she would be admired rather than admonished for looking so attractive when she arrived at the tea party, which was to be in her honour and certainly not to celebrate her birthday. Perhaps she could add a hair ornament, to finish her preparations in style, or a choker around her neck, like she had done for the opera. This was a special party.

A table had been booked at the Narcissus, the fine restaurant at Marshall Field's department store, which was decorated with columns inlaid with flowered frescos, thick carpet to warm heeled feet, and a grand circular fountain. Chamber music always accompanied the food.

Lola had been invited. She and Jane Addams had returned to Chicago from their peace mission to The Hague in April, for they believed—like Rose Scott, who still waited for her spirit child to come home—that women were messengers of peace. Miles had written an article celebrating their mission for *Life and Labor.* It had turned out to be one of her last for that publication, because Margaret Dreier Robins had finally run out of cheques.

Lola was hardening her heart against her husband, who had become more obviously attracted to Miles, who still accepted his invitations to the opera and restaurants, but nothing more.

Her friends were coming to the party. Rose would have called them her *fellow women.* They were like sisters to her. Her real sisters—Linda and darling little Laurel—were irreplaceable, and she carried her memories of them with her always. She would do likewise with all these friends—her sisters—whom she had found in the world since leaving Stillwater with her two dresses and a debut book more than a decade ago.

She wrote the guest list in her diary:

Miss Margery Currey Dell, who, in 1913, had separated from Floyd. He'd left Chicago for New York, as jealousy and fights took over from proclamations of free love as liberation. Miles had resisted telling her 'I told you so', because friendship was more important than petty triumphs.

Miss Editha Phelps, who, like Alice, was an older sister and who wanted to write about Shakespeare's wife as the real reason for his genius. They had become especially close when they travelled together to London in 1911. Miles had proudly introduced her to Vida.

Miss Agnes Nestor, once a singing factory glove-maker and now president of the Chicago branch of the WTUL, helping 'overworked and underpaid women' in the city. Miles envied her ability to be 'free from inner turbulence'.

Miss Emma Pischel, whose brother Fred was such a 'donkey'. Miles had written to Rose in 1913 that women who serve men like Fred were fools: 'They are happier serving men than some of the rest of us [who] are in hot demand for our freedom and a system of society which will nurture self-respect . . .' she paused.

'Do you suppose we are really ahead of our time? Are we deluded fools or are we merely conceited?'

Alice, who did not suffer fools and was not deluded, would meet her in New York. True to her hats, Zelie had already been in London four years, and she'd endured jail and force feeding after hunger strikes in solidarity with Sylvia Pankhurst.

Do not be afraid, a scientist had once warned, as a comet streaked through the sky. Sylvia, Zelie, Alice and her sisters in Chicago; Vida and Rose in Australia. They were all comets. Not adrift in the darkness, but tracking their own orbits, leaving a trail of light for others to follow.

She was not afraid of the dark. She did not fear solitude. She too was a comet.

She touched her hair and put on her fall coat. Then she squinted down the stairs. It was her farewell party, and she would not wear glasses.

~

In London, Sylvia Pankhurst cared for mothers and children, providing milk and clothes at her East End headquarters, rather than work in the munitions factory that was opposite their building. Not that the government would send her to a factory, she said, 'because they knew there will be trouble' if they did.

'You can't send me to war', she taunted the government. 'I'm not a man.'

And in Chicago, Miles stowed her bags on the train and settled into her seat, at the start of her long journey to London, via New York, where her ship, the *St Paul*, was docked, preparing for the perilous transatlantic journey ahead.

There had been more intimate farewells that were yet more intimate after the Narcissus party. She and Bill Lloyd had had one last dinner at the Chicago Automobile Club, where they had often gone so she could meet him in the safety of a crowded room, and where she picked up a postcard on which she wrote to her mother a note to assure her she was safe, so safe, she was in an elite club, surrounded by the security of status and wealth.

'You are the most complex mortal I have ever met,' Bill said, fascinated and exasperated. He implied that, if she had been prepared to wait, he would have married her, because he saw divorce from Lola as inevitable. He had hinted more than once that, if only she would give him a key to her hotel door, he could make her terribly comfortable and she could concentrate on her writing.

'I could not undertake the heavy burden of competing with all your sporting women,' Miles told him.

'I have not been with such sporting women, as you say, since I wanted to be with you,' Bill had assured her, but Miles had not believed him.

For one final night of theatregoing together, they saw *One Last Step* by Irving Berlin. Miles went home, alone. One day many years later, reflecting on her wealthy suitors, she would say, 'I could have had money with a man attached several times over.'

Yet it would have come at a cost to herself and her friendships. She had always known that.

~

Miles did not say goodbye to Demy. He was now divorced, and it had been possible for her to have joined the Lloyd family officially without losing Lola's friendship. She could have been an aunt to Lola and Bill's children, and never worried about money again. She could have been like Zelie Emerson and Margaret Dreier Robins who were able to advocate with money and the power of a name, and swap countries and cities with the flick of a hat.

If only Demy wasn't such a *silly ass*. She'd based a character called Bobby on him in her new novel, *On Dearborn Street*. The book was named after one of the main streets in Chicago, and the League's office address. It now had a playboy.

In the beginning, the joie de vivre flirtation had been so much fun, as it always is. They had exchanged letters; Demy had called her 'little rascal'. The letters were word games, jolts of pleasure in the mail. He never spoke of a constricting future or that he couldn't live without her, as Edwin had done, and he took her automobiling in his sports cars.

Then, while on League business in Boston, she had met him one night in his sailing mecca, Rhode Island, where they had danced fast. And then he drove fast, made uninhibited by his wealth and too much champagne. The car careered around corners.

'Stop!' she demanded. He only stopped the car.

'He was desperate and brutal . . . escaped death or tragedy by a v. small margin,' she wrote afterwards in her diary in her cryptic way. She vowed never to see him again. *You work it out*, she implied to her future reader, for Miles knew she would be remembered. She was more like Marie Bashkirtseff than the critic had given her credit for.

I am my own heroine.

Her trunk, now stowed on the train, is lighter, for some of her manuscripts have already been turned into books, like *Some Everyday Folk and Dawn. The Net of Circumstance*, her book about Constance, the single working woman in Chicago, has just been published in London by the fledgling book company Mills & Boon, which, she is proud to note, published Jack London's UK editions. She is in his orbit now. Her novel should be in bookstores now, although the war had greatly rationed books and other luxuries. The publication of a new book is a proud moment, given the circumstances of war.

It is time to leave. That sense, like it had been leaving Australia, has grown stronger over the past months. The war. The end of *Life and Labor.* What had once been glamorous and exciting is now routine. Zelie would be waiting for her. So would the war. She will volunteer and work as a foreign correspondent, writing articles from London. She will write an article about Sylvia Pankhurst. She'd had experience as a regular columnist for Australian papers, there and in America, and as the co-editor of *Life and Labor.* She is ready for London; after all, it was the ultimate test of fame for any writer.

Why do I write? For what does anyone write?

Her heroine, Sybylla, had asked herself this in *My Brilliant Career.*

She knows the answer now.

Miles takes one last look at her friends gathered on the platform, holding bouquets of violets and wiping their eyes. Sybylla had told her readers: *To hot young hearts beating passionately in strong breasts, the sweetest thing is motion.*

The train bell rings. She waves and blows kisses, shouting goodbyes into the glass of the carriage window.

What the future holds, I know not.

Her friends throw the violets into the grey air, and the purple petals float onto the tracks.

Coda

Miles reached London on 7 November 1915, where she reconnected with Sylvia Pankhurst and Zelie Emerson; who together had founded a journal called *The Woman's Dreadnought* (later *Workers' Dreadnought*) and both had been force-fed in prison as part of hunger strike protests over women's suffrage. Miles worked as a freelance journalist until 1917 when she volunteered with the Scottish Women's Hospital and served in the Balkans as a cook, evoking her Mary Anne experiences. She wrote of her wartime experiences in an unpublished nonfiction work called 'It Matters Nothing'. For a fictionalised account of her service in the Balkans during WWI see Gail Jones's beautifully vivid *Salonika Burning* (Text, 2022).

Miles returned to Australia in 1927 and published a well-received historical saga series under another eccentric pseudonym, 'Brent of Bin Bin'. She finally reclaimed her name, Miles Franklin, in the detective potboiler *Bring the Monkey* in 1933, and in 1936 with the acclaimed *All That Swagger*, and maintained lively correspondence with her dearest friends, including Alice 'Pops' Henry and the Goldsteins until her death in 1954. As Franklin wrote in her literary notebook, 'I am glad I am not young now, I don't desire to stagnate inside outworn customs, and the monogamous marriage, so far, has been monogamous for women only'.

Franklin bequeathed her estate to establishing the Miles Franklin Literary Award to ensure her legacy after her death. It remains Australia's most prestigious prize for fiction.

Author's note

Stella Miles Franklin is one of Australia's best-known writers, and her *My Brilliant Career* alter ego, Sybylla Melvyn, is one of our best-loved heroines. Miles bequeathed her estate to create Australia's most prestigious literary prize, the Miles Franklin Literary Award, and gave a voluminous collection of her personal papers and drafts to the State Library of New South Wales.

In the archive, two brown leather volumes are titled 'When I Was Mary Anne, a Slavey'. The thick pages of manuscript, inked in the author's curling script, are amended with glued paper inserts from the diary that she kept for a year in 1903–04 as she worked as a domestic servant to research 'literary material'.

There is a picture in the archive of Miles in a teasing pose and dressed in her 'get-up' of a lacy parlour cap pinned atop her thick brunette hair, and a black-and-white tunic. She is unrecognisable as the author of *My Brilliant Career* who had dazzled Australia in 1901 and inspired young women across the nation to write to her about their own frustrations and dreams.

There is another trace of 'Mary Anne' in the archives: a scratchy microfilm of her handwritten summary of her year working as a servant. The summary, titled, 'Concerning

Maryann', was the basis of a short letter to *The Bulletin* in 1904, and which was the only published work from her year as a servant.

I wondered: how did she do it, and why?

I knew she was broke, and that sales of *My Brilliant Career* had given her little in royalties. 'Mary Anne' was as much about her real, material need of money as it was about 'literary material'.

The servant work was gruelling; a 60-hour-plus working week was common. Still, she persevered for the year. Her resulting manuscript remains unpublished, 120 years later. Jill Roe, Miles' biographer, suggests defamation was the reason for the non-publication, as the identities of the people she served were only veiled behind pseudonyms as thin as chiffon. At the time, being found guilty of defamation could mean a jail sentence.

With the threat of defamation now six feet under, given that more than a century has passed, I initially tried to revive the manuscript intact, with an introduction and edit of the original text of 'Mary Anne'. However, there were problems. The existing manuscript was likely not the final draft she submitted to the publisher George Robertson and possibly other publishers. Miles changed the point of view from 'I' to 'Mary Anne' abruptly mid-manuscript, as if she had merged with Mary Anne the character. And her attitudes—towards sex workers, tradies and First Nations Australians—are jarringly of their time. It had not 'aged well', I was told. Leave it alone.

To put 'Mary Anne' away in the archive again was like avoiding a sometimes embarrassing relative in an aged care home, despite them still having so much wisdom and wit to give. Miles' enduring commitment to her writing, her adventurous spirit, her deep and enduring friendships, her courage to reject security and marriage, and her confrontations of her worst habits and prejudices were as timeless as Sybylla's feisty innocence. The manuscript set her later years in motion, especially her decision to try her luck in the United States.

I thought, too, that her investigation of 'the servant question' was timeless. When Miles began her year as a servant in 1903, domestic service was a constant newspaper topic. The country was growing on the sheep's back, but in the cities it was expanding on the toil of factory work, which gave women an alternative to domestic service. For the aspirational, employing 'help' in the home may have reflected their prosperity, but this was not shared with their servants, who bristled at the class dynamics underneath the myth of equality. It was an especially cruel myth for the young First Nations women who were forced into indentured domestic service.

Appliances have changed from washing mangles, hand-heated irons, and melting ice boxes, to sleek stainless-steel and glossy white machines that glow, hum and beep in the background. Yet our demand for casual domestic workers remains relentless. In our 21st-century apartment buildings, renovated homes and office blocks, they are still there. They are in the shadows of our outsourced lives, in the gig economy. Low-wage childcare workers welcome our children. Chefs on call cook meals that are delivered by mobile waiters on electric bikes weighed down with branded paper bags, who are hit by headlights or worse as they speed from door to door. At the bottom of a prestigious skyscraper in the city, not far from where Miles sought servant work in the employment agencies of Elizabeth Street, cleaners push carts filled with disinfectants into the foyer.

At its core, Miles' investigation of the servant question hasn't aged at all.

I decided a different approach was needed to tell Miles' story as a servant. As they stand, traditional biographies rarely draw breath as they take in big lives such as Miles'. I instead begin at the start of her *Brilliant Career*—1901, when she was 21—and end in 1915. It is a slice-of-life biography rather than cradle-to-the-grave, allowing it to fully breathe through these critical years in which she experienced the exciting success of her acclaimed debut novel, then struggled with failure and tragedy, and triumphed as a single woman embarking on a life that few women in her era contemplated alone. She was only in her twenties, so she flirted, dated and romanced. She would always choose risk over security.

Rather than the 'dispassionate' voice of a historian or biographer, I have dramatised Miles' world, in which she defied the status quo for Edwardian women and formed the Miles we know today. The author who was the heroine of her own story.

This book, however, is not fiction—although it might read as such. Think of *Miles Franklin Undercover* as a literary lacework of Edwardian sources, stitched together to create Miles' life and her world. I relied on Miles' archive in the Mitchell Library (State Library of New South Wales), which contains her letters, and those from her family, friends, confidants, publishers and admirers; her diaries, notebooks and scrapbooks; her unpublished manuscript 'When I Was Mary Anne, a Slavey'; and other unpublished early works in the same collection. I drew from *My Brilliant Career*, that as much as Miles denied it, is agreed to be based closely on her own life—as well as the early drafts of the sequel to *My Brilliant Career* that was published late in life as *My Career Goes Bung*; her later published novels, her journalism in *The Sydney Morning Herald*, and other periodicals; and the biographies of Franklin that have intermittently appeared since her death in 1954. Jill Roe, author of the exhaustively researched *Stella Miles Franklin*, was a valued guide. If Roe was a floodlight on Miles' life, this book is a spotlight on these formative years post *My Brilliant Career*.

I built her wider world, and that of her friends, from international archives in New York and Chicago, where she lived, and historical newspaper archives from Australia and the United States. For a full list of sources, including where 'speculation' has been used to fill in some gaps based on what was happening in Miles' life at the time, there are extensive source notes at the end of the book.

Although Miles called herself 'Mary Anne' when she attempted to publish the book, in the servant chapters (Part Two), I use the pseudonym Miles used with her employers—'Sarah Frankling'—and, where known, her employers' actual identities to show the authenticity of her actual experience as it happened. Whether she also gave other servants pseudonyms is unknown, so I have kept their names as used in the 'Mary Anne' text, honouring their ghosts as well as the ghosts whose names we know.

Acknowledgements

A book is written in solitude and in a crowd, at night, in the early morning, on weekends, and in thoughts and in dreams. There are those in my life who may not put words on the page, however they have contributed to the book as it appears now.

Firstly, though, I am not the first to write about Miles Franklin, and I doubt I will be the last. Of Miles Franklin's biographers, Jill Roe's extraordinary research covering the 'cradle to grave' of Franklin's life in *Stella Miles Franklin* provided a map for me to follow, as did her edited collection of Franklin's letters and her co-edited collection of Franklin's non-fiction writing. For those wanting to know what happened next in Franklin's life after 1915, Roe's biography of Franklin is rich reading.

Miles Franklin Undercover first began in 2019, thanks to permission from Rachel Franks and Richard Neville at the State Library of New South Wales (SLNSW), to transcribe the two-volume manuscript for 'When I was Mary Anne, a Slavey' and publish it. Later, the SLNSW's visiting fellowship position afforded me space to work on the book in this historic literary building with Mitchell librarians who provided guidance. Blanche De Winter assisted with the transcription, funded by the School of the Arts & Media UNSW, and has remained a reader and supporter of the book through its draft iterations until today. Author and friend Dan Kaufman was another early reader, and Powerhouse Museum Senior Curator Roger Leong shared his Edwardian fashion expertise. Thank you to H.C. and A. Glad, Estate of Norman Lindsay, for extracts from *Bohemians of the Bulletin*.

Allen & Unwin publisher Richard Walsh encouraged me to write creative non-fiction and saw the potential of the book beyond the initial edit of the 'When I as Mary Anne, A Slavey' manuscript. He advised me through the first drafts as I expanded the story to include the lead-up to Franklin's year as a servant, and the years after to show her arc of resilience. Richard's contribution to identifying and mentoring Australian authors, me among them, is invaluable to the Australian literary landscape.

Allen & Unwin publisher Elizabeth Weiss, editor Samantha Kent and freelance editor Emma Driver's fresh eyes and insights further refined the text. Internationally, I'm grateful for the expertise of Meagan McChesney at Winnetka Historical Society, the curators of Hull House, Newberry Library, and the Northwestern Memorial Hospital Archives, all in Chicago; the Loma Linda Sanatorium Archives, California, and the New York Public Library Brooke Russell Reading Room, New York.

My colleagues at UNSW Sydney School of Arts & Media were tolerant of me muttering about Miles Franklin in the corridors and in meetings, especially Professor Brigitta Olubus, author of *Shirley Hazzard: A writing life*.

I am lucky to have friends who understand the unique obsession that is writing a book. Associate Professor Camilla Nelson has also ridden the Miles Franklin wave with me from these early days, and Isabel McIntosh was a decisive sounding board.

Most supportive of all was Ollie—my portrait photographer, and the first relationship to survive a book. It's not easy being married to a writer, and it requires wit, patience and love. Together we have a chaotic life between Sydney and Ballina/Byron Bay with our dogs Loki and Ursa, who, like Ollie, have patiently listened to my endless fretting if the book will be okay.

Notes on sources and further reading

This guide indicates the sources used to recreate Miles Franklin and her world. Principal sources include correspondence, notebooks, manuscripts and diaries in the voluminous Miles Franklin collection in the State Library of New South Wales; diaries and correspondence within the Lola Maverick Lloyd Papers, New York Public Library; digitised Australian archival newspapers accessed via Trove (1903–15); the *San Francisco Examiner* and *Chicago Daily Tribune* online archives via newspapers.com (1906–15); Franklin and others' creative works, essays and interviews; and published biographies and anthologies.

Sources are cited in full in the first instance, then in shortened form for subsequent references. Abbreviations used are noted.

'Speculation' is noted on the following pages where it fills in gaps and is based on suggestions from existing research into Franklin's life and emotions at that time, and into the lives of her family and friends.

Abbreviations used in sources

ABP	Andrew Barton 'Banjo' Paterson
AGS	A.G. Stephens
AH	Alice Henry
CG	Charles Graham
DL	Demarest 'Demy' Lloyd
EB	Edwin Bridle
GR	George Robertson
HL	Henry Lawson
JF	Joseph Furphy
JL	Jack London
JP	Jessie Paterson (Banjo Paterson's sister)
LG	Linda Graham, nee Franklin (sister)
LML	Lola Maverick Lloyd
MDR	Margaret Dreier Robins
MF	Miles Franklin
MFFC	Miles Franklin Family Correspondence
MFGC	Miles Frankin General Correspondence
ML MSS	Mitchell Library, SLNSW
NL	Norman Lindsay
NYPL	New York Public Library
RS	Rose Scott
RSCM	Rose Scott Correspondence, miscellaneous
SF	Susannah Franklin (mother)
SL	Sarah Lampe ('Granny')
SLNSW	State Library of New South Wales
SMH	*The Sydney Morning Herald*
VG	Vida Goldstein
WL	William 'Bill' Lloyd

Prologue

'Arriving in the metropolis'; *'I had armed'*: 'Miles Franklin, 'Sketch II: The struggle to gain a footing', in 'When I Was Mary Anne, a Slavey', Vol. 1, Sketches 1–4 (c. 1904), 4. Miles Franklin papers, mainly literary manuscripts [1900–1954?]. SLNSW, ML MSS 445/23.

'I left a purse'; *'He eyed me'*: Franklin, 'The struggle to gain a footing', 5.

'Are you trying': Franklin, 'The struggle to gain a footing', 10.

'You'll find it terrible': Franklin, 'The struggle to gain a footing', 11. Miles narrates the woman's history.

'A very superior'; *'Through the back window'*: Franklin, 'The struggle to gain a footing', 10.

'I changed the only': Miles Franklin, 'Sketch 1: Introductory', in 'When I Was Mary Anne, a Slavey', Vol. 1, Sketches 1–4 (c. 1904), 5.

Part One: Miles

1

Stillwater: Possum Gully in *My Brilliant Career* (A&R Classics, 2013 [1901]) was based on Stillwater. The Federation drought lasted from 1895 to 1902.

mailman; 'sweepstake'; kerosene tin: Miles Franklin, *My Career Goes Bung* (A&R Classics, 2013 [1946]), 305. It is speculation that the mailman was the same one described in *My Career Goes Bung*, though Miles wrote close to home.

'red marauder': Henry Lawson, 'Andy's gone with cattle', in *In the Days When the World Was Wide and Other Verses* (Angus & Robertson, 1896), 57.

'I have lived such a secluded life': MF to HL, 19 Nov 1899. File 1: MFGC, 1887–1951, SLNSW, ML MSS 364/6. Published in Jill Roe, *My Congenials: Miles Franklin and Friends in Letters* (Angus & Robertson, 1993), 9–10.

'more than skimmed'; *'Will you write and tell me'*: HL to MF, 'Wednesday January 1900'. File 1: MFGC, 1887–1951. Published in Roe, *My Congenials*, 10–11.

'Words of thanks are tame': MF to HL, 17 Oct 1900. File 1: MFGC, 1887–1951. Published in Roe, *My Congenials*, 11–12.

'Please on no account': MF to James B. Pinker (agent), 6 Feb 1901. Published in Roe, *My Congenials*, 12–13.

She would question that: See MF to James B Pinker, 18 Nov 1901. Published in Roe, *My Congenials*, 18–19.

'A few months before': Henry Lawson, 'Preface', in Franklin, *My Brilliant Career.*

'You run about': Jill Roe, *Stella Miles Franklin: A Biography* (HarperCollins, 2008), 30.

froward: The *Macquarie Dictionary* defines 'froward' as 'perverse; wilfully contrary; refractory; not easily managed'. Quoted in Roe, *Stella Miles Franklin*, 19.

Talbingo: called 'Caddagat' *in My Brilliant Career.*

'big and sunburnt'; *'chestnut moustache'*; *'six foot three'*; *'mighty well-shaped filly'*: Franklin, *My Brilliant Career*, 88.

'lovely, lovely present'; *'great excitement in the camp'*; *'The Lordly Phillip'*; *'I can hear'*; *'When I read it right through'*: LG to MF, 16 Sep 1901. File 3: MFFC, Graham-Lampe, 1897–1954. SLNSW, ML MSS 364/49. Published in Roe, *My Congenials*, 14–16.

'To weary hearts'; *'I see it and'*: Franklin, *My Brilliant Career*, 264–65.

'Stella of St Kilda': Stella Simpson to MF, undated ('Saturday'). Miles replied, and 'Stella of St Kilda' responded, thrilled, on 27 Dec 1901. File 2: MFGC, 1901–1936. SLNSW, ML MSS 364/7.

'sets all the English world': Martha Garnett to MF, undated. File 2: MFGC, 1901–1936. Franklin has noted 'answered'.

'It is absurd': Based on Franklin, 'Preface', *My Career Goes Bung*, 270. It is speculation that the location of this conversation Franklin records in the preface was by a fence.

Ned Kelly beard: 'Franklin Family, 1894', Photographs of Miles Franklin, c. 1879–1954. SLNSW, PX*D 250.1 (Vol. 1), file no. FL3250519.

2

'My Brilliant (?) Career': MF to JF Archibald, 5 Sep 1901. File 2: MFGC, 1901–1936. Published in Roe, *My Congenials*, 14–15.

'divided skirts': See 'Sydney sidelights', *Evening News*, 20 Aug 1901, 8.

'A Bookful of Sunlight': 'The Red Page', *The Bulletin*, 28 Sep 1901, 2. Attributed to A.G. Stephens.

'Brontë': A profile of Miles Franklin in *The Sunday Sun*, 13 April 1904, 4, refers to English critics' comparisons of Franklin to Charlotte Brontë and *Jane Eyre*. See also Roe, *Stella Miles Franklin*, 81.

'"Marie Bashkirtseff" of the bush': Quoted in Martha Garnett's letter, cited in ch. 1 above; also quoted in Roe, *Stella Miles Franklin*, 81.

'It's perhaps silly': Marie Bashkirtseff, *The Journal of Marie Bashkirtseff*, trans. Mathilde Blinde (Cassell & Company, 1890), 40.

'Bashkirtseff cult': Sonia Wilson, 'I am my own heroine', *Public Domain Review*, 2 Sep 2020, https://publicdomainreview.org. See also Sonia Wilson, *Personal Effects: The Journal of Marie Bashkirtseff* (Routledge, 2010).

'A man's love is a fire': Olive Schreiner, *The Story of an African Farm* (Roberts Brothers, 1888), 216.

'You are pretty hot': LG to MF, 16 Sep 1901. File 3: MFFC, Graham-Lampe, 1897–1954. Published in Roe, *My Congenials*, 14–15.

'all malicious lies'; *'your letter to hand'*: MF to unnamed uncle, 21 Oct 1901. Published in Roe, *My Congenials*, 17–18.

'There is one dreadful': MF to AGS, 10 Oct 1901. Published in Roe, *My Congenials*, 16–17.

Miles' next book: Initially called 'On the outside track', published as *Cockatoos* (Angus & Robertson, 1954).

'shouting at the top': Franklin, *Cockatoos*, 292. Quoted in Roe, *Stella Miles Franklin*, 79.

3

'I think I am jealous': CG to MF, 14 Oct 1901. File 3: MFFC, Graham-Lampe, 1897–1954.

Baxter boys: Photograph of Miles on horse, in Colin Roderick, *Miles Franklin: Her Brilliant Career* (Rigby, 1982), 68. Miles sometimes rode bareback; see Roe, *Stella Miles Franklin*, 47.

'I would have seen'; *'I want you to ride'*: CG to MF, 'Sunday', 19 Sep 1901. File 3: MFFC, Graham-Lampe, 1897–1954.

'it seems to me': CG to MF, 14 Oct 1901. File 3: MFFC, Graham-Lampe, 1897–1954.

'I want you to try': CG to MF, 9 Dec 1901. File 3: MFFC, Graham-Lampe, 1897–1954.

'Uncle Theo calls us': LG to MF, 12 Jan 1902. File 3: MFFC, Graham-Lampe, 1897–1954.

4

a hurricane wind: 'Dust storm', *Goulburn Penny Post*, 23 Jan 1902, 4.

'inflammation of the brain': 'Fatalities and accidents', *SMH*, 10 Jan 1902, 7.

sudden summer squall: 'The gale on the harbor [sic]', *Evening News*, 15 Jan 1902, 3.

Lynton: The site, in Woollahra, is now an aged-care home, with a plaque dedicated to Scott.

Rose Scott dressed: Speculation. Rose referred to servants in interviews. For Lynton's interior details, see Judith A. Allen, *Rose Scott: Vision and Revision in Feminism* (Oxford University Press, 1994), 74.

'We speak for those'; *'one of our most earnest'*: Animals' Protection Society of New South Wales to RS, 17 Apr 1902, Vol. 23: Scott family papers, RSCM, 1884–1904. SLNSW, ML MSS A 2282.

'but please I want': AH to RS, 15 Feb 1902, Vol. 23: Scott family papers, RSCM, 1884–1904.

she wanted 'men's respect': M. Forrest, 'With Rose Scott', *Daily Mail* (Brisbane), 18 Feb 1922, 11.

Often tired of writing letters: 'Prominent Australian women', *The Sun*, 13 Apr 1913, 20.

install a bigger letterbox: Allen, 'Preface', in *Rose Scott*.

Charity; justice: 'Prominent Australian women', *The Sun*.

'I have just read': RS to MF, 31 Mar 1902. File 3: MFGC, 1902–1953. SLNSW, ML MSS 364/8.

'milk, rosemary, postmaster': Fragment written on letter, undated, (file 466), Vol. 3: Scott family papers, RSCM, 1884–1904.

God save the Queen: Allen, *Rose Scott*, 98. Speculation that she missed her mother singing.

5

water buffalo: See Jim Angell & Brian Fletcher, *The Australian Club: 1828–2013* (Allen & Unwin, 2013).

Suggestions and Complaints Book: Australian Club (Sydney, N.S.W.) records, 1838–1963. 'Suggestions and Complaints' book, 1895–1902. SLNSW, ML MSS 1836.

war correspondent: 'Life on board the S.S. *Kent* by our Special War Correspondent, A.B. Paterson', *SMH*, 29 Dec 1899, 7. 'With the S.S. *Kent* contingent. By our Special War Correspondent, A.B. Paterson', *SMH*, 28 Dec 1899, 5.

'trained horses like machinery'; *'Don't look at them'*: A.B. Paterson, 'A day under fire. A battlefield sketch', *SMH*, 11 Aug 1900, 7.

lectures: 'Mr Paterson's war lectures', *SMH*, 15 Sep 1900, 12.

suits, shoes: Rose Lindsay (nee Soady) recalls Paterson in *Rose Lindsay: A Model Life*, (ed.) Lin Bloomfield (Odana Editions, 2001), 210.

he will write to her: ABP to MF, 25 Mar 1902. File 2: MFGC, 1901–1936. SLNSW, ML MSS 364/7.

6

'I should like': RS to MF, 31 Mar 1902. File 3: MFGC, 1902–1953. SLNSW, ML MSS 364/8.

'elegancy'; *Weigel's Journal of Fashion*: Miles Franklin papers, literary notebooks, volumes I–XV, 1934–c. 1948, Vol. X, 'Odds and ends', pp. 451–498, Item 11, 461. SLNSW, ML MSS 364/3.

meeting place: Pejar Local Aboriginal Land Council notes that the Goulburn region was known as a meeting place. This means that Goulburn wasn't inhabited by just one group of people, but it had many: Mulwaree, Wollondilly, Wiradjuri, Gundungarra, Dharrook (Dharug), Tharawal (Dharawal), Tarlo, Lachlan, Pajong, Parramarragoo, Cookmal, Burra Burra and Ngunawal.

white cockatoos: A nineteenth-century dictionary of slang defines 'cockatoo' as 'farmer or settler, a small settler . . . So called to compare them with the common sulphur-crested white cockatoos, which come down on the newly sown cornfields in myriads'. Albert Barrere & Charles Godfrey Leland, 'Cockatoos', in *A Dictionary of Slang, Jargon & Cant*, Vol. 1 (The Ballantyne Press, 1889–90), 259.

7

the artist is in his studio: Norman Lindsay, *My Mask: For What Little I Know of the Man Behind It, An Autobiography* (Angus & Robertson, 1970), 179.

the plague: N. Lindsay, *My Mask*, 178–79; see also 'Plague precautions', *SMH*, 20 Feb 1902, 6; 'Outbreak of plague: Fumigation of sewers', *Evening News*, 21 Feb 1902, 3.

boxing lesson: R. Lindsay, *Rose Lindsay*, 179–80, refers to Norman Lindsay's boxing.

locked diary: R. Lindsay, *Rose Lindsay*, 178.

drips in ink: Speculation. They later became lovers, then married.

'sad looking person': ABP to MF, 7 Apr 1902. File 2: MFGC, 1901–1936.

A.B.C. tearoom: A.B.C. was an upmarket tearoom run by the Aerated Bread Company, who took the site over from Shadler's Cafe. See 'Shadler's Café', *Sunday Times*, 25 Nov 1900, 5.

reflux: Norman Lindsay, 'Banjo Paterson', in *Bohemians of The Bulletin* (Angus & Robertson, 1965), 77–83.

'embodiment of destructiveness': Paterson, 'A day under fire'. Miles spoke against using men as cannon fodder in *Cockatoos*.

guarded, shy: Paterson noted their different personalities in ABP to MF, 30 July 1902. File 2: MFGC, 1901–1936.

Banjo: The 'Banjo' nickname was from a family racehorse, not the musical instrument.

'free as air': ABP to MF, 2 Apr 1902. File 2: MFGC, 1901–1936.

8

flowered hat: N. Lindsay, 'Miles Franklin', in *Bohemians of The Bulletin*, 143.

'charmed'; *'Marie B was a self-conscious'*: AGS to MF, 2 Feb 1902. File 2: MFGC, 1901–1936.

'Was it true?': Franklin, *The End of My Career*, 413. Note: 'He' is based on A.B. Paterson.

In her mind: Franklin dramatised the *Bulletin* meeting, Stephen's reticence and her admiration for Lindsay in *My Career Goes Bung*. See also N. Lindsay, 'Miles Franklin', and N. Lindsay, 'Meeting on the stairs', *The Bulletin*, 18 Sep 1946, in which Lindsay remembered Miles as a 'rebellious minx'.

'Stephens—poof—crap—bum': Norman Lindsay to Lionel Lindsay, 'Sydney, circa 1901', in Norman Lindsay, Robert Guy Howarth & Anthony Barker, *Letters of Norman Lindsay* (Angus & Robertson, 1979), 28–29.

'pert nose'; *'pert rump'*: N. Lindsay, 'Miles Franklin', 143.

'another Marie': N. Lindsay, *'Miles Franklin'*, 144.

'Damn it, I was only': N. Lindsay, 'Miles Franklin', 144. Re Stephens blocking Lindsay, see N. Lindsay, 'Meeting on the stairs'.

Dis aliter visum: N. Lindsay, 'Miles Franklin', 145.

'The best love affairs': N. Lindsay, 'Miles Franklin', 145.

'saturnine': N. Lindsay, 'Banjo Paterson', 80.

'I'll buy that horse': N. Lindsay, 'Banjo Paterson', 80. Lindsay's horse later threw the groom and smashed into a carriage, and sadly was shot due to its injuries.

9

Women thronged: see e.g. 'Melbourne Letter'. *Gippsland Times*, 14 Apr 1902, 3.

light April rain: 'The weather', *The Argus*, 8 Apr 1902. Canberra was built in 1913.

'I see no reason': Australian Senate, *Debates*, 9 Apr 1902, 11451–52, parlinfo.aph.gov.au.

'Really!': Australian Senate, *Debates*, 9 Apr 1902.

'I say again that everywhere': Australian Senate, *Debates*, 9 Apr 1902.

'It would be a monstrous': Australian Senate, *Debates*, 10 Apr 1902, 11587. The objecting senator was Sir Alexander Matheson, 3rd baronet.

'the nastiest things of men': 'Our Public Women Miss Rose Scott'. *The Daily Telegraph*, 10 Mar 1915, 6.

'Where do you dig us': Allen, *Rose Scott*, 214.

refused a glass of wine: Miles did not drink and was open about her distaste for alcohol. See ch. 32.

'Dear girl': Rose had a number of affectionate names for Miles.

'white puddings': Speculation. Sybylla in *My Career Goes Bung* calls Mrs Crasterton's breasts 'white puddings' and is fixated by bosoms bulging from dresses everywhere.

10

made of possum fur: Grantlee Kieza, *Banjo* (HarperCollins, 2020), 205.

'sheer drivel': ABP to MF, 12 Apr 1902. File 2: MFGC, 1901–1936.

broken engagement: Kieza, *Banjo*, 326. Paterson wrote the lyrics to Waltzing Matilda, composed by Christine Macpherson.

'Your note & mine': ABP to MF, 2 May 1902. File 2: MFGC, 1901–1936.

'You lucky fellow': MF to AB, undated. File 1: MFGC, 1887–1951. Note filed with Lawson correspondence.

writes at a time of the day: Franklin suffered insomnia. Roe cites a scene from 'On the Outside Track' in which the heroine, Ignez, writes after putting her young sister to bed, and suggests Franklin similarly wrote after she put Laurel to bed. See Roe, *Stella Miles Franklin*, 90.

'On the Outside Track': Published as *Cockatoos* (Angus & Robertson, 1954).

the snake: Franklin recalls her recurring visions of the snake in Miles Franklin, *Childhood at Brindabella* (Angus & Robertson, 1963), 19. Quoted in Roe, *Stella Miles Franklin*, 31.

S.S. Mambare; expedition: A.B. Paterson, 'The New Hebrides. Voyage of the pilgrims. No. 1', *SMH*, 1 Jul 1902, 5–7. The New Hebrides is now Vanuatu.

sheep; a pig: A.B. Paterson, 'The New Hebrides Voyage of the Pilgrims. IV. At New Caledonia'. *SMH*, 15 Jul 1902, 7.

All have little capital: A.B. Paterson, 'The New Hebrides. Voyage of the pilgrims. No. 1', *SMH*, 1 Jul 1902, 5.

'Pilgrim Fathers': Paterson, 'The New Hebrides . . . No. 1'.

'There are farmers': Paterson, 'The New Hebrides . . . No. 1'.

'I am leaving': ABP to MF, 31 May 1902. File 2: MFGC,1901–1936.

'He desired my collaboration': MF to JP, 3 Jun 1902, File 3: MFGC, 1902–1953. SLNSW, ML MSS 364/8.

'I quite agree': JP to MF, 13 Jun 1902. File 3: MFGC, 1902-1953.

'I agree with you': JP to MF, 22 Jul 1902. File 3: MFGC, 1902–1953.

'being rather fond': JP to MF, 12 Nov 1902. File 3: MFGC, 1902–1953.

'I don't know': LG to MF, 30 Jun 1902. File 3: MFFC, Graham-Lampe, 1897–1954.

'Aunt Sara's advice': LG to MF, 30 Jun 1902. File 3: MFFC, Graham-Lampe, 1897–1954.

'I have just got back': ABP to MF, 25 Jul 1902. File 2: MFGC, 1901–1936.

'brother's terribly tragic death': 'Personal items. Death of Mr H.H. Paterson', *SMH*, 25 Jul 1902, 5.

'finale': Finale is written in Franklin's handwriting on the 25 July 1902 letter.

11

'I know all about': Frederick W. Maudsley to MF, 8 Jun 1902. File 2: MFGC, 1901–1936., File 3: MFGC, 1902–1953.

'you too have lost': JP to MF, 2 Aug 1902. File 3 MFGC, 1902–1953.

'A young, strong life': JF to MF, 2 Aug 1902, File 3: MFGC, 1902–1953.

'I don't think my brother': JP to MF, 2 Aug 1902. File 3: MFGC, 1902–1953.

'very taken with the idea': ABP to MF, 30 Jul 1902. File 2:MFGC, 1901–1936.

'It is queer': ABP to MF, 30 July 1902. File 2: MFGC, 1901–1936.

'you err I think': ABP to MF, 30 July 1902. File 2: MFGC, 1901–1936.

'I mean to take a spell': ABP to MF, 30 July 1902. File 2: MFGC, 1901–1936.

'I think I understand': ABP to MF, 30 July 1902. File 2: MFGC, 1901–1936.

'We can do our work': ABP to MF, 7 Aug 1902. File 2: MFGC, 1901–1936.

'Have all the glory': LG to MF, 30 June 1902. File 3: MFFC, Graham-Lampe, 1897–1954.

'When are you going to be Mrs Banjo?': LG to MF, undated. c. 1902. File 3: MFFC, Graham-Lampe, 1897–1954.

'I am sorry to worry': MF to RS, 19 Aug 1902. File 3: MFGC, 1902–1953. Published in Roe, *My Congenials*, 23.

'I think American men': 'Miss Vida Goldstein', *SMH*, 18 Aug 1902, 5.

'Welcome, Welcome': RS to MF (telegram), 20 Aug 1902. File 3: MFGC, 1902–1953.

prominent Chinese merchant: 'A city sensation', *SMH*, 20 Aug 1902, 9. The merchant was Mei Quong Tart.

fallen from a tram: 'Fatal tram accident', *SMH*, 1 Aug 1902, 8. See also Franklin, *Cockatoos*.

'Sent up here hurriedly': ABP to MF (telegram), 25 Aug 1902. File 2: MFGC, 1901–1936.

12

the shearers' camp: A.B. Paterson, 'Conditions at Coonamble', *SMH*, 26 Aug 1902, 5.

'If any man wants': reconstructed from A.B. Paterson, 'Trouble at Coonamble', *SMH*, 27 Aug 1902, 10.

town besieged: In 'Trouble at Coonamble', Paterson compares the shearing camp and neighbouring town to Ladysmith, South Africa, referencing the Boer War.

police inspector: See A.B. Paterson, 'Trouble at Wingadee Station', *SMH*, 29 Aug 1902, 5.

13

'he be a cad or a lad': CG to MF, undated ('Sunday evening'). File 3: MFFC, Graham-Lampe, 1897–1954. See also Roe, *Stella Miles Franklin*, 98. Note: Roe's text is 'if he be a cad or a man?'.

'I was thinking over something': CG to MF, undated ('Sunday evening'). File 3: MFFC, Graham-Lampe, 1897–1954.

She felt plain: Miles was self-conscious about her looks, especially compared to Linda. Speculation she felt pressure; she was shy and anxious underneath her charm.

14

follows the man from Snowy River: Reconstructed from Miles' recollection of being with Paterson in his flat. Miles Franklin Personal papers 1880–1954, Diaries, notebooks and indexes, 1909–1954, literary note-books, volumes I–XV, 1934–c. 1948, 'Vol. I . . . pp. 1–50', Item. 1, 34. SLNSW, Box ML MSS 364/3.

'revelations'; *'shrivelled all inspiration'*; *'shell sealed up'*; *'the most sophisticated man'*: Miles Franklin literary notebooks, volumes I–XV, 1934–c. 1948, 'Vol. I . . . pp. 1-50', Item 1, 34.

'Dear girl': Speculation. Miles would have been clearly upset, and Rose mothered her. It is unclear if she told Rose directly about Paterson's attempted seduction.

'Mrs Lawson just received': HL to MF, 5 Sep 1902. File 1: MFGC, 1887–1951.

departing actor: 'Rignold send-off supper', *SMH*, 11 Sep 1902, 4.

golf: See 'Golf notes by Jock', *Referee*, 24 Sep 1902, 9.

'The long day passes': A.B. Paterson, 'He giveth his beloved sleep', in *Rio Grande's Last Race and Other Verses* (Angus & Robertson, 1902).

'You are my fairy'; *'spirit child'*: Speculation. Miles recalled her 'fairy days' with Rose Scott, and the events mentioned. Rose introduced Miles as 'her spirit child'. See Roe, *Stella Miles Franklin*, 97, 124–125.

Mrs E. O'Sullivan: Franklin refers to Mrs E. O'Sullivan's offer of help in 'Concerning Maryann, First draft' Ms. 1904, 2.

'Special Correspondent'; *'She is most shy'*: 'Thalia', 'Gossip for women', *The Week*, 26 Sep 1902, 4. Speculation that Miles read these reviews; syndication of articles was common, and news travelled.

aristocratic like Linda's: Miles thought Linda was prettier; she disliked her own nose. See Roe, *Stella Miles Franklin*, 46.

'holding daily receptions': 'Woman's column', *The Newsletter*, 6 Sep 1902, 13.

Thank God for sleep: A.B. Paterson, 'He giveth his beloved sleep'.

15

'superior': MF to GR, 20 Jul 1902. Published in Roe, *My Congenials*, 23.

'toning': Quoted in Roe, *Stella Miles Franklin*, 77.

'Am I wrong': Bertha Lawson to MF, undated. File 1: MFGC, 1887–1951.

'But be very careful': Bertha Lawson to MF, undated. File 1:MFGC, 1887–1951.

'I am sad': RS to MF, 26 Sep 1902. File 3: MFGC, 1902–1953.

'I believe that you': JP to MF, 17 Oct 1902. File 3, MFGC, 1902–1953.

Selina Sangal: See 'Dandenong tragedy', *SMH*, 27 Sep 1902, 9; 'Selina Sangal her expected baby', *Truth*, 19 Oct 1902, 4; (Rose Scott), 'Sydney day by day', *Australian Star*, 4 Nov 1902, 3; 'Death sentence on Selina Sangal', *SMH*, 26 Nov 1902, 9.

'represented the rebellious'; *'saved from the death penalty'*: 'The case of Mrs Sangal,' *SMH*, 6 Nov 1902, 8.

16

fever: Frederick W. Maudsley to MF, 8 Jun 1902. File 2: MFGC, 1901–1936.

'Sybylla asleep': The seduction is likely based on her experience with Paterson, given Miles' recollection of what happened at his flat (see ch. 14), and her later note stating to George Robertson that she thought she had disguised Paterson (see note in ch. 18).

She quotes a poem: See 'The End of My Career', manuscript fragments. Miles Franklin papers, mainly literary manuscripts [1900–1954?].

'So you think': 'Ambrose Pratt, The woman speaks', First published in *The Bulletin*, 26 May 1900, 11.

'The End of My Career', manuscript fragments, Miles Franklin papers, mainly literary manuscripts [1900–1954?]. The reworked published version of the sequel appeared as *My Career Goes Bung* in 1946, without the slap scene; however Franklin refers to the Paterson-like character as a 'rampant stallion', 416 [2013].

no spring lambs: 'The drought', *Sydney Wool and Stock Journal*, 23 Sep 1902, 1.

17

The publisher's home: See 'Reminiscences of George Robertson and Angus & Robertson Ltd by Rebecca Wiley. Memories of over 43 years, 1894–1938 (1945)'. SLNSW, ML MSS 5238.

'serious mistake': Quoted in Roe, *Stella Miles Franklin*, 68.

'Re some stuff I've written': MF to GR, 10 Nov 1902. Published in A.W. Barker (ed.), *Dear Robertson: Letters to an Australian Publisher* (Angus & Robertson, 1982), 34–35.

'No need to fear'; *'Do not be afraid'*: '300,000 mile tail. Extraordinary facts about a new comet', *The Telegraph*, 1 Nov 1902, 5.

'for the war has': 'Rio Grande's Last Race', *SMH*, 6 Dec 1902, 4.

'a favourite among': 'A.B. Paterson's latest verses', *The Age*, 6 Dec 1902, 4.

'Occasionally the writer drops': A.B. Paterson's latest verses', *The Age*.

Longed for: speculation. Most writers want critical as well as commercial success.

'What do you think of a poet as a lover?': 'The End of My Career', manuscript fragments, Miles Franklin papers, mainly literary manuscripts [1900–1954].

'dark brilliancy'; *'She takes no pains'*: Reviewer quoted in Roe, *Stella Miles Franklin*, 102.

'I had no difficulty': GR to MF, 30 Nov 1902. Published in Barker, *Dear Robertson*, 35. The sequel was eventually published in 1946 as *My Career Goes Bung*.

promised to send: GR to MF, 30 Nov 1902. Published in Barker, *Dear Robertson*, 35.

18

southern districts; rain; circus cart: 'The rainfall', *Goulburn Herald*, 19 Dec 1902, 5; 'Fine rain'; *Goulburn Evening Penny Post*, 18 Dec 1902, 2; 'The rain. General over the state. Some splendid falls', *Daily Telegraph*, 17 Dec 1902, 8.

'My dear, dear, little Stella': RS to MF, 15 Dec 1902. File 3: MFGC, 1902–1953.

Selina Sangal: 'Petition for reprieve', *Truth*, 30 Nov 1902, 5; 'Her life spared', *SMH*, 1 Dec 1902, 4.

Myrtle: Jenny Boyer, 'Murder Most Foul', *Spreading Branches*, Narre Warren & District Family History Group Inc., Issue 55, Feb 2003: 4–5.

'Alas, Alack': MF to GR, 4 Dec 1902. Published in Barker, *Dear Robertson*, 35–36. In her reply, Miles says 'I thought I had him [Paterson] well disguised'.

lyrebird tail feather: RS to MF, 6 Jan 1903. File 3: MFGC, 1902–1953.

church services; 'wisdom and necessity': 'Thanksgiving for rain', *SMH*, 30 Dec 1902, 5. Speculation that Miles attended a service; despite her cynicism, she would have been expected to go to church.

royalties: Franklin only sold around 1000 copies a year of *My Brilliant Career*, mainly in Australia; these were subject to import royalty so her earnings were meagre.

'Many thanks for the cheque': ABP to MF, 16 Dec 1902. File 2: MFGC, 1901–1936.

pigsty: Hiding the manuscript behind the pigsty is referred to in Roe, *Stella Miles Franklin*, 105. Speculation her mother retrieved it; in the preface to *My Career Goes Bung*, Franklin writes the manuscript was put in a suitcase with other manuscripts and taken to Chicago.

'Strange, is it not': Omar Khayyam, *Rubáiyát of Omar Khayyam, the Astronomer-Poet of Persia*, trans. Edward FitzGerald (Bernard Quaritch, 1859 [1120]), quoted in ABP to MF, undated. File 2: MFGC, 1901–1936.

19

'came bounding at me': 'The Marulan Tiger', *Queanbeyan Age*, 11 Mar 1903, 2.

pet leopard: 'Explained', *The Evening News*, 9 Mar 1903, 4.

local clergyman: 'The Marulan Tiger, Goulburn, Saturday', *SMH*, 2 Mar 1903, 2.

clearing-out sale: 'short notice', *Goulburn Evening Penny Post*, 14 Mar 1903, 3. Referred to in Roe, *Stella Miles Franklin*, 107.

farewell picnic: 'Picnic and Presentation', *Goulburn Herald*. 2 Feb 1903, 2.

'He's no businessman': LG to MF, Undated. File 3: MFFC, Graham-Lampe 1887–1954. Quoted in Roe, *Stella Miles Franklin*, 106.

'How is Graham getting on?': SL to MF, 30 Mar 1903. File 3: MFFC, Graham-Lampe 1887–1954.

20

Surprised and amused: JP to MF, 27 Sep 1903. File 3: MFGC, 1902–1953.

Tenterfield Station: 'Tenterfield Station A noted cattle run'. *Australian Town and Country Journal*, 6 May 1899, 30.

Alice Walker: Grantlee Kieza profiles their relationship in *Banjo*, 443.

'Am very anxious': RS to MF, 18 Mar 1903. File 3: MFGC, 1902–1953.

'you were breaking up': JP to MF, 27 Sep 1903. File 3: MFGC, 1902–1953.

Penrith: Miles describes the then orchard town in *Some Everyday Folk and Dawn* (Blackwood, 1909), which she calls 'Noonoon'. Penrith is now a major city centre of Sydney.

Farmers rang bells: 'Penrith'. *South Coast Times and Wollongong Argus*, 28 Mar 1903, 5.

'land o' lots o' time': MF to J.F. Archibald, 5 Sep 1901.Published in Roe, *My Congenials*, 14.

'land of melons': Franklin, *Some Everyday Folk and Dawn*, 3.

meteor: 'A Meteor at Penrith', *The Daily Telegraph*, 4 May 1903, 7.

'Be sure and catch one': SL to MF, 30 Mar 1903. File 3: MFFC, Graham-Lampe 1887–1954. See also Roe, *My Congenials*, 25.

'selling what does not belong': SL to MF, 6 Apr 1903. File 3: MFFC, Graham-Lampe 1887–1954.

'Now Dear Stella': SL to MF, 27 Apr 1903. File 3: MFFC, Graham-Lampe 1887–1954.

'No, I would not advise': SL to MF, 4 May 1903. File 3: MFFC, Graham-Lampe 1887–1954.

'It has rained': SL to MF, 27 Apr 1903. File 3: MFFC, Graham-Lampe 1887–1954.

21

wedding in Tenterfield: 'Banjo's wedding', *The Leader* (Orange), 20 Apr 1903, 2.

'a queer man': RS to MF, 27 Apr 1903. File 3: MFGC, 1902–1953.

'I always thought you might': LG to MF, 16 May 1903. File 3: MFFC, Graham-Lampe 1887–1954.

'What a life his poor wife': LG to MF, 16 May 1903. File 3: MFFC, Graham-Lampe 1887–1954.
'His wife is very nice': JP to MF, 27 Sep 1903. File 3: MFGC, 1902–1953.
Camping: Roe quotes a postcard MF to LG while camping en-route, 19 Mar 1903. Roe, *Stella Miles Franklin*, 107.

Part Two: Sarah

Note: All real identities are provided in the text where known. Miles' actual pseudonym, 'Sarah Frankling', is used, rather than 'Mary Anne' which was used in the manuscript 'When I Was Mary Anne, a Slavey'.

22

Easter Show: 'The Royal Easter Show', *SMH*, 30 Mar 1903, 5.
back alleys of the city: 'Poverty stricken Sydney', *Blue Mountains Gazette*, 31 Jul 1903, 3.
first reviews; *poodle*: Elizabeth L. Banks, *The Autobiography of a 'Newspaper Girl'* (Methuen, 1902), 71.
'Sarah Frankling': Identified from correspondence sent to Franklin. Quoted in Roe, *Stella Miles Franklin*. 110.
Mrs O'Sullivan; *'fairy'*: Miles Franklin, 'Concerning Maryann. First draft' Ms. 1904, 2. Sub-series 1: Miles Franklin literary manuscripts and related papers, 1887–1954. Essays and Articles 189- –c. 1950. SLNSW, Vol. ML MSS 364/59.
'Mother and father': reconstructed from Franklin, 'Concerning Maryann. First draft' Ms. 1904, 2. Mrs O'Sullivan's queries are speculation; she would have been concerned for Miles' welfare.
'The idea of a hospital nurse': Franklin, 'Sketch 1: Introductory', in 'When I Was Mary Anne, a Slavey', Vol. 1, Sketches 1–4 (c. 1904), 4.
'Waitress wanted': Franklin, 'The struggle to gain a footing', 7.
THOROUGH general: 'Servants wanted', *SMH*, 15 Apr 1903, 12.
She wondered if the reports: Franklin, 'The struggle to gain a footing', 8.
'lose sight of the fact': 'The domestic servant question', *Tasmanian News*, 18 Nov 1903, 2.
'The mistress may be a she-dragon': 'The domestic servant question', *Sunday Press* (Perth), 29 Mar 1903, 3. See also 'The domestic servant problem', *The Argus*, 14 Jun 1902, 18; and 'Letterbox', *Catholic Press*, 13 Aug 1903, 24. For context on the 'servant problem', see Beverley Kingston, *My Wife, My Daughter, and Poor Mary Ann: Women and Work in Australia* (Thomas Nelson, 1975).
suspicious glances: Franklin, 'The struggle to gain a footing', 7.
'it was imperative': Franklin, 'The struggle to gain a footing', 8.

COOKS and L'dresses: 'Servants wanted', *SMH*, 15 Apr 1903, 12. Speculation the agency was Hittman's. Franklin does not name the actual agency. Hittmann's was a prominent advertiser in 1903, and located in the city, where Miles went to the first employment office.

It is evening: Franklin, 'The struggle to gain a footing', 15.

her mother is wearily awake: Speculation. Her mother would have been worried. Franklin, 'The struggle to gain a footing', 15.

too over-strung for sleep: Franklin, 'The struggle to gain a footing', 15.

a doctor's wife; Mrs Finlayson; equestrians : Franklin, 'The struggle to gain a footing', 9, 14–15. Mrs Finlayson was identified by correspondence to Miles care of the address. See also Roe, *Stella Miles Franklin*, 110.

23

Her hand froze; 'Come right in'; paws; fastidiousness: Miles Franklin, 'Sketch II [repeated]: Through inexperienced spectacles', in 'When I Was Mary Anne, a Slavey', Vol. 1, Sketches 1–4 (c. 1904), 16. The Finlaysons are renamed 'The Tomlinsons' in the text.

'My nervousness beats': Franklin, 'Third and fourth days' (diary extracts), in 'Through inexperienced spectacles', 19.

'aggressively bald'; *'self-important voice'*: Franklin, 'Third and fourth days' (diary extracts), in 'Through inexperienced spectacles', 18.

'boss of his backyard'; *'beetle on the fence'*: Franklin, 'Through inexperienced spectacles', 25, 26.

'I was glad to hear': RS to MF, 22 May 1903. File 3: MFGC, 1902–1953. Published in Roe, *My Congenials*, 26.

'blindly' leading women: See 'Voice of women', *Australian Star*, 16 May 2022, 2; 'Country versus town', *SMH*, 26 May 1903, 7.

What a shame: Speculation. Rose clearly missed Miles in her life.

'Ye Gods!'; *'The next Saturday'*: RS to MF, 'Wednesday' (c. May 1903). File 3: MFGC, 1902–1953.

'How clever': In her letter of 22 May 1903, Rose said Mrs O'Sullivan told her where Miles had disappeared.

24

miners: 'Victorian coal strike—women arrested', *Sunday Times*, 10 May 1903, 8.

petition: 'The uprising domestic', *Daily Telegraph*, 28 Sep 1901, 8. The Domestic Service and Houseworker Association was briefly formed and ineffective.

bacon; searing skin: Franklin, 'Fifth Day' (diary extract), 'When I Was Mary Anne', 20.

'Dear me, how terribly': Franklin, 'Through inexperienced spectacles', 22.

'the absence of economy': 'Engineering Association', *Daily Telegraph*, 15 May 1903, 7. Mentions 'R.W. Finlayson'.
sauce, piano; loose gas taps: Franklin, 'Through inexperienced spectacles', 22.
hanging more loosely: See Franklin, 'Concerning Maryanne. First draft' Ms. 1904.
'my dear girl where are you': SL to MF, 14 May 1903. File 3: MFFC, Graham-Lampe 1887–1954.
'Be sure to tell me': LG to MF, 16 May 1903. File 3: MFFC, Graham-Lampe 1887–1954.

25

When she woke: Franklin, 'Through inexperienced spectacles', 26.
boiled blue; corroded her skin: Early 1900s washing powder, like 'Recketts', was harsh and blue.
'It's easy to see': Franklin, 'Through inexperienced spectacles', 27. Miles' original text mimics the laundress's accent; removed here for clarity.
'reflection of its mistress': Franklin, 'Through inexperienced spectacles', 43.
'playing cubby house': Franklin, 'Third and fourth days' (diary extract), in 'Through inexperienced spectacles', 19.
forest of class; *stand-offishness*: Franklin's 'diary extract' in 'Through inexperienced spectacles' refers to Miles describing her curiosity meeting 'denizens of beyond the pale—people in trade', 17.
'dazzling teeth': Franklin, 'Through inexperienced spectacles', 35.
'Hullo! You forgot your jug!': Franklin, 'Through inexperienced spectacles', 35.
'Oh dear, no': Franklin, 'Through inexperienced spectacles', 37.
She had never felt so alone: See 'any company is preferable to loneliness', in Franklin, 'Through inexperienced spectacles', 35.
'You make her': Franklin, 'Through inexperienced spectacles', 38.
swings herself onto: Franklin, 'Through inexperienced spectacles', 40.
'Give it to her': Franklin, 'Through inexperienced spectacles', 41.

26

Rupert: Franklin, 'Through inexperienced spectacles', 50. Unclear if real name or a pseudonym.
'I wish a fellow'; *'Every fellow is at heart'*: Franklin, 'Through inexperienced spectacles', 33.
'Very good': Franklin, 'Through inexperienced spectacles', 44.
'Don't begin to invite': Franklin, 'Through inexperienced spectacles', 46.
'Charlie was thinking': LG to MF, 9 Jun 1903. File 3: MFFC, Graham-Lampe 1887–1954.

In the privacy: Franklin, 'Diary extracts' in 'Through inexperienced spectacles', 18 describes her room next to the laundry.

fuzz: Franklin describes the partial loss of her front hair in (diary extract) 'Fifth Day', 20.

hopes Linda knows: Speculation. Miles never indicated jealousy over her sister's happiness.

27

her desire to leave; 'very well I can easily': Franklin, 'Through inexperienced spectacles, 46.

'Did you ever have a row'; 'Now don't you think': Franklin, 'Through inexperienced spectacles', 47.

'who walks about'; this 'suppression': Franklin, 'Through inexperienced spectacles', 39.

Tuesday of her last week: Franklin, 'Through inexperienced spectacles', 48.

'Here's the bill': Franklin, 'Through inexperienced spectacles', 48.

verged on telling him: 'I contemplated telling him who I was', in Franklin, 'Through inexperienced spectacles', 49.

She still blushed: Speculation. The episode had stayed vividly with her, given her memory of Paterson's flat years later.

'No one has a claim': Franklin, 'Through inexperienced spectacles', 49.

reference: See Franklin, 'Through inexperienced spectacles', 49. Note that the original manuscript replaces 'Sarah Frankling' with 'Mary-Anne Smith' and 'Finlayson' with 'Tomlinson'.

Sunday; tram: Franklin, 'Through inexperienced spectacles', 50.

The next morning: Speculation. It is unlikely being a Sunday that Mrs Finlayson would have got a replacement maid to start so soon.

28

a baby girl, Ruby; a servant, Nellie: 'Summons court, Dubbo', *Dubbo Liberal and Macquarie Advocate*, 20 Jun 1903, 2; 'Tragedy at Annandale, Sydney', *Newcastle Morning Herald and Miners Advocate*, 10 Jun 1903, 5.

'accident to Miles Franklin': 'Accident to Miles Franklin', *Queanbeyan Observer*, 23 Jun 1903, 2. Attributed to *The Book Lover*.

wondered how the newspaper: Speculation. Likely it was Rose.

ferry to Mrs O'Sullivan's: Miles wrote that she rested 'between acts' with Mrs O'Sullivan, or with Rose. See 'Concerning Maryann. First draft' Ms. 1904. The O'Sullivans lived in Mosman, Sydney, on the north shore of the harbour.

eyed the new guest curiously: Speculation: the staff would question a guest who wore plain clothes.

a tight winter; *God help anyone*; *one of her pet places*: Miles Franklin, 'Sketch III: Some registry offices and a Jewess', in 'When I Was Mary Anne, a Slavey', Vol. 1, Sketches 1–4 (c. 1904), 51.

dogs; *She shivered*: Franklin, 'Some registry offices', 54–55.

The son, 'Levy': Franklin, 'Some registry offices', 53. The son's actual first name is unknown, as is the family's so Franklin's pseudonyms are used as per the manuscript.

'What's the Master like?': Franklin, 'Some registry offices', 53.

siesta: Franklin, 'Some registry offices', 54.

Inside her new space: Franklin, 'Some registry offices', 54.

winter-cold water; *numb*; *wrinkled*: Franklin, 'Some registry offices', 57–59.

dog kennels: Franklin, 'Some registry offices', 54.

feeling fretful; *The house was a muddle*: Franklin, 'Some registry offices', 58.

'You said my house': Franklin, 'Some registry offices', 59.

struck a match: Franklin, 'Some registry offices', 59.

Rose's home: Franklin, 'Some registry offices', 65. Rose Scott lived close to Darling Point, the location of the 'Michelstein' villa. See earlier note re Franklin stating she rested with Mrs O'Sullivan or Rose 'between acts'.

'not quite strong enough': Franklin, 'Some registry offices', 65.

29

'No fear': Franklin, 'Some registry offices', 68.

boarding house: See Seamus O'Hanlon, '"All found" they used to call it': Genteel boarding houses in early twentieth-century Melbourne', *Urban History*, 2002, 29(2): 239–53.

'Let's try each other out': Franklin, 'Some registry offices', 69. Mrs Vance and the boarding house are identified from correspondence sent to Miles while at the boarding house.

Elsiemere; *'Look at her pretty cap'*: Franklin, 'Sketch IV Maria's Dingle', in 'When I Was Mary Anne, a Slavey', Vol. 1, Sketches 1–4 (c. 1904), 70. Elsiemere is called 'Maria's Dingle' in original text, and Mrs Vance is 'Mrs Bordinghaus'. Despite half the street being bulldozed for the Harbour Bridge, Elsiemere still stands as a luxury apartment building. Maids' actual names unknown, or Miles did not use pseudonyms for maids.

'badge of slavery': Franklin, 'Maria's Dingle', 164.

dark rings: Franklin, 'Maria's Dingle', 136.

'These women': Franklin, 'Maria's Dingle', 136.

her first day; *'zoo'*: Franklin, 'Maria's Dingle', 77.

The Old Goat: Franklin, 'Maria's Dingle', 80.

'I knew from the start'; *held back her name*: Franklin, 'Maria's Dingle', 88. Miles does not disclose whether she gave her real name to Alice.

shock of recognition: Franklin, 'Maria's Dingle', 83.

'a head and shoulders': Franklin, 'Maria's Dingle', 96.

instead was irritated: See 'his stupidity irritated her', Franklin, 'Maria's Dingle', 98.

rush to their nests; *officers leer*; *Alice snaps*: Franklin, 'Maria's Dingle', 106, 108.

30

a letter from 'Mother': 'Royal commission on the birth rate', *Evening News*, 29 Aug 1903, 3. Paterson was *Evening News* editor from 1903 to 1908.

In the harbour: 'Steamer collision, Sydney', *The Week*, 7 Aug 1903, 16; 'Sultan Johore's experience', *Australian Star*, 1 Aug 1903, 7.

'Oh, fascinating brass-buttoned uniforms and naval caps': Franklin, 'Maria's Dingle', 129. Possibly a diary extract as sub-titled: 'Tuesday'. Fanshawe was the vice-admiral in 1903; the officers are given pseudonyms in 'Mary Anne'. See note below about the identity of 'Brownie'. Franklin includes other diary entries in 'Maria's Dingle', 133.

'The sickening paralysing'; *'Worry, worry'*: Franklin, 'Maria's Dingle', 129–30. Franklin's description suggests she suffered panic attacks.

'I tried that once': Franklin, 'Maria's Dingle', 141. Original text refers to officer as 'Brownie'. He is possibly Arthur Bedford, a young flag lieutenant attached to Fanshawe's staff and son of the Western Australian governor.

Shakespearean banter: Franklin, 'Maria's Dingle', 132.

'game little kid': Franklin, 'Maria's Dingle', 88.

'You must be wonderfully brave': Franklin, 'Maria's Dingle', 127. Original text refers to guests as 'Romeo and Juliet'.

On payday; *pay cheque*; *half-sovereign coin*: Equal to ten shillings. The ten-shilling note did not appear until 1910. See Franklin, 'Maria's Dingle', 144.

'I haven't got enough': Franklin, 'Maria Dingle's', 152.

'I have business': Franklin, 'Maria's Dingle', 152. See SF to MF, 1 Aug 1903, which mentions bad colds. MFFC, Franklin family, 1896–1954, SLNSW, ML MSS 364/48.

'Her name is Mrs Free': Laurel Franklin to MF, 1 Aug 1903 (likely enclosed with her mother's letter, also 1 Aug 1903). File 2: MFFC, Franklin family, 1896–1954.

'divinity'; *'fat'*; *'little fairy'*: Franklin, 'Maria's Dingle', 163.

'They are a pack': Franklin, 'Maria's Dingle', 150.

winter morning: Franklin, 'Maria's Dingle', 163.

'Sarah! I will speak to you!': Franklin, 'Maria's Dingle', 164. Note original has 'Mary!' and 'Mr Browne!'.

'Always that slur': Franklin, 'Maria's Dingle', 164.

Bedford was still: See Franklin, 'Maria's Dingle', 165. Original text is 'Brownie'.

Penrith address: Correspondence from F. Vance, 8 Sep 1903. File 4: MFGC, 1903–1953. SLNSW, ML MSS 364/9A.

'You did give me hope': Franklin, 'Maria's Dingle', 174.

Influenza Fiend; *Kissing Peril*: See 'The kissing peril', *Albury Banner and Wodonga Express*, 27 Feb 1903, 11; 'The influenza fiend', *Leader*, 28 Mar 1903, 39. For influenza outbreak, see 'The country', *Australian Star*, 24 Sep 1903, 3.

Miles strokes her sister's head: Speculation. Miles was home so would have cared for her sister.

'Dear little sister': LG to MF, 30 Sep 1903. File 3: MFGC, 1902–1953.

two children: 'Precocious children', *Maffra Spectator*, 5 Oct 1903, 3.

lion tamer: 'Attacked by a lion', *Newcastle Morning Herald and Miners' Advocate*, 5 Oct 1903, 5.

Selina Sangal: See 'Her life spared. Selina Sangal's doom', *The Herald*, 2 Dec 1902, 4.

Rose Scott: 'Miss Rose Scott. Her tour through Queensland. Some impressions', *Australian Star*, 9 Nov 1903, 4.

the artist Norman Lindsay: Speculation. They regularly rode together in Centennial Park. See N. Lindsay, 'Banjo Paterson', 80.

Alice and the maids: Speculation. They had been close friends.

sister as she passes: 4 Oct 1903, cause of death recorded as 'inflammation of the heart'. See RootsWeb, 'Laurel Susannah FRANKLIN (1892–1903)', https://freepages.rootsweb.com/~hanhorg/genealogy/ind_narrative/ind799.html.

31

Granny's local paper: 'Tumut', *Adelong and Tumut Express and Tumbarumba Post*, 16 Oct 1903, 4. Article notes death was on 4 Oct.

ill with influenza; *Working and Factory Girls' Club*: Miles Franklin, 'Sketch V: Geebung Villa', in 'When I Was Mary Anne, a Slavey,' Vol. 2, Sketches V & VI (c. 1904), 1. Miles Franklin papers, mainly literary manuscripts [1900–1954?]. SLNSW, ML MSS 445/24. See also 'Working and Factory Girls' Club', *SMH*, 9 Jun 1899, 3, which lists donors like Arnott's.

'slimy'; *food tuned in her stomach*; *sleeping cook*; *home of a clergyman's wife*: Franklin, 'Geebung Villa', 1, 2.

Keston: Original text refers to 'Geebung Villa' as the O'Connor residence in Kirribilli, Sydney.

Richard Edward O'Connor: Identified by correspondence sent to Miles at Keston. For a biography of O'Connor, see Martha Rutledge, 'Richard Edward (Dick) O'Connor (1851–1912)', *Australian Dictionary of Biography*, 1988, https://adb.anu.edu.au. Original text calls the family 'Kingscounsil'.

'No necessity to work so hard': SF to MF, 29 Oct 1903. File 2: MFFC, Franklin family, 1896–1954.

'Jane': See Franklin, 'Geebung Villa', 1. Original text notes that 'Mary' has the same name as the 'Mistress', (Sarah O'Connor, and Franklin was using 'Sarah Frankling').

Linda wrote to Keston: LG to MF, undated ('Friday 1903'). File 3: MFFC, Graham-Lampe 1887–1954.

'She is a perfect wreck': SF to MF, 15 Nov 1904. File 2: MFFC, Franklin family, 1896–1954.

'I am glad to hear'; *'It is dreadfully lonely'*: LG to MF, undated ('Friday 1903'). File 3: MFFC, Graham-Lampe, 1887–1954.

'Come here, little chicken!'; *'Little doll!'*, *'Old Demon'*: Franklin, 'Geebung Villa', 7, 10, 11. Original text mimics Honore's Irish accent.

Kathleen; Richard; the little boys'; *Winifred*: Original text uses pseudonyms for children. For the identities of the O'Connor children, see 'Amateurs in "As You Like It"', *Sydney Mail & New South Wales Advertiser*, 16 Dec 1903, 1595. (Note that the youngest was also known as Roderick Alan.)

not a 'tattler': Franklin, 'Geebung Villa', 11.

learning to cook: Franklin, 'Geebung Villa', 19. Original text uses Kathleen's pseudonym 'Millicent'.

'disgusting': Franklin, 'Geebung Villa', 16. Miles abhorred waste.

'I am too!': Franklin, 'Geebung Villa', 9. Original text uses sons' pseudonyms.

'I think the government': Franklin, 'Geebung Villa', 26. Original text has spelling reflecting mimicking Irish accent pronunciation.

'Sure, I knew your hair': Franklin, 'Geebung Villa', 21.

'must have magnificent health': Franklin (diary extract), 'Geebung Villa', 59.

library: Speculation. Miles inspected the library of each home she was in; see Miles Franklin, 'Sketch VI: Mary Anne's enchanted city', in 'When I Was Mary Anne, a Slavey,' Vol. 2, Sketches V & VI (c. 1904), 153.

Melbourne: Miles was in Melbourne by Christmas.

32

stripes of a zebra: 'The extraordinary summer', *The Age*, 13 Feb 1904, 4.

Melbourne employment agencies: Franklin, 'Mary Anne's enchanted city', 64.

the women accompanying them: See Franklin, 'The struggle to gain a footing', 10–17, and 'Mary Anne's enchanted city', 144, 172. Miles was horrified by sex workers and, like Rose Scott, subscribed to the ideas of social purity feminism.

Toorak: Original text refers to the home as 'Nabob Hall' in Toorak. Family's identity is unknown but the Governor-General visited, as did the captain of the English cricket team, so they were very well connected.

nauseous fluid: Franklin, 'Mary Anne's enchanted city', 78.

photography studio: Miles Franklin, author-portrait, 1902 [dated from internal evidence 1904], Cole's Studio Book Arcade. Photographs of Miles Franklin, c. 1879–1954. SLNSW, PX*D 250 (Vol. 1).

'I received your letter': SL to MF, 1 Feb 1904. File 3: MFFC, Graham-Lampe 1887–1954.

'I don't know how': SL to MF, 29 Feb 1904. File 3: MFFC, Graham-Lampe 1887–1954.

'I suppose poor Linda': SL to MF, 1 Feb 1904. File 3: MFFC, Graham-Lampe 1887–1954.

feigned an illness: Franklin, 'Mary Anne's enchanted city', 103. See also note re letter to Rose Scott below.

The doctor: Franklin refers to the doctor in MF to RS, 3 Mar 1903. Published in Roe, *My Congenials*, 30–31.

draw a circle; *'person with a well-balanced'*: Speculation. A maid claiming to be a famous author? For mental health test see 'How do you draw a circle?', *Northern Argus* (Clare, SA), 6 Nov 1903, 2.

'woes of the flesh': see 'Our Doctor. Woes of the flesh. What is advised', *The Herald*, 1 Oct 1903, 3.

the doctor laughed: MF to RS, 3 Mar 1903. Published in Roe, *My Congenials*, 30–31.

elderly cook; *kerosene oil*: Franklin, 'Mary Anne's enchanted city', 154. Miles was confronted by ageing.

The critic has heard: AGS to MF, 29 Jul 1903. Published in Roe, *My Congenials*, 27–28.

'Jemimas', 'Mary Anns': See 'Our Jemima', *The Advocate* (Melbourne), 6 Sep 1902, 29; 'Poor Mary Ann', *Australian Star*, 29 Dec 1900, 13.

'The Butterfly': 'Where are the servant maids?', *The Quiz*, 25 Apr 1901.

33

Easter 1904: 'Easter thoughts', *Sunday Times*, 3 Apr 1904.

members' stand: 'Dresses and attendance', *SMH*, 4 Apr 1904; 'A.J.C. races', *Australian Town and Country Journal*, 6 Apr 1904.

'horsey section': See earlier note re review of *Rio Grande's Last Race* (1902).

weather: 'Melbourne lady's letter', *Australian Town and Country Journal*, 20 Apr 1904.

'I tried Christian Science': 'Mark Twain on faith healing', *Muswellbrook Chronicle*, 7 Feb 1903.

'It is odd and strange': Mark Twain, *Christian Science* (Harper & Brothers, 1907), 186.

invited Miles to their meetings: Goldstein family letters to Miles refer to encouraging her to join Christian Science. Aileen Goldstein to MF, 24 May 1904. File 6: MFGC, 1904–1954. SLNSW, ML MSS 364/10. Published in Roe, *My Congenials*, 34–35.

'cult'; *'aristocratic craze'*: 'An aristocratic craze', *The Leader*, 12 Nov 1904, 34; 'Christian Science', *Daily Mail* (Brisbane), 24 Oct 1903, 11.

'The most exclusive people': MF to Mrs E. O'Sullivan, 'Tuesday' (c. Apr 1904). Published in Roe, *My Congenials*, 32–33.

loaned her dresses: Speculation. 'I only have Mary-Anne clothes,' Miles wrote. MF to Mrs E. O'Sullivan, 'Tuesday' (c. Apr 1904). Published in Roe, *My Congenials*, 32–33.

a photograph that framed them: 'Miles Franklin [and] Vida Goldstein [picture]', c. 1900–1920, State Library of Victoria, H42756a.

'Most seductive': AGS to MF, 8 Mar 1904. File 2: MFGC, 1901–1936.

'dear inconsistent girl': AGS to MF, 24 Mar 1904. File 2: MFGC, 1901–1936.

disconcerted: Speculation. Miles was flirty but self-conscious and moral.

'dashing housemaid': 'The Red Page', *The Bulletin*, 31 Mar 1904. Attributed to A.G Stephens.

Alexandra Club; *'Maryantics'*: 'A woman's letter', *The Bulletin*, 21 Apr 1904; 'Mainly about people', *The Newsletter*, 30 Apr 1904, 9.

'One of my Mistresses'; *'I think this speaks'*: MF to RS, 3 Mar 1903. Published in Roe, *My Congenials*, 30–31.

Tom Collins: Pen name of Joseph Furphy. See Roe, *Stella Miles Franklin*, 114–15.

Kate Baker: See Roe, *Stella Miles Franklin*, 114.

'frankness': JF to MF, 21 Mar 1904. File 5: MFGC, 1904–1907. SLNSW, ML MSS 364/9B.

'I haven't got a tack': MF to JF, 23 Mar 1904. Published in Roe, *My Congenials*, 31–32.

gallery in the State Library: See Roe, *Stella Miles Franklin*, 114–15; John Barnes, *The Order of Things: A Life of Joseph Furphy* (Oxford University Press, 1990), 342. Now the National Gallery of Victoria.

'flesh and blood'; *'I conceived you'*: Kate Baker to MF, 17 Apr 1904. Published in Roe, *My Congenials*, 33.

soulful; poetic; slangy: 'Tom Collins' (Joseph Furphy) to William Cathels, quoted in Roe, *Stella Miles Franklin*, 114.

Every interviewer: 'Miss Miles Franklin and "My Brilliant Career"', *Sunday Sun* (Sydney), 24 Apr 1904, 4.

'Be a nice interviewer': 'Miss Miles Franklin', *Sunday Sun* (Sydney), 24 Apr 1904, 4.

'no-one dares to mention': 'Miss Miles Franklin', *Yass Courier*, 29 Apr 1904, 2.

a carriage; *SS Peregrine*; *roses*; *The Roadmender*: Roe describes Franklin's farewell from her 'Enchanted City' in *Stella Miles Franklin*, 113.

snake: speculation. Miles felt the snake was always with her. See Franklin, *Childhood at Brindabella*, 119. Quoted in Roe, *Stella Miles Franklin*, 31.

34

zoo: See 'Woman's Letter', *The Bulletin*, 7 Apr 1904, 16; and Roe, *Stella Miles Franklin*, 113, quotes a maid 'bursting into tears'. Speculation this is Alice.

'Dearest, it was good': MF to RS, 3 Mar 1904. Published in Roe, *My Congenials*, 30–31.

'This is only a line': RS to MF, 3 May 1904, File 3: MFGC, 1902–1953.

'deliberate interference with reproduction': 'Royal Commission on the Birth Rate', *SMH*, 5 Mar 1904. See also Kingston, *My Wife, My Daughter, and Poor Mary Ann*, 8.

Northern Rivers; *'the brutal outrages'*: 'Women's Political League. Lecture by Miss Rose Scott', *Richmond River Express and Tweed Advertiser*, 17 May 1904.

Ngurra Country: The Blue Mountains is located within the Ngurra (Country) of the Dharug and Gundungurra people.

cult of vegetarianism: 'Vegetarian infancy', *Queanbeyan Observer*, 3 May 1904.

migraines; *dumbbells*; *tattoos*; *Fijian princess*: See Carol Cantrell, 'Caroline Martha (Cara) David', *Australian Dictionary of Biography*, 1993, https://adb.anu.edu.au/biography.

in their house: 'Interview with Mrs David. Professor David's letters, with the Nimrod', *SMH*, 9 Jan 1908, 3. See also Caroline (Cara) David to MF, undated. File 4: MFGC, 1903–1953.

On walks: Speculation.

unending flatness: Isabella Goldstein mentions Miles' discouragement in Isabella Goldstein to MF, 20 May 1904. File 6: MFGC, 1904–1954.

'anti-hell': See 'Cantrell, 'Caroline Martha (Cara) David'.

'I have been worried'; 'Do you ever hear'; 'You can be their old cranky maiden aunt': LG to MF, 23 July 1904. 03: MFFC, Graham-Lampe 1887–1954.

35

'I had against me': 'Vida Goldstein: The Australian women in politics', *Review of Reviews*, 1904. See Jacqueline Kent, *Vida* (Penguin, 2020), 141.

'No-one thinks': 'Miss Vida Goldstein', *Benalla Standard*, 1 Dec 1903, 2.

'women do not always support': Kent, *Vida*, 121.

'I am passing through': VG to MF, 16 May 1904. File 6: MFGC, 1904–1954. Also quoted in Kent, *Vida*, 148.

'You are a real brick': VG to MF, quoted in Kent, *Vida*, 148.

'I am glad to hear': Isabella Goldstein to MF, 20 May 1904. File 6: MFGC, 1904–1954.

'Christian Science'; *'We glean spiritual harvests'*: 'Christian Science in relation to Christian character', *Christian Science Journal*, Apr 1904.

rain streamed: 'Wintry blasts', *Daily Telegraph*, 2 Jul 1904, 10.

mignonette; *'the most charming of all'*: 'Ladies' column', *Queanbeyan Observer*, 8 Apr 1904, 2.

'Tell your sister': LG to MF, 5 Aug 1904. File 3: MFGC, 1902–1953.

Pollice Verso; *'an imagination in an advanced'*: See Kirsty Grant, 'Thumbs up or thumbs down? The trials and tribulations of Norman Lindsay's *Pollice verso*', *NGV Art Journal*, 2 Jun 2014, 42, www.ngv.vic.gov.au.

his brother Lionel: Lionel Lindsay wrote a letter on Norman's behalf, at his request, to *The Bulletin* in defence of *Pollice Verso*. See Grant, 'Thumbs up or thumbs down?'.

bats feasting: 'Local and general', *Nepean Times*, 22 Nov 1904, 4.

'I am grieved': VG to MF, 16 Oct 1904. File 6 MFGC, 1904–1954. Quoted in Kent, *Vida*, 148.

successful American tour: Kent, *Vida*, 101. See also Jill Roe (ed.), *To America and Back: January–June 1902. A Lecture by Vida Goldstein* (Australian History Museum, 2002).

'was in the hands': V. Goldstein, *Australian Women's Sphere*, May 1902, quoted in Kent, *Vida*, 101.

lack of preparation: VG to MF, 16 Oct 1904. File 6:MFGC, 1904–1954. Quoted in Kent, *Vida*, 149.

box of jumping fleas: See Franklin, 'Maria's Dingle' in 'When I Was Mary Anne, a Slavey', 102: 'You remind me of a box of fleas.'

royalty cheque: Only 1399 copies of *My Brilliant Career* were sold in 1901; the majority of them were sold in Australia, for which Miles received lower royalties. By 1904, Roe records that Miles had only made 27 pounds, eight shillings from *My Brilliant Career.* See Roe, *Stella Miles Franklin*, 125.

the fittings irritated her: Speculation. See note above that Miles was like a box of fleas.

'I fear I may have offended'; *Discourses of Epictetus*: MF to JF, 15 Nov 1904. Published in Roe, *My Congenials*, 38–40.

'merrily Miles': See Roe, *Stella Miles Franklin*, 115.

chatter became an idea: Speculation. Roe suggests Miles was inspired by the NSW election and Linda's wedding. See Roe, *Stella Miles Franklin*, 118.

St Stephen the Martyr: 'Wedding', *Tumut and Adelong Times*, 16 Dec 1904; family wedding picture, 23 Nov 1904. Photographs of Miles Franklin, c. 1860–1954. SLNSW, PX*D 250 (Vol. 1), no. 32.

Linda lies in bed: Speculation. See below re: her veiled reference to sex.

Miles falls asleep: Speculation. Miles would have been at home in Penrith after the big wedding day.

36

'tornado of fierce fire'; *'demon of destruction'*; *'martyrs'*: 'Swept by flame', *Freeman's Journal*, 7 Jan 1905, 20.

'I have everything'; *'I never want'*: LG to MF, undated; soon after the wedding in 1904. File 3: MFFC, Graham-Lampe 1887–1954.

'Well, it's this way': Miles Franklin, *Some Everyday Folk and Dawn* (Blackwood, 1909), 49.

George Robertson: Speculation. All publishers rejected it on defamation grounds, and Roe also suggests defamation curtailed the manuscript. Roe, *Stella Miles Franklin*, 117. The archived draft suggests structural and point-of-view issues as well.

cricket: See Rebecca Wiley, 'Reminiscences of George Robertson and Angus & Robertson Ltd by Rebecca Wiley. Memories of over 43 years, 1894–1938', 1945. SLNSW, ML MSS 5238.

sulked and curled up: Speculation. Miles referred to sulking at the post and rejection in her letter to MF to Joseph Furphy (JF), 15 Nov 1904. Published in Roe, *My Congenials*, 38–39.

'Well, my old demon': MF to AGS, 30 Mar 1905. Published in Roe, *My Congenials*, 41.

he worried: Speculation. See letter below.

Friday-night literary soirees: See Verna Coleman, *Her Unknown (Brilliant) Career: Miles Franklin in America* (Angus & Robertson, 1981), 67.

'Do you think of me': AGS to MF, 31 Mar 1905. Published in Roe, *My Congenials*, 41–42. Most Australian women journalists were confined to the women's pages. *New Idea* began in 1902.

'debris': 'Towrang', *Goulburn Herald*, 15 Mar 1905.

'Vernacular': Speculation that the editor 'reluctantly' agreed, given A.B. Paterson had been a celebrity correspondent in an era when bylines were rare.

Paterson; Evening News: See Roe, *Stella Miles Franklin*, 134.

'They were typical': 'Vernacular' [Miles Franklin], 'The lads from the land', *SMH*, 27 May 1905, 9.

palm reader: Franklin recalls the palm reader in Miles Franklin personal papers, miscellaneous notebooks 19-, 1927–1940, 'Notes mainly books read, 19-', Item 13, 10. SLNSW, ML MSS 364/5.

'small beer': Quoted in Roe, *Stella Miles Franklin*, 118.

She wondered: Speculation. Miles was anxious about more success for financial reasons as much as her reputation.

From her window seat: 'Vernacular' [Miles Franklin], 'A Kiandra holiday', *SMH*, 12 Aug 1905, 6.

'Have you found anyone': SL to MF, 1 Feb 1903. File 3: MFFC, Graham-Lampe 1887–1954

At Cooma: Franklin, 'A Kiandra holiday'.

cattle muster: 'Vernacular' [Miles Franklin], 'A mountain cattle muster II', *SMH*, 26 Aug 1905; 'Vernacular' [Miles Franklin], 'The woods of the west', *SMH*, 14 Oct 1905, 9.

As she rides along: Franklin, 'A Kiandra holiday', 6.

Part Three: Stella

37

It was April 1906: 'An overdue barque, Sydney, Thursday', *The Age*, 6 Apr 1906, 4; 'A South African stowaway', *The Age*, 6 Apr 1906, 6.

RMS Ventura: The *Ventura* left Sydney on 6 Apr 1906. See *SMH*, 9 Apr 1906, 8; Roe, *Stella Miles Franklin*, 137; and ship postcard, MF to LG, 12 Apr 1906, in Roe, *My Congenials*, 45. It is speculation that she did not promote her book, in line with her previous reticence to discuss it publicly.

And on 18 April: 'Earthquake and fire: San Francisco in ruins', *Call-Chronicle-Examiner*, 19 Apr 1906, 1. Special edition combining the *San Francisco Examiner, The San Francisco Chronicle* and *The San Francisco Call.*

he rode his horse: JL to Merle Maddern (niece), 1 May 1906, in Earle Labor, Robert C. Leitz III & I. Milo Shepard (eds), *Letters of Jack London*, Vol. 2 1906–1912, (Stanford, 1988), 572–73.

A fortnight after the earthquake: Miles Franklin, 'San Francisco. A fortnight after', *SMH*, 23 Jun 1906, 11. Republished in Jill Roe & Margaret Bettison, *A Gregarious Culture: Topical Writings of Miles Franklin* (UQP, 2001), 25–30.

'pulsated like a living thing': 'Earthquake special', *Signs of the Times* (Seventh Day Adventist periodical), 2 May 1906, 5.

Aboard the Ventura: Franklin, 'San Francisco a fortnight after'.

60 pounds: Roe records Franklin's earnings from her journalism, estimating Franklin earned two guineas per article (a guinea was equal to one pound and one shilling) and Franklin wrote a total of 31 articles. Roe, *Stella Miles Franklin*, 131.

She told Miles: Speculation they discussed Chicago; Miles was influenced by Vida Goldstein's experience in the United States. Vida describes Chicago in V. Goldstein, *Australian Women's Sphere*, May 1902, quoted in Kent, *Vida*, 97.

As that year moved on: Speculation. Ship and agents' advertisements were common. See e.g. *Sunday Times* (Sydney), 18 Jun 1905, 1.

'I can only hope': Aileen Goldstein to MF, 25 May 1904. File 6: MFGC, 1904–1954.

'having a happy time'; *'Well, my dear'*: Isabella Goldstein to MF, 26 Nov 1904. File 6: MFGC, 1904–1954.

'Be sure you don't go': LG to MF, 16 May 1904. File 3: MFFC, Graham-Lampe 1887–1954.

It was still stultifying: Miles visited the city for breaks and to stay 'in the swim'. Quoted in Roe, *Stella Miles Franklin*, 124.

confided in Joseph Furphy: JF to MF, 31 July 1904. File 5: MFGC, 1904–1907. See also MF to JF, 15 Nov 1904. Published in Roe, *My Congenials*, 38–41.

'happiest day': EB to MF, 27 Oct 1905. File 1: MFFC, Barton-Cotterill, 1901–1954. SLNSW, ML MSS 364/47.

'I am yours forever: EB to MF, 22 Aug 1906. File 1: MFFC, Barton-Cotterill, 1901–1954.

'guiding star': EB to MF 30 Oct 1905. File 1: MFFC, Barton-Cotterill, 1901–1954.

'I know nothing': RS to MF, 5 Apr 1904; quoted in Roe, *Stella Miles Franklin*, 126.

'I have been getting a fair amount': EB to MF, 30 Oct 1905. File 1: MFFC, Barton-Cotterill, 1901–1954.

'Is it true you are': SL to MF, 24 Sep 1906. File 3: MFFC, Graham-Lampe 1887–1954. Also quoted in Roe, *Stella Miles Franklin*, 129. Speculation that Granny had asked earlier; it's likely Granny heard about the romance well before 1906.

'I can hardly bear': EB to MF, Oct 27 1905. File 1: MFFC, Barton-Cotterill, 1901–1954.

'It was only men': Franklin, *My Brilliant Career.*

'weighed too heavily': EB to MF, 24 Nov 1905, File 1: MFFC, Barton-Cotterill, 1901–1954. Published in Roe, *My Congenials*, 44–45.

'It is only a few short days': EB to MF 24 Nov 1905. File 1: MFFC, Barton-Cotterill, 1901–1954. Published in Roe, *My Congenials*, 44–45.

'I had longed to go': See Roe, *Stella Miles Franklin*, 135, quoting MF to Henrietta Drake-Brockman, 1950.

38

Miles' mother calculated: Speculation. The *SMH* reported the earthquake on 20 Apr 1906; her daughter was sailing into a disaster. The voyage took 21 days and fares ranged from sixteen to twenty pounds. See Roe, *Stella Miles Franklin*, 137.

'I keep thinking': Mark Twain to Robert Reid, 30 Apr 1906. Reproduced in 'Mark Twain on the San Francisco earthquake and a picture he cannot get out of his mind', Shapell Manuscript Foundation, www.shapell.org/manuscript/mark-twain-earthquake-1906/.

a man preached: See Richard Pittard, 'San Francisco earthquake of 1906, a report'. See also Richard Bruce Pittack, 'San Francisco earthquake of April 18 1906,' (PhD thesis, Andrews University, November 1972), via Ellen G. White Estate, https://ellenwhite.org/media/document/8780

'humped into ridges'; *'all the shrewd contrivances'*: Jack London, 'The story of an eyewitness', *Collier's*, 12 May 1906.

'Do not worry': Speculation. Miles was chronically anxious despite her extroverted exterior.

'Jonesie': Miss E.B. Jones was listed on the *SMH* passenger report, 9 Apr 1906, 8. See also Roe, *Stella Miles Franklin*, 138.

Loma Linda: Loma Linda's 1906 patient ledger includes 'Stella Franklin'. '1906 Patient Ledger', Department of Archives and Special Collections, Loma Linda University Library, Loma Linda, California.

relief camp: See Coleman, *Her Unknown (Brilliant) Career*, 74.

'there is not more'; *'pathetically overworked'*; *'some of the gaunt'*; *bridegroom*; *'little malicious'*: Franklin, 'San Francisco. A fortnight after'.

'There is word from Carrie!': Roe writes that Whelan's sister arranged the tugboat. Many years later, Franklin thanked Carrie Whelan as 'her first American friend' and Carrie's sister: 'opened up a whole new world' quoted in Roe, *Stella Miles Franklin*, 138. Edwin Bridle also addressed his letters to 1217 Sixth Avenue, East Oakland.

Oakland had been damaged: 'Five killed at Oakland Theatre', *San Francisco Examiner*, 19 Apr 1906.

Berkeley: See Mike Rosen-Molina, 'East Bay aftershocks', *The Monthly*, Apr 2006, https://themonthly.com/feature2-04-06/.

Miles read Jack London's: Speculation she read the article—they'd both written about the earthquake; there was no other connection between Miles and the famous author to warrant her writing to him (see note below re correspondence between London and MF). Speculation that she asked Carrie about his address.

At his Sonoma Mountain ranch: Jack 's home is now Jack London State Historic Park.

'Wolf': See JL to George Sterling, 22 Mar 1906, signed 'Wolf', in Labor et al., *Letters of Jack London*, 557–558, and the 'Wolf House Ruins', Jack London State Historic Park, California.

'After having some irritable': JL to MF, 28 May 1906. File 6: MFGC, 1904–1954.

Miles is grateful: Speculation. Miles packed her manuscripts, hoping for publication in the United States. Jonesie was religious, so would have prayed nightly. Miles likely unpacked rather than prayed.

39

San Francisco: Franklin, 'San Francisco. A fortnight after'.

in southern California: See Patti Morrison, 'Southern California's curious history as the Sanatorium Capital of America', *LA Times*, 30 Aug 2022, www.latimes.com/california/story/2022-08-30/explaining-l-a-with-patt-morrison-los-angeles-as-lourdes-by-the-sea.

Twenty dollars for the month; *Miles sent a brochure*: LG to MF, 17 Jul 1907. File 3: MFFC, Graham-Lampe 1887–1954. Miles (stella) Franklin is listed in the 'patient ledger, 1906' at Loma Linda and the Loma Linda pamphlet lists accommodation rates. Archives and Special Collections, Loma Linda University Library.

'could never tell how delighted'; *'You bad girl'*: LG to MF, undated (c. 1906). File 3: MFFC, Graham-Lampe 1887–1954.

'Mother was here': LG to MF, 17 Jul 1906. File 3: MFFC, Graham-Lampe 1887–1954.

'Everyone thinks of her as so young': LG to MF, 17 Jul 1906. File 3: MFFC, Graham-Lampe 1887–1954.

Loma Linda's nursing school: See 'Until the daybreak' [obituary: McKenzie, Edith Beatrix, (nee Jones)], *Australasian Record and Advent World Survey*, 1965, 69(35):7. The obituary notes that in 1910 Jonesie was the first Australian nurse to graduate from Loma Linda.

parks were still populated: 'Thousands are living in tents', *San Francisco Examiner*, 24 Apr 1906.

'You can stay here': Carrie Whelan then suggested Chicago. See Roe, *Stella Miles Franklin*.

'The greatest charge': See *Arena-Sun*, 11 Feb 1904, 7; 'On child labor', *The Worker*, 19 Mar 1904, 4.

'Just this inst. received'; strip photo; going for a swim: MF to LG, 20 Aug 1906; File 3: MFFC, Graham-Lampe 1887–1954. Published in Roe, *My Congenials*, 48–49.

'darling Stella': EB to MF, 23 May 1906. MFFC, Barton-Cotterill, 1901–1954. Published in Roe, *My Congenials*, 46–47.

'My love for you': EB to MF, 28 Jun 1906. MFFC, Barton-Cotterill, 1901–1954.

Kenyon Hotel staff uniform: referenced in Roe, *Stella Miles Franklin*, 141.

'I received yr welcome': SL to MF, 24 Sep 1906. File 3: MFFC, Graham-Lampe 1887–1954.

Roaring Fork Valley; she aims at the nearest log; strongman: See MF to Bruce Sutherland, 18 Mar 1954, quoted in Roe, *Stella Miles Franklin*, 152.

40

Mary Kelly: 'Refugee march', 31 Jul 1906. See also Alexandra Rae, 'The 1906 earthquake survivor who fought for San Francisco's homeless', KQED, 28 Jun 2021, https://kqed.org.

'We expect lots of action': JL to Bailey Millard (editor of *Cosmopolitan*), 18 Feb 1906. Labor et al, 'The letters of Jack London', 549.

spring snow: 'The weather', *Chicago Daily Tribune*, 30 Oct 1906, 1.

streetcar: Speculation, Miles does not mention being met at the train station.

river; Lovers: See Jane Addams, *Twenty Years at Hull-House with autobiographical notes* (The MacMillan Company 1912), 115, https://digital.library.upenn.edu/women/addams/hullhouse/hullhouse.html. For a description of the surrounds and waste boxes; see also John Matthew Corpolongo, 'Refuse, reform and reversal: The environmental history of the Chicago River, 1830–1910' (PhD thesis, University of Oklahoma, 2020).

Upton Sinclair's The Jungle: Published as a serial in November 1905, and in book form February 1906 (Doubleday, Page & Company). The book contributed to the beginning of the US Food and Drug Administration (FDA).

anti-wage slavery: London compared *The Jungle* to the 'Uncle Tom's Cabin of wage slavery'. See Michael Brester Folsom, 'Upton Sinclair's escape from the jungle', in Harold Bloom (ed.), *Upton Sinclair's The Jungle* (Chelsea House Publishers, 2002), 47.

'It is alive and warm': R.N. Mookerjee, 'Muckraking and fame: *The Jungle*' in Harold Bloom (ed.), *Upton Sinclair's The Jungle*, 72.

Hilda Polacheck: Hilda Satt Polacheck, *I Came a Stranger*, (ed.) Dena J. Polacheck Epstein (University of Illinois Press, 1991). Speculation she was there at the time of Miles' visit; Polacheck conducted tours of Hull House and acted as translator as an adult. She was 24 in 1906.

'Miss Addams'; did not believe in drop-in charity: See Terri Kapalis, *Jane Addams' Travel Medicine Kit* (Hull House/University of Illinois College of Architecture and Art, 2011).

9000 locals a week; class or meeting; Hull House theatre: are all mentioned in the *Hull House Yearbook 1906–1907* (Hull House, 1907), https://archive.org/. Hull House is now a museum on the grounds of the University of Illinois.

Florence Kelley: fled domestic violence with her children to Hull House and was instrumental in reforming child labour and sweatshop conditions. See Alisha Norwood, 'Florence Kelley', National Women's History Museum, 2017, www.womenshistory.org.

clubs: *Hull House Yearbook 1960–1907* (Hull House, 1907, https://archive.org.

American heroine: 'Speed Read Jane Addams', The Nobel Prize, nobelprize.org and Allen Davis, *American Heroine* (Oxford University Press, 1973).

back was permanently crooked; medical school training: See Kapalis, *Jane Addams' Travel Medicine Kit*. See also Peter Gibbon, *'Jane Addams a hero for our time'*, Humanities, Fall 2021 (42)4: online.

Jane Club: Hull House's accommodation for single, working women.

Alice Henry: Miles Franklin, 'Letter from Chicago', *Book Lover*, Sep 1907, republished in Roe & Bettison, *A Gregarious Culture*, University of Queensland Press, 2001, 29–33. See also Coleman, *Her Unknown (Brilliant) Career*, 81–88. For a biography of Alice Henry, see Diane Kirkby, *Alice Henry: The Power of Pen and Voice* (Cambridge University Press, 1991).

'clever but unpleasant': Spence is quoted in Kirkby, *Alice Henry*, 75.

moved with Alice to rooms: See Roe, *Stella Miles Franklin*, 145.

Miles was envious: Speculation. Alice had a career.

investigate department stores: Coleman, *Her Unknown (Brilliant) Career*, 89.

secretarial course: see Roe, *Stella Miles Franklin*, 145.

policeman saved: 'Christmas "mob" throngs streets', *Chicago Daily Tribune*, 25 Dec 1906, 5.

'Christmas Baby': 'Christmas Baby rules hospital', *Chicago Daily Tribune*, 24 Dec 1906, 5.

Charles and Linda: Speculation that Miles was thinking of them. It was her first Christmas away from Australia.

window displays: See Daniel Hautzinger, 'From the archive: Marshall Field's Christmas windows', WTTW, 1 Dec 2017, https://wttw.com; speculation that Alice and Miles went Christmas shopping.

bushfire: EB to MF, 12 Dec 1906. File 1: MFFC, Barton-Cotterill, 1901–1954.

'You came into my life': EB to MF, 9 Nov 1906. File 1: MFFC, Barton-Cotterill, 1901–1954.

'We could live together': EB to MF, 9 Nov 1906. The implication was that she would not consummate the marriage. File 1: MFFC, Barton-Cotterill, 1901–1954.

'Only love'; *'I would not like to see'*: EB to MF, undated (Roe cites 10 Dec 1906). The federal election was 12 Dec 1906 and Edwin's letter mentions election day. File 1: MFFC, Barton-Cotterill, 1901–1954. Published in Roe, *My Congenials*, 51–52.

At Wilga Vale: Speculation; these would be normal Christmas preparations.

Anna Strunsky; *William Walling*: *The Chicago Daily Tribune* reported on Walling and Strunsky's speech at Hull House. See 'Socialistic world as result of Russian revolt', *Chicago Daily Tribune*, 6 Dec 1906, 8.

'speechifying': Franklin, 'Letter from Chicago', in Roe & Bettison, *A Gregarious Culture*, 32.

'Miss Strunsky'; *'I believe in the freedom'*: 'Wife calls "Mrs" obsolete', *Chicago Daily Tribune*, 2 Dec 1906, 4.

'Millionaire Red': See Susan O'Connor Davis, *Historic Illinois, A Tour of the State's Top National Landmarks* (Globe Pequot, 2022), 82. In 1920, William Bross Lloyd was found guilty in a group trial of conspiring to overthrow the US Government. He was later pardoned.

petted lions: See Janet Lee, '"Early flower" meets "petted lion": The New Woman and New Man in Miles Franklin's "lost" novel, *The Net of Circumstance*', *Women: A Cultural Review*, 2017, 28(3): 193–216.

'I wish more Australians': Franklin, 'Letter from Chicago'.

41

in the city's courts: '200 court cases against Welchers', *San Francisco Examiner*, 19 Apr 1907, 1. The article mentions 1700 suits to compel payment by insurance companies since the earthquake.

the Snark: Jack London, *The Cruise of the Snark* (Macmillan, 1935 [1911]).

banned the colour red: 'Veto on red flags', *Chicago Daily Tribune*, 21 May 1907, 4; 'Bar Jaxon and red', *Chicago Daily Tribune*, 19 May 1907, 8.

The mayor sacked: 'Mayor Busse sets forth his reasons for firing School Board radicals', *Chicago Daily Tribune*, 28 May 1907, 2.

small column on page 57: Franklin, 'No dignity in domestic service'. *Chicago Daily Tribune*, 14 Apr 1907, 57.

The Sydney Morning Herald: Miles Franklin, 'Concerning "helps"—raise the status', *SMH*, 13 Apr 1907, 8.

over the winter: MF mentions the cold in her letter to RS, quoted in 'Page for women', *SMH*, 29 May 1907.

dragon's breath; hissed under her skirts: 'Mr & Mrs Ogniblat L'Artsau' [Miles Franklin], *The Net of Circumstance* (Mills & Boon, 1915), 1–4.

department store: See Coleman, *Her Unknown (Brilliant) Career*, 89.

she would wash the snow: Franklin, *Net of Circumstance*, 9.

weeping with tiredness: Speculation. Exhaustion.

secretarial course: Franklin, *Net of Circumstance*, 19.

the Sonoma; He fretted; Perhaps, if he did well: EB to MF, 20 Mar 1907. File 1 MFFC, Barton-Cotterill, 1901–1954. See also 'The *Sonoma* crew', *SMH*, 27 Feb 1907, 5.

'literary wings'; 'If I was doing the thing'; 'Will you come': EB to MF, 20 Mar 1907. File 1: MFFC, Barton-Cotterill, 1901–1954.

wrinkles her nose: Franklin, *Net of Circumstance*, 19, which describes Chicago public transport's 'fetid smells'.

'greatest and grandest place on the globe': MF to RS, quoted in 'A Page for Women', 29 May 1907, 5.

she is thinking; homesickness: Miles Franklin, 'The old house on the corner' (unpublished). See also Roe, *Stella Miles Franklin*, 155, re: Miles' periodic homesickness.

She thinks of Edwin: Speculation. Miles would have sent a reply; all letters then stop. It is reasonable to think she would have thought of him given their relationship, and the fact that she kept his letters.

'I know too well': EB to MF, 20 Mar 1907. File 1: MFFC, Barton-Cotterill, 1901–1954.

42

'like being thrown': Jack London, *Cruise of the Snark*, 82.

heatwave: 'Temperature', *Chicago Daily Tribune*, 24 Jun 1907, 2.

magic 'May' party: See *Hull House Year Book 1906–1907*, 18.

Ice cream: Franklin, 'Letter from Chicago'.

'amateur night evil': 'Hull House opens its model show', *Chicago Daily Tribune*, 16 Jun 1907. See also 'Traces crime to nickel theater', *Chicago Daily Tribune*, 14 Apr 1907; 'Efforts to lure school children', *Chicago Daily Tribune*, 26 Apr 1907, 4.

new pure food laws: 'Chicago center of pure food laws', *Chicago Daily Tribune*, 17 Feb 1907, 3.

'by your photo': SL to MF, 24 Sep 1906. File 3: MFFC, Graham-Lampe 1887–1954.

three-piece bathing suits; sailor collars: See summer fashion advertisements such as 'Mandel Brothers', *Chicago Daily Tribune*, 19 Jun 1907, 18.

pack up the house: Speculation. It is clear from the letter (see below) Linda is with her mother in Penrith.

'My very dear sister'; *'Penrith is the same'*; *'Scribbles on the page'*: LG to MF, 6 Jun 1907. File 3: MFFC, Graham-Lampe 1887–1954.

Miles did not know: Miles' conflict with her mother inspired the relationship of Sybylla and her mother in *My Brilliant Career* and *My Career Goes Bung*.

jilted: Franklin, *On Dearborn Street*, 120, quoted in Roe, *Stella Miles Franklin*, 156.

She liked that he was: Speculation. Miles enjoyed attention but seemingly at a distance.

'I am determined': 'Carnage begins on holiday eve', *Chicago Daily Tribune*, 4 Jul 1907, 4.

Miles could feel; *This is insanity*: See Franklin, 'Letter from Chicago'.

Chicago's telegraphers; *Women's Trade Union League*: 'Appeals to the telegraph strikers for and against the steps they have taken', *Chicago Daily Tribune*, 11 Aug 1907, 2.

spreading her parasol: 'Picket armed with parasol braves the police all day', *Chicago Daily Tribune*, 11 Aug 1907.

'Look after your health': LG to MF, 6 Jun 1907. File 3: MFFC, Graham-Lampe 1887–1954.

'dens': Franklin, 'Letter from Chicago'.

tired; *frazzled*; *machine*: Franklin, *Net of Circumstance*, 19.

'automobiling': See 'Matrimony chances for Chicago girls', *Chicago Daily Tribune*, 14 Apr 1907, in which eligible men cite 'automobiling' as an interest.

'I got your letter': SF to MF, 30 Aug 1907. File 2: MFFC, 1896–1954.

43

'wilds of America'; *'We fancy'*; *'having a very good time'*; *'delightful'*; *'sociable'*: Franklin, 'Letter from Chicago'.

'shows no intention': Franklin, 'Letter from Chicago.

Penrith; *'Charlie, poor boy'*: SF to MF, 30 Aug 1907. File 2: MFFC, Franklin family, 1896–1954.

Miss Alice Henry; Miss Addams: Alice would have sought advice from Jane Addams, who was close to the Lloyd family. See Roe, *Stella Miles Franklin*; Coleman, *Her Unknown (Brilliant) Career.*

Passavant Memorial Hospital: Franklin personal papers 1880–1954. Diaries, notebooks and indexes, 1909–1954. Literary notebooks, volumes I–XV, 1934–c. 1948, Vol. XV, Item 14, 761–762. Re: Dr Allen Johnson, the Northwestern Memorial Hospital Archives has no record of him; see later note re: sacking and death. Roe spells it as 'Johnston'.

'dungeon of despair': MF to AH, undated, c. 1934 (marked 'Extra Private'). File 7: MFGC, 1908–1949. SLNSW, ML MSS 364/11.

'I resent death': MF to AH, 29 Jan 1942 (on the death of her brother, Norman). File 7: MFGC, 1908–1949.

'her milk left her'; *'cease from troubling'*; *'It was very sad'*: SF to MF, 30 Aug 1907. File 2: MFFC, Franklin family, 1896–1954.

Passavant pastor: Speculation. As Passavant was a Christian hospital, a pastor would have routinely done rounds of patients.

'neurasthenia'; *'fashionable disease'*: 'Take a tub for Neurasthenia', *Chicago Daily Tribune*, 27 Dec 1908, 32; 'Light, complexion and nerves', *Chicago Daily Tribune*, 4 Dec 1905, 8; G.L Kerr Pringle, 'Hydrotherapy and Electricity in the treatment of Neurasthenia', *Edinburgh Medical Journal*, 1907, 320–324.

Mitchell's Rest Cure: Charlotte Perkins Gilman, *The Yellow Wallpaper.* First published in *The New England Magazine*, in January 1892. Also see Kapalis, *Jane Addams' Travel Medicine Kit*, 6, 11. Franklin became friends with Perkins Gilman.

'To be put to bed': Jane Addams, 'Democracy and social ethics', quoted in Kapalis, *Jane Addams' Travel Medicine Kit*, 19.

operating theatre; *scalp and eyebrow*: Miles Franklin Personal papers 1880–1954; Diaries, notebooks and indexes, 1909–1954; literary notebooks, volumes I–XV, 1934–c. 1948, Vol. XV, Item 13, 761–762.

'psychic rebellion': Franklin, *Net of Circumstance*, 244.

'cursed by feeling'; *'terror to herself'*; *'divine sensitiveness'*: Franklin, *Net of Circumstance*, 272.

'Why . . . should I continue': Franklin, *Net of Circumstance*, 269.

'before I could be . . .': Franklin, *Net of Circumstance*, 269.

44

tried not to think: Speculation. Lola and William Bross Lloyd later divorced in 1916, with Lola citing infidelity.

sealskin jackets: William and Lola's son, William Lloyd Jnr, unpublished recollections, Winnetka Historical Society, Winnetka, Illinois.

Samuel Maverick: Paula Mitchell Marks, 'Maverick, Samuel Augustus', Texas State Historical Association, August 2023 [1952].

engraved Weber: See Winnetka Historical Society Collection.

shopping: LML, diary, 14 Nov 1907. Lola Maverick Lloyd Papers, 1856–1949, Series II, b. 41 v. 2–17A: Diaries 1895–1909. NYPL, Mss Col 6233.

'Miss H brought me': MF to SF, 14 Nov 1907 (postcard). Published in Roe, *My Congenials*, 61.

'dreadfully disappointed': VG to MF, 1907. File 6: MFGC, 1904–1954.

32nd birthday; *alligator-skin bag*; *nervous*; *cross*; *Miss Henry would be here*:

LML, diary, 24 Nov 1907. Lola Maverick Lloyd Papers, 1856–1949, Diaries 1895–1909.

'My heart': WL to LML, 7 Dec 1908. Lola Maverick Lloyd Papers, Series I, b. 35 f. 6–7; Lloyd, William Bross: 1908–1935, undated. NYPL, Mss Col 6233.

her aunt Helena . . . had sent her: Helena Franklin (Aunt Lena) to MF, c. Oct 1907; Roe, *Stella Miles Franklin*, 158.

'Demy' Lloyd: LML, diary, 15 Nov 1907. Lola Maverick Lloyd Papers, 1856–1949, Diaries 1895–1909.

'dude': Franklin, *Net of Circumstance*, 43; Roe, *Stella Miles Franklin*, 213.

hell; damn: Franklin, *On Dearborn Street*, 100, quoted in Janet Lee, *Fallen Among Reformers: Miles Franklin, Modernity and the New Woman* (Sydney University Press, Sydney), 86.

'When a man becomes': Franklin, *On Dearborn Street*, 120, quoted in Roe, *Stella Miles Franklin*, 156.

Walks: LML, diary, 10 Nov 1907. Lola Maverick Lloyd Papers, 1856–1949, Diaries 1895–1909.

moustache: Franklin, *On Dearborn Street*, 168.

Part Four: The Survivor

The Survivor: See Lee, *Fallen Among Reformers*, 35.

45

anxious to know: JL to George P. Brett, 15 Feb 1908, Published in Labor et al, *The letters of Jack London*, 734.

In Samoa, 'Apia, Samoa, the Snark', photograph, undated. Published in Labor et al, *The letters of Jack London*, '1908'.

ice skates; mother: MF to SF, 9 Mar 1908. Published in Roe, *My Congenials*, 62.

too old to write: SL to MF, 24 Sep 1906. Granny died in 1912, aged 81. File 3: MFFC, Graham-Lampe 1887–1954. Published in Roe, *My Congenials*, 49.

God forbid that anyone: Franklin, *Net of Circumstance*, 235. Miles dwelled on ageing.

rickety houses: Mary Dreier, *'Margaret Dreier Robins'* (1950, Island Press), 25.

'the existence of charity': Jane Addams, 'Democracy and social ethics' (1902); *The Greatest Works of Jane Addams* (Maddison & Adams Press, 2019), 18.

William 'Big Bill' Hayward: See 'Haywood, William 'Big Bill' Dudley, Social Welfare History Project, Victoria Commonwealth University, https://socialwelfare.library.vcu.edu/organizations/labor/haywood-william-big-bill-dudley/.

'The feeling against Margaret': M. Dreier, 'Margaret Dreier Robins', 44

average working week: See SueEllen Hoy, 'Chicago working women's struggle for a shorter day, 1908–1911', *Journal of the Illinois State Historical Society*, 2014, 107(1):9–44.

'The more I work': MDR to MF, 29 Oct 1907. File 6: MFGC, 1904–1954. Published in Roe, *My Congenials*, 60–61.

'Hello Girls': 'Wooed by phone, ends in cell. Hello Girl appears in court', *Chicago Daily Tribune*, 25 Oct 1907, 6.

talked about it with Alice: Speculation. She would have discussed the offer with Alice, a close friend, and especially as Alice had worked with Margaret Dreier Robins.

'Fine to see': LML, diary, 4 Apr 1908. Lola Maverick Lloyd Papers, 1856–1949, Diaries 1895–1909.

Winnetka spa: 'North Shore Health Resort', *Chicago Daily Tribune*, 12 Jan 1911, 22.

Loma Linda: Jonesie to MF, postcard, undated; quoted in Roe, *Stella Miles Franklin*, 148. They reunited in 1950.

corner offices: See Coleman, *Her Unknown (Brilliant) Career*, 110–11.

Agnes Nestor had voted: see Coleman, *Her Unknown (Brilliant) Career*, 110–11; Agnes Nestor, *Woman's Labor Leader* (Bellevue Books, 1954).

'built for war': Raymond Robins, 'John Fitzpatrick', *Life and Labor*, Feb 1911, 41–43.

mapped out a code: Coleman, *Her Unknown (Brilliant) Career*, 110–11.

'Lieutenant Franklin': See Coleman, *Her Unknown (Brilliant) Career*, 110. Speculation that she cheekily saluted; Miles was flirty and charming.

'dearest little Stella-girl': MDR to MF, 18 Apr 1911. Published in Roe, *My Congenials*, 65.

'women adrift': See Joanne Meyerowitz, *Women Adrift: Independent Wage Earners in Chicago, 1880–1930*. See also Roe, *Stella Miles Franklin*, 152.

'all last winter': MDR to AH, undated. Franklin incidental papers. Papers received from the estate of Alice Henry, 1903–1946. File 3. Correspondence with Margaret Dreier Robins, 10 February 1920–6 July 1940. SLNSW, ML MSS 364/116.

'You have the right': MF, quoted in Coleman, *Her Unknown (Brilliant) Career*, 110.

'I was so tired': Agnes Nestor, *Woman's Labor Leader* (Bellevue Books 1954), 28.

'Daisy Bell': Harry Dacre, 'A Bicycle Built for Two', 1892.

Fred: Roe refers to Franklin's relationship with Emma's brother, Fred Pischel. Roe, *Stella Miles Franklin*, 198. The modest café and paying for herself insistence features in Franklin *On Dearborn Street*, 23.

'an ecstasy of expense': MF to AH, 7 Oct 1942. For a short bio of Zelie, see 'Miss Zelie Passavant Emerson', Women's Suffrage, n.d., www.suffrageresources.org.uk/database.

Australian whip-cracking; *'proposed to a patient'*: Franklin personal papers 1880–1954. Diaries, notebooks and indexes, 1909–1954. Literary notebooks, volumes I–XV, 1934–c. 1948, Vol. XV, Item 15, 762. Dr Allen Johnson died from pneumonia in 1908.

'If you do not move': MDR to AH, undated. Franklin incidental papers. Papers received from the estate of Alice Henry.

Harvard Hotel: Roe, *Stella Miles Franklin*, 151.

she arranges her typewriter: See Coleman, *Her Unknown (Brilliant) Career*, 114. Miles wrote constantly at the hotel.

'the house of dreams': Jane Addams, 'The spirit of youth and the city streets', in *The Greatest Works of Jane Addams*, 96.

'The Survivors': See Lee, *Fallen Among Reformers*, for a critical analysis of the play. It was not produced.

'quiet as a mouse': quoted in Roe, *Stella Miles Franklin*, 155.

46

the wreck: JL to Ninetta Eames, 22 Jan 1909. Published in Labor et al, *The letters of Jack London*, 785.

'deep sorrow'; *'I am at times practically helpless'*: JL to George P. Brett, 22 Dec 1908. Published in Labor et al, *The letters of Jack London*, 774.

Pollice Verso: The National Gallery of Victoria bought *Pollice Verso* in 1907 for 150 guineas and ten shillings; Lindsay went to London in 1910. See Grant, 'Thumbs up or thumbs down?'.

Charlie Graham and his new fiancée: 'Wedding Graham-Johnstone', *Brisbane Courier*, 30 Mar 1909, 7.

his new wife, Traillie: See Roe, *Stella Miles Franklin*, 156. Roe cites Edwin's wedding date as 27 May 1908.

'woman of great wealth': 'A page for women', *SMH*, 29 Jan 1908, 5.

League chorus: Franklin, pocket diary, 6 Jan 1909. Franklin personal papers, 1880–1954. Diaries, notebooks and indexes, 1909–1954. Franklin pocket diaries, 1909–1953, Item 1. SLNSW, ML MSS 364/Box 2.

new baby; *San Antonio*: LML, diary, Jan–Feb 1909. Lola Maverick Lloyd Papers, 1856–1949, Diaries 1895–1909.

bought a diary: Franklin, pocket diary, 1 Jan 1909. Franklin pocket diaries, 1909–1953, Item 1. Miles' unbroken diary records begin from 1909.

went to the Robins': Franklin, pocket diary, 2 Jan 1909. Franklin pocket diaries, 1909–1953, Item 1.

'Came back to Harvard': Franklin, pocket diary, 10 Mar 1909. Franklin pocket diaries, 1909–1953, Item 1.

Louise Dresden; *Ludwig Wüllner*: Franklin, pocket diary, 13 Mar 1909. Franklin pocket diaries, 1909–1953, Item 1.

chorus; *Garden of Flowers*: Franklin, pocket diary, 9 May 1909. Franklin pocket diaries, 1909–1953, Item 1.

storming parliament: 'Suffragist rows. Storming the House of Commons', *The Argus*, 1 Dec 1908, 9.

took off her wool underjacket: Franklin, pocket diary, 20 Jun 1909. Franklin pocket diaries, 1909–1953, Item 1.

a walk; *The Dresdens*; *tennis*: Franklin, pocket diary, 21–23 Jun 1909. Franklin pocket diaries, 1909–1953, Item 1.

Kappa Kappa Gamma House: Franklin, pocket diary, 26 Jun 1909. Franklin pocket diaries, 1909–1953, Item 1.

French classes; *Tennyson's poetry*: Franklin, pocket diary, 29 Jun 1909. Franklin pocket diaries, 1909–1953, Item 1.

lectures: Miles mentions in her diary hearing Earl Barnes, who would publish his book *Woman in Modern Society* in 1912, and Felix Adler, founder of the Ethical Culture movement, whom she found 'uninteresting and unattractive'. Franklin pocket diaries, 1909–1953, Item 1.

'Van brought his chair': Franklin, pocket diary, 16 Aug 1909. Franklin pocket diaries, 1909–1953, Item 1.

paddling in canoes: Franklin, pocket diary, 1 Aug 1909. Franklin pocket diaries, 1909–1953, Item 1.

the lotus eaters: Alfred Tennyson, 'The Lotos-eaters' (1832), in *Poems of Alfred Tennyson in Two Volumes*, Vol. I (Edward Moxon, 1842), 180–81.

'right cute': MF to Blackwood, 2 Aug 1909. Published in Roe, *My Congenials*, 63.

'Happy days': Franklin, pocket diary, 4 Aug 1909. Franklin pocket diaries, 1909–1953, Item 1.

typeset proofs: Franklin, pocket diary, 16 Aug 1909. Franklin pocket diaries, 1909–1953, Item 1.

'I am in receipt': MF to Blackwood, 2 Aug 1909. Published in Roe, *My Congenials*, 63–64.

'Van gave me his handkerchief': Franklin, pocket diary, 6 Aug 1909. Franklin pocket diaries, 1909–1953, Item 1.

'Ulysses': Alfred Tennyson, 'Ulysses' (1842), in *Poems of Alfred Tennyson in Two Volumes*, Vol. II (Edward Moxon, 1842), 91.

telegraph poles: See a similar description in Theodore Dreiser, *Sister Carrie* (Doubleday, 1900), 9.

Instead, she sits: Speculation that she wrote in her room on the night of her birthday—there is no special dinner mentioned in her diary.

47

Man from Snowy River: 'Vehicle swept down river', *SMH*, 13 Jan 1910, 6.

swirling snowstorm: 'Snow shies off; cold wave due', *Chicago Daily Tribune*, 14 Jan 1910, 5.

Fur was on sale: See advertising, e.g. 'A purchase of fur coats', *Chicago Daily Tribune*, 5 Dec 1909, 41.

'Red Queen'; *Emma Goldman*: Franklin, pocket diary, 16 Jan 1910. Franklin personal papers, 1880–1954. Diaries, notebooks and indexes, 1909–1954. Franklin pocket diaries, 1909–1953, Item 2. SLNSW, ML MSS 364/Box 2. Speculation she browsed; there was likely merchandise on sale at talks. Re: Goldman's nickname, see 'May bar Emma Goldman Red Queen', *Chicago Daily Tribune*, 9 Apr 1909.

'The Angel of Discontent': See *Mother Earth*, Mar 1909, 4(1):1, www.archive.org.

Eleanor Club; *'self-respecting, self-supporting girl'*: see Franklin, *Net of Circumstance*, 33–34; Coleman, *Her Unknown (Brilliant) Career*, 115; and Ron Grossman, 'Flashback: A lifeline in the big city: Women's clubs, started in Chicago in 1898, gave women a home and an instant support network', *Chicago Daily Tribune*, 23 Apr 2020, www.chicagotribune.com.

refuge on the rooftop: Roe dates the photo of Miles on rooftop, Indiana Street, to c. 1910. See Roe, *Stella Miles Franklin*, 160.

Halley's Comet: 'Watcher falls off roof', *Chicago Daily Tribune*, 18 May 1910; 'Society, clubs, entertainments', *Chicago Daily Tribune*, 9 May 1910, 8.

Miles did not look; *Lola scanned*: Miles does not mention watching the comet in her 1910 diary; LML's 26 May 1910 diary records watching the comet; NYPL Lola Maverick Lloyd Papers 1856–1949, Series II, b. 42 v. 18–29; Diaries 1910–1919. NYPL, MssCol 6233.

Some Everyday Folk: Reviews were lukewarm. See Roe, *Stella Miles Franklin*, 123, 156.

'beastly' headaches: LML, diary, 10 Dec 1907. Lola regularly wrote of severe headaches in her diaries, suggesting a migraine condition. Lola Maverick Lloyd Papers, 1856–1949; Diaries 1895–1909.

Cyathus stercoreus: LML, diary, 1909b. See gathering notes: 3 Jun, 27 Jun, 10–11 Sep, 18 Sep 1909. Lola Maverick Lloyd Papers, 1856–1949, Series II, b. 41 v. 2–17A; Diaries 1895–1909. NYPL, MssCol 6233.

'tired and cross'; *'W. never forgives me'*; *'I escaped to cry alone'*: LML, diary, 13 Nov 1910. Lola Maverick Lloyd Papers 1856–1949.

dear heart: WL to LML, 7 Dec 1908. Lola Maverick Lloyd Papers, Series I, b. 35 f. 6–7: Lloyd, William Bross: 1908–1935, undated. NYPL, MssCol 6233.

'I am always the one': LML, diary, 5 May 1911. Lola Maverick Lloyd Papers 1856–1949; Diaries 1910–1919.

his automobile: William Lloyd Jnr, unpublished recollections.

She could see: Speculation. See previous note about Bill Lloyd's infidelity. Lola seemingly trusted Miles; see guest list in ch. 49, and letters.

'gay dawg': MF to LML, undated ('Tuesday in the "oasif"'). NYPL Lola Maverick Lloyd, Series I. Correspondence 1893–1949, undated; A. General correspondence 1895–1949, undated, b. 1 f. 1-6 1895–1915 May.

Automobile Club: See *Chicago Daily Tribune*, 12 Jan 1908, 21.

Stemonitis: LML, diary 1909b, 27 Jun 1909. Lola Maverick Lloyd Papers, 1856–1949; Diaries 1895–1909.

Women such a sport: See Roe, *Stella Miles Franklin*, 198.

oculist: Franklin, pocket diary, 1911. An oculist was an optometrist. Not to be confused with an occultist. Franklin pocket diaries, 1909–1953, Item 3.

'We swap husbands'; *'teach virgins'*: Reconstructed from Franklin's recollections using these quotations in Franklin literary notebooks volumes I–XV, 1934–c. 1948; 'Vol. XIII . . . p. 591–709 . . . Minor works, trivia, tripe, etc. etc [sic]'. Item 13, 614.

'experiments in living': Franklin literary notebooks volumes I–XV, 1934–c. 1948; 'Vol. XIII . . . pp. 591–709 . . . Minor works, trivia, tripe, etc. etc [sic]'. Item 13, 614.

'They are a thimbleful': Franklin personal papers. Literary notebooks, volumes I–XV, 1934–c. 1948. 'Vol. XIII . . . pp. 591–709 . . . Minor works, trivia, tripe, etc. etc [sic]'. Item 13, 614. SLNSW Box ML MSS 364/3.

wanted to dig: Franklin, *On Dearborn Street*, 26.

'You are denying life': Franklin literary notebooks volumes I–XV, 1934–c. 1948; 'Vol. XIII . . . pp. 591–709 . . . Minor works, trivia, tripe, etc. etc [sic]'. Item 13, 614.

'What you offer': Reconstructed from Franklin's recollections using these quotations in Franklin literary notebooks volumes I–XV, 1934–c. 1948; 'Vol. XIII . . . pp. 591–709 . . . Minor works, trivia, tripe, etc. etc [sic]'. Item 13, 614.

'You will become an old maid'; *'harridan'*; *'What do you want'*: Franklin literary notebooks volumes I–XV 1934–c. 1948; 'Vol. XIII . . . pp. 591–709 . . . Minor works, trivia, tripe, etc. etc [sic]'. Item 13, 614.

'death was preferable': Franklin literary notebooks volumes I–XV, 1934–c. 1948; 'Vol. XIII . . . pp. 591–709 . . . Minor works, trivia, tripe, etc. etc [sic]'. Item 13, 614.

'code'; *'sensitiveness'*: Franklin literary notebooks volumes I–XV, 1934–c. 1948; 'Vol. XIII . . . pp. 591–709 . . . Minor works, trivia, tripe, etc. etc [sic]'. Item 13, 614.

'initiation': Franklin literary notebooks volumes I–XV, 1934–c. 1948, 'Vol. XIII . . . pp. 591–709 . . . Minor works, trivia, tripe, etc. etc [sic]'. Item 13, 614.

She wrote to Blackwood: MF to Blackwood, 4 Apr 1910. Quoted in Roe, *Stella Miles Franklin*, 159.

her suitcase: Speculation. The manuscript remained unpublished until 1946.

all copies to be withdrawn: MF to Blackwood, 4 Apr 1910. *The End of My Career* (*My Career Goes Bung*) was evidently rejected for the second time. Roe records that Franklin received sixteen pounds, twelve shillings in royalties in 1910 (from *Some Everyday Folk and Dawn*). See Roe, *Stella Miles Franklin*, 159.

48

It was November 1910: See 'Architect visits to discuss Wolf House, November 1910', in Labor et al., 'Chronology', *Letters of Jack London*, x–xi. In 1913, when it was near completion, the house burned down and London never rebuilt. Ruins remain at Jack London State Historic Park.

Jonesie made plans: Jonesie stayed five years at Loma Linda. They reunited in 1950.

police; *riot*: Franklin, pocket diary, 1–2 Nov 1910. Franklin pocket diaries, 1909–1953, Item 2. See also Coleman, *Her Unknown (Brilliant) Career*, 120. Also see 'Armed mob led by girl', *Chicago Daily Tribune*, 3 Nov 1910, 1.

'aristocratic picketers': See 'Armed mob led by girl', 3 Nov 1910, 1. See also 'Mrs Raymond Robins and "cabinet" in strike conference: Armed patrolmen on guard in vicinity of a "storm center"', 4 Nov 1910, 4.

milk fund; *40,000 on strike*: 'Milk is promised for strike babies', *Chicago Daily Tribune*, 28 Nov 1910, 3; 'City intervenes in strike to end deadlock', *Chicago Daily Tribune*, 29 Nov 1910, 1.

John Fitzpatrick's Federation men; landlords: Miles Franklin, 'Chicago at the front', *Life and Labor*, Jan 1911, 1(1):4–14.

Day after freezing day: Franklin, pocket diary, 11 Nov 1910. Franklin pocket diaries, 1909–1953, Item 2.

'The workers in the garment trades': Franklin, 'Chicago at the front'.

Miles slept in: Franklin, pocket diary, 25 Dec 1910. Franklin pocket diaries, 1909–1953, Item 2.

posters: See the badge designed by Sylvia Pankhurst at The National Archives (UK), www.nationalarchives.gov.uk/.

'Waited for Sylvia': Franklin, pocket diary, 21 Jan 1911. Franklin personal papers, 1880–1954. Diaries, notebooks and indexes 1909–1954. Franklin pocket diaries, 1909–1953, Item 3. SLNSW, ML MSS 364/Box 2.

'slender, gentle': 'Sylvia Pankhurst comes ready for martyrdom', *Chicago Daily Tribune*, 6 Jan 1911, 5.

caricatured her: 'Young London suffragette who doubts success of militant plan in America', *Chicago Daily Tribune*, 20 Jan 1911, 3.

Hull House: See the account of Sylvia Pankhurst's Chicago visit and dinner at Hull House with Zelie and Miles after the prison visit in Rachel Holmes, *Sylvia Pankhurst: Natural Born Rebel* (Bloomsbury, 2020), 389.

Harrison Street prison: 'Sylvia Pankhurst, suffraget [*sic*] chief, assails Harrison Street Station', *Chicago Sunday Tribune*, 22 Jan 1911, 7.

Sylvia made a point: 'Jail suits heartless fits', *Chicago Daily Tribune*, 29 Jan 1911, 7.

'Come to London': Speculation. See Holmes, *Sylvia Pankhurst*, which details Sylvia's friendship with Zelie and Miles. Zelie joined Sylvia later in the year.

'dark and dreadful day': 'A Line o' type or two', *Chicago Daily Tribune*, 24 Apr 1911, 5.

'I have my own switch': MF to Aunt 'Annie', quoted in Roe, *Stella Miles Franklin*, 172.

Miles still wrote at night: Miles noted her insomnia in her diaries and in specialist appointments.

'The Love Machine': See Roe, *Stella Miles Franklin*, 157.

London holiday: Franklin returned to Chicago two months later, and stayed in Chicago until 1915.

sleep on the floor: Franklin, pocket diary, 29 May 1911. Franklin pocket diaries, 1909–1953, Item 3.

rooftop: Speculation she took a moment on the rooftop before leaving; it was a warm May. See 'May hottest in years', *Chicago Daily Tribune*, 29 May 1911, 2.

'Oh for some refuge': See Sandra Knowles, '"Oh, for some refuge—for myself—to be myself": The search for gender neutrality in the diaries of Miles Franklin', *Australian Feminist Studies*, 2010, 25(63):63–77.

49

Searchlights: 'Searchlights in war', *The Argus*, 28 Oct 1915, 6; 'Chlorine gas on the battlefield', *Daily News* (Perth), 21 Jul 1915, 7.

Lusitania had sunk: 'Tuesday 11 May 1915', *The Argus*, 11 May 1915, 8.

Egypt; *'take charge of the horses'*: 'Banjo Paterson for Egypt', *Evening Telegraph* (Queensland), 23 Oct 1915, 5.

'More men': 'Latest war news', *Evening Telegraph* (Queensland), 23 Oct 1915, 5.

'Don't look at them': Paterson, 'A day under fire. A battlefield sketch', *SMH*, 11 Aug 1900, 7.

in Kirribilli: Speculation. She had three sons fighting in the war. Justice Richard O'Connor died in 1912. Their eldest son, Richard Jnr, died in France in 1916.

tea party; the Narcissus: see Leslie Goddard, *Remembering Marshall Field's* (Arcadia Publishing, 2011), 46. Franklin, pocket diary, 18 Sep 1915. Franklin pocket diaries, 1909–1953, Item 8. Franklin personal papers, 1880–1954. Diaries, notebooks and indexes 1909–1954. Franklin pocket diaries, 1909–1953, Item 8. SLNSW, ML MSS 364/2.

Lola had been invited: MF to LML, 9 Sep 1915. File 9: MFGC, 1915–1950. SLNSW, ML MSS 364/13. It is unclear if Lola attended.

guest list: Franklin, pocket diary, 1915; written under 'Memoranda' at diary's end. Franklin pocket diaries, 1909–1953, Item 8.

'donkey': Franklin, pocket diary, 5 Dec 1914. Franklin personal papers, 1880–1954. Diaries, notebooks and indexes 1909–1954. Franklin pocket diaries, 1909–1953, Item 7. SLNSW, ML MSS 364/2. Quoted in Roe, *Stella Miles Franklin*, 213.

'They are happier'; *'deluded fools?'*: MF to RS, 19 Jun 1913, quoted in Roe, *Stella Miles Franklin*, 163.

She was not afraid of the dark: Franklin personal papers 1880–1954. Diaries, notebooks and indexes, 1909–1954, literary notebooks, volumes I–XV, 1934–c. 1948, 'Vol. I . . . pp. 1–50', Item 1, 55. SLNSW, ML MSS 364/3.

'You can't send me to war': 'Sylvia Pankhurst again refuses to register', *The Sun*, 17 Aug 1915, 5.

'You are the most complex': See Roe, *Stella Miles Franklin*, 198.

'I could not undertake'; *'I have not been with'*: See Roe, *Stella Miles Franklin*, 198.

One Last Step: Franklin, pocket diary, 13 Oct 1915. Franklin pocket diaries, 1909–1953, Item 8.

silly ass: Franklin, *Net of Circumstance*, 43.

'little rascal': See DL to MF, and MF to DL, 9 Dec 1912–16 Oct 1914. File 8: MFGC, 1909–1954. SLNSW, ML MSS 364/12.

'He was desperate and brutal': Franklin, pocket diary, 14 Oct 1914. Franklin pocket diaries, 1909–1953, Item 7. See Roe, *Stella Miles Franklin*, 202.

Demy remarried in 1916 and became foreign editor of *The Christian Science Monitor.*

I am my own heroine: Bashkirtseff, *Journal of Marie Bashkirtseff*, 52.

'Why do I write?': Franklin, *My Brilliant Career*, 254.

'To hot young hearts': Franklin, *My Brilliant Career*, 253.

'What the future holds': Franklin, *My Brilliant Career*, 256.

throw violets: Franklin, pocket diary, 22 Oct 1915. Franklin pocket diaries, 1909–1953, Item 8.

Coda

'I am glad I am not young': Franklin literary notebooks volumes I–XV, 1934–c. 1948, XIII, Item 13 pages 591–709, Item 13, 621.

Author's Note

Note: 'Mary Anne' and 'Maryann' are spelled inconsistently in original manuscripts. The spellings used are those that appear in original documents.

Note: Original page numbering on the Mary Anne manuscript is used in sources.

diary: See Miles Franklin, 'Concerning Maryann. First draft' Ms. 1904. Sub-series 1: Miles Franklin literary manuscripts and related papers, 1887–1954. File 12: Essays and articles 189-–c. 1950. SLNSW, ML MSS 364/59. In this document, Miles refers to keeping an original diary that 'I carefully kept during that period' (1903–1904), and she also includes extracts in 'When I Was Mary Anne, a Slavey'. This 1903–1904 diary is missing (Miles' existing diaries begin from 1909—see sources Part 3 and 4), but is recreated in the prologue.

Select bibliography

Manuscripts

Miles Franklin—Papers, 1841–1954, State Library of NSW

'Concerning Maryann. First draft' Ms. 1904. Sub-series 1: Miles Franklin literary manuscripts and related papers, 1887–1954. File 12: Essays and articles 189-–c. 1950. SLNSW, ML MSS 364/59.

Miles Franklin incidental papers. Papers received from the estate of Alice Henry, 1903–1946.

- File 3: Correspondence with Margaret Dreier Robins, 10 February 1920–6 July 1940. SLNSW, ML MSS 364/116.

Miles Franklin personal papers, 1880–1954. Diaries, notebooks and indexes, 1909–1954. File 1: Miles Franklin pocket diaries, 1909–1953. SLNSW, ML MSS 364/Box 2:

- 1909, Item 1
- 1910, Item 2
- 1911, Item 3
- 1914, Item 7
- 1915, Item 8.

Miles Franklin personal papers, 1880–1954. Diaries, notebooks and indexes, 1909–1954. Literary notebooks, volumes I–XV, 1934–c. 1948. SLNSW, ML MSS 364/3:

- Vol. I, pp. 1–50, Item 1
- Vol. XI, Odds and ends, pp. 451–498, Item 11
- Vol. XIII, pp. 591–709, Minor works, trivia, tripe, etc. etc [*sic*], Item 13
- Vol. XV, pp. 761–762, Item 15.

Miles Franklin personal papers, 1880–1954. Miscellaneous notebooks, 19–, 1927–1940, SLNSW Box ML MSS 364/5:

- Notes mainly re books read, 19–, Item 13.

Miles Franklin Family Correspondence, 1896–1954:

- File 1: Miles Franklin Family Correspondence, Barton-Cotterill, 1901–1954. SLNSW, ML MSS 364/47
- File 2: Miles Franklin Family Correspondence, Franklin family, 1896–1954. SLNSW, ML MSS 364/48
- File 3: Miles Franklin Family Correspondence, Graham-Lampe, 1897–1954. SLNSW, ML MSS 364/49.

Miles Franklin personal papers, 1880–1954. Miles Franklin general correspondence, 1887–1954:

- File 1: Miles Franklin General Correspondence, 1887–1951. Note filed with Lawson correspondence. SLNSW, ML MSS 364/7
- File 2: Miles Franklin General Correspondence, 1901–1936. SLNSW, ML MSS 364/7
- File 3: Miles Franklin General Correspondence, 1902–1953. SLNSW, ML MSS 364/8
- File 4: Miles Franklin General Correspondence, 1903–1953. SLNSW, ML MSS 364/9A
- File 5: Miles Franklin General Correspondence, 1904–1907. SLNSW, ML MSS 364/9B
- File 6: Miles Franklin General Correspondence, 1904–1954. SLNSW, ML MSS 364/10
- File 7: Miles Franklin General Correspondence, 1908–1949. SLNSW, ML MSS 364/11.

Other Miles Franklin manuscripts, State Library of NSW

Miles Franklin papers, mainly literary manuscripts [1900–1954?]. 'Novel "The end of my career", 190–, MS and typescript', SLNSW, ML MSS 445/2. (CY 879)

Miles Franklin literary manuscripts and related papers. 'Untitled Ms., c. 189-–19- incomplete sections. Contains some characters and incidents used in *My Career Goes Bung*, published 1946'. Volume ML MSS 364/55.

Miles Franklin family photographs, c. 1868–1952. SLNSW, PX*D 250 (Vol. 2).

Photographs of Miles Franklin, c. 1879–1954. SLNSW, PX*D 250 (Vol. 1).

'When I Was Mary Anne, a Slavey':

- Vol. 1. Sketches I–IV (c. 1904). Miles Franklin papers, mainly literary manuscripts [1900–1954?]. SLNSW, ML MSS 445/23.
- Vol. 2. Sketches V–VI (c. 1904). Miles Franklin papers, mainly literary manuscripts [1900–1954?]. SLNSW, ML MSS 445/24.

Other manuscripts

Australian Club (Sydney, NSW) records, 1838–1963. 'Suggestions and Complaints' book, 1895–1902. SLNSW, ML MSS 1836.

Lola Maverick Lloyd Papers, 1856–1949. New York Public Library, Mss Col 6233:

- Series II, Diaries and address books 1894–1933, undated, b. 41 v. 2–17a: Diaries 1895–1909
- Series II, Diaries and address books 1894–1933, undated, b. 42 v. 18–29: Diaries 1910–1919

- Series I, Correspondence 1893–1949. B. Family Correspondence. b. 35 f. 6–7: Lloyd, William Bross: 1908–1935, undated
- Series I, Correspondence, A. General correspondence, b. 1 f. 1–6: 1895–1915, May.

Loma Linda, '1906 Patient Archive'. Department of Archives and Special Collections, Loma Linda University, Loma Linda, California. (No ledger file name given.)

'Mark Twain to Robert Reid, 30 Apr 1906'. Reproduced in 'Mark Twain on the San Francisco earthquake and a picture he cannot get out of his mind', Shapell Manuscript Foundation, n.d., www.shapell.org/manuscript/mark-twain-earthquake-1906/.

Miles Franklin [and] Vida Goldstein [picture], c. 1900–1920. State Library of Victoria, H42756a.

Rebecca Wiley, 'Reminiscences of George Robertson and Angus & Robertson Ltd by Rebecca Wiley. Memories of over 43 years, 1894–1938 (1945)'. SLNSW, ML MSS 5238.

Scott family papers. Vol. 23: Scott family papers, Rose Scott correspondence, miscellaneous, 1884–1904. SLNSW, A2284.

William Lloyd Jnr, unpublished recollections. Winnetka Historical Society, Winnetka. (No file name given.)

Published books and journals

Addams, J. 'The spirit of youth and the city streets' (1902), in *The Greatest Works of Jane Addams*, Prague: Maddison & Adams Press, 2019.

—— 'Democracy and social ethics' (1902), in *The Greatest Works of Jane Addams*, Prague: Maddison & Adams Press, 2019.

—— *Twenty Years at Hull-House with Autobiographical Notes*, New York: The MacMillan Company, 1912.

Allen, J.A. *Rose Scott: Vision and Revision in Feminism*, Oxford: Oxford University Press, 1994.

Angell, J. & Fletcher, B. *The Australian Club: 1828–2013*, Sydney: Allen & Unwin, 2013.

Banks, E. L. *The Autobiography of a 'Newspaper Girl'*, London: Methuen, 1902.

Barker A.W. (ed.), *Dear Robertson: Letters to an Australian Publisher*, Sydney: Angus & Robertson, 1982.

Barnes, J. *The Order of Things: A Life of Joseph Furphy*, Oxford: Oxford University Press, 1990.

Barrere, A. & Leland, C. *A Dictionary of Slang, Jargon & Cant*, Vol. 1. Edinburgh: The Ballantyne Press, 1889–90.

Bashkirtseff, M. *The Journal of Marie Bashkirtseff*, trans. Mathilde Blinde, London: Cassell & Company, 1890.

Cantrell, C. 'Caroline Martha (Cara) David (1856–1951)', *Australian Dictionary of Biography*, 1993, https://adb.anu.edu.au/biography/david-caroline-martha-cara-9906.

Coleman, V. *Her Unknown (Brilliant) Career: Miles Franklin in America*, Sydney: Angus & Robertson, 1981.

Davis, A.F. *American Heroine: The Life and Legend of Jane Addams*, New York: Oxford University Press, 1973.

Dreier, M.E. *Margaret Dreier Robins: Her Life, Letters and Work*, New York: Island Press, 1950.

Dreiser, T. *Sister Carrie*, New York: Doubleday, 1900.

Epictetus. *The Discourses of Epictetus*, trans. George Long, London: George Bell and Sons, 1902.

Folsom, M.B. 'Upton Sinclair's escape from the jungle', in H. Bloom (ed.), *Upton Sinclair's The Jungle*, New York: Chelsea House Publishers, 2002.

Foss, S.W. 'Angel of discontent', *Mother Earth*, 1909, 4(1): 1, https://archive.org/stream/motherearthvol4/.

Franklin, M. *My Brilliant Career*, Sydney: A&R Classics, 2013 [1901].

—— *Some Everyday Folk and Dawn*, Edinburgh: Blackwood, 1909.

—— 'Chicago at the front', *Life and Labor*, 1911, 1(1): 4–14.

—— [as 'Mr & Mrs Ogniblat L'Artsau'] *The Net of Circumstance*, London: Mills & Boon, 1915.

—— *My Career Goes Bung*, Sydney: A&R Classics, 2013 [1946].

—— *Cockatoos*, Sydney: Angus & Robertson, 1954.

—— *Childhood at Brindabella*, Sydney: Angus & Robertson, 1963.

—— *On Dearborn Street*, Brisbane: UQP, 1982.

Gibbon, P. 'Jane Addams: A hero for our time', *Humanities*, 2021, (42)4, www.neh.gov/article/jane-addams-hero-our-time.

Goddard, L. *Remembering Marshall Field's*. Mount Pleasant, NC: Arcadia Publishing, 2011.

Grant, K. 'Thumbs up or thumbs down? The trials and tribulations of Norman Lindsay's *Pollice Verso*', *NGV Art Journal*, 2014, 42, www.ngv.vic.gov.au/journal_edition/edition-42/.

Holmes, R. *Sylvia Pankhurst: Natural Born Rebel*, London: Bloomsbury, 2020.

Hoy, S. 'Chicago working women's struggle for a shorter day, 1908–1911', *Journal of the Illinois State Historical Society*, 2014, 107(1): 9–44.

Hull House. *Hull House Yearbook 1906–1907*, Chicago: Hull House, 1907.

Kapalis, T. *Jane Addams' Travel Medicine Kit*. Chicago: Hull House/University of Illinois College of Architecture and Art, 2011.

Khayyam, O. *Rubáiyát of Omar Khayyam, the Astronomer–Poet of Persia*, trans. Edward FitzGerald, London: Bernard Quaritch, 1859 [1120].

Kent, J. *Vida: A Woman for Our Time*, Melbourne: Penguin, 2020.

Kerr Pringle, G.L. 'Hydrotherapy and electricity in the treatment of neurasthenia', *Edinburgh Medical Journal*, 1907: 320–324.

Kieza, G. *Banjo*, Sydney: HarperCollins, 2020.

Kingston, B. *My Wife, My Daughter, and Poor Mary Ann*, Melbourne: Thomas Nelson, 1975.

Kirkby, D. *Alice Henry: The Power of Pen and Voice*, Cambridge: Cambridge University Press, 1991.

Knowles, S. '"Oh, for some refuge—for myself—to be myself": The search for gender neutrality in the diaries of Miles Franklin', *Australian Feminist Studies*, 2010, 25(63): 63–77.

Labor, E., Leitz, Robert C. III & Shepard, I.M. (eds), *Letters of Jack London*, Vol. 2 1906–1912, Stanford, CA: Stanford, 1988.

Lawson, H. *In the Days When the World Was Wide and Other Verses*, Sydney: Angus & Robertson, 1896.

Lee, J. *Fallen Among Reformers: Miles Franklin, Modernity and the New Woman*, Sydney: Sydney University Press, 2020.

—— '"Early flower" meets "petted lion": The New Woman and New Man in Miles Franklin's "lost" novel, *The Net of Circumstance*', *Women: A Cultural Review*, 2017, 28(3): 193–216.

Lindsay, N. *Bohemians of The Bulletin*, Sydney: Angus & Robertson, 1963.

—— *My Mask: For What Little I Know of the Man Behind It, An Autobiography*, Sydney: Angus & Robertson, 1970.

Lindsay, N., Howarth, R.G. & Barker, A. *Letters of Norman Lindsay*, Sydney: Angus & Robertson, 1979.

Lindsay, R. *Rose Lindsay: A Model Life*, (ed.) Lin Bloomfield, Sydney: *Odana* Editions, 2001.

London, J. *The Cruise of the Snark*. New York: Macmillan, 1935 [1911].

Meyerowitz, J. *Women Adrift: Independent Wage Earners in Chicago, 1880–1930*, Chicago: University of Chicago Press, 1988.

Mookerjee, R.N. 'Muckraking and fame: *The Jungle*', in H. Bloom (ed.), *Upton Sinclair's The Jungle*, New York: Chelsea House Publishers, 2002.

Nestor, A. *Woman's Labor Leader: An Autobiography of Agnes Nestor*. Rockford, IL: Bellevue Books, 1954.

O'Connor Davis, S. *Historic Illinois: A Tour of the State's Top National Landmarks*, Blue Ridge Summit, PA: Globe Pequot Press, 2022.

O'Hanlon, S. '"All found" they used to call it: Genteel boarding houses in early twentieth-century Melbourne', *Urban History*, 2002, 29(2): 239–53.

Paterson, A.B. *The Man from Snowy River and Other Verses*, Sydney: Angus & Robertson, 1895.

—— *Rio Grande's Last Race and Other Verses*, Sydney: Angus & Robertson, 1902.

Perkins Gilman, C. 'The yellow wallpaper', *The New England Magazine*, January 1892.

—— *The Yellow Wallpaper and Other Writings*, New York: Penguin Random House, 1999.

Robins, R. 'John Fitzpatrick', *Life and Labor*, Feb 1911, 41–43.

Roderick, C. *Miles Franklin: Her Brilliant Career*, Adelaide: Rigby, 1982.

Roe, J. (ed.), *My Congenials: Miles Franklin and friends in letters*. Sydney: Angus & Robertson, 1993.

—— (ed.), *To America and Back: January–June 1902. A lecture by Vida Goldstein*, Sydney: Australian History Museum, 2002.

—— *Stella Miles Franklin*, Sydney: HarperCollins, 2008.

Roe, J. & Bettison, M. (eds), *A Gregarious Culture: Topical Writings of Miles Franklin*, Brisbane: UQP, 2001.

Rosen-Molina, M. 'East Bay aftershocks', *The Monthly*, April 2006, https://themonthly.com/feature2-04-06/.

Rutledge, M. 'Richard Edward (Dick) O'Connor (1851–1912)', *Australian Dictionary of Biography*, 1988, https://adb.anu.edu.au/biography/oconnor-richard-edward-dick-1102.

Satt Polacheck, H. *I Came a Stranger*, (ed.) D.J. Polacheck Epstein, Champaign, IL: University of Illinois Press, 1991.

Schreiner, O. *The Story of an African Farm*, Boston: Roberts Brothers, 1888.

Sinclair, U. *The Jungle*, New York: Doubleday Page & Company, 1906.

Tennyson, A. *Poems of Alfred Tennyson in Two Volumes*, London: Edward Moxon, 1842.

Twain, M. *Christian Science*, New York: Harper & Brothers, 1907.

'Until the daybreak' [obituary: McKenzie, Edith Beatrix, (nee Jones)], *Australasian Record and Advent World Survey*, 1965, 69(35): 7.

Wilson, S. *Personal Effects: Reading the Journal of Marie Bashkirtseff*, Leeds: Routledge, 2009.

—— '"I am my own heroine": How Marie Bashkirtseff rewrote the route to fame', *Public Domain Review*, 2 Sep 2020, https://publicdomainreview.org/essay/marie-bashkirtseff/.

Newspapers and periodicals

Attributed authors

Forrest, M. 'With Rose Scott', *Daily Mail* (Brisbane), 18 Feb 1922, 11.

Franklin, M. 'San Francisco. A fortnight after', *The Sydney Morning Herald*, 23 Jun 1906, 11.

—— 'Letter from Melbourne', 'The Red Page', *The Bulletin*, 31 Mar 1904, 2. Republished in Roe & Bettison (eds), *A Gregarious Culture*, 8–10.

—— 'No dignity in domestic service', *Chicago Tribune,* 14 Apr 1907, 57.

—— 'Concerning "helps"—raise the status', *The Sydney Morning Herald*, 13 Apr 1907, 8.

—— ['Vernacular'] 'The lads from the land', *The Sydney Morning Herald*, 27 May 1905, 9.

—— ['Vernacular'] 'A Kiandra holiday', *The Sydney Morning Herald*, 12 Aug 1905, 6.

—— ['Vernacular'] 'A mountain cattle muster I', *The Sydney Morning Herald*, 19 Aug 1905, 6.

—— ['Vernacular'] 'A mountain cattle muster II', *The Sydney Morning Herald*, 26 Aug 1905, 6.

—— ['Vernacular'] 'The woods of the west', *The Sydney Morning Herald*, 14 Oct 1905, 9.

Grossman, R. 'Flashback: A lifeline in the big city: Women's clubs, started in Chicago in 1898, gave women a home and an instant support network', *Chicago Daily Tribune*, 23 Apr 2020, www.chicagotribune.com/2020/04/10/flashback-a-lifeline-in-the-big-city-womens-clubs-started-in-chicago-in-1898-gave-women-a-home-and-an-instant-support-network/.

Lindsay, N. 'Meeting on the stairs', *The Bulletin*, 18 Sep 1946, 2.

Morrison, P. 'Southern California's curious history as the sanitarium capital of America', *Los Angeles Times*, 30 Aug 2022, www.latimes.com/california/story/2022-08-30/explaining-l-a-with-patt-morrison-los-angeles-as-lourdes-by-the-sea.

Paterson, A.B. 'Life on board the S.S. *Kent* by our Special War Correspondent, A.B. Paterson', *The Sydney Morning Herald*, 29 Dec 1899, 7.

—— 'With the S.S. *Kent* contingent. By our Special War Correspondent, A.B. Paterson', *The Sydney Morning Herald*, 28 Dec 1899, 5.

—— 'A day under fire. A battlefield sketch', *The Sydney Morning Herald*, 11 Aug 1900, 7.

—— 'The New Hebrides. Voyage of the pilgrims. No. I', *The Sydney Morning Herald*, 1 Jul 1902, 5–7.

—— 'The New Hebrides. Voyage of the pilgrims. No. IV. At New Caledonia', *The Sydney Morning Herald*, 15 Jul 1902, 7.

—— 'Conditions at Coonamble', *The Sydney Morning Herald*, 26 Aug 1902, 5.

—— 'Trouble at Coonamble', *The Sydney Morning Herald*, 27 Aug 1902, 5.

—— 'Trouble at Wingadee Station', *The Sydney Morning Herald*, 29 Aug 1902, 5.

Pratt, A. 'The woman speaks', *The Bulletin*, 26 May 1900, 11.

'Thalia', 'Gossip for women', *The Week*, 26 Sep 1902, 4.

Unattributed authors

Articles by unattributed authors were drawn from the following newspapers and periodicals. All Australian titles listed here are available online via Trove at the National Library of Australia (www.trove.nla.gov.au). See notes on sources for specific references to articles.

Adelong and Tumut Express and Tumbarumba Post (NSW)
Advocate (Melbourne)
The Age (Melbourne)
The Argus (Melbourne)
The Australian Star (Sydney)
Bendigo Advertiser (Victoria)
The Bulletin (Sydney)
The Call-Chronicle-Examiner (San Francisco)
Chicago Daily Tribune (Chicago)
Chicago Sunday Tribune (Chicago)
The Christian Science Journal (Boston)
The Daily Mail (Brisbane)
The Daily Telegraph (Sydney)
The Dubbo Liberal and Macquarie Advocate (NSW)
Evening News (Sydney)
The Freeman's Journal (Sydney)
The Gippsland Times (Victoria)
Goulburn Evening Penny Post (NSW)
The Goulburn Herald (NSW)
The Leader (Orange, NSW)
The Maffra Spectator (Victoria)
The Muswellbrook Chronicle (NSW)
The Nepean Times (Penrith, NSW)
Newcastle Morning Herald and Miners' Advocate (NSW)
The Newsletter: An Australian Paper for Australian People (Sydney)
The Northern Argus (Clare, SA)

The Queanbeyan Age (NSW)
The Queanbeyan Observer (NSW)
Quiz (Adelaide)
The Referee (Sydney)
The Richmond River Express and Tweed Advertiser (NSW)
The San Francisco Examiner (San Francisco)
Signs of the Times (Australia)
South Coast Times and Wollongong Argus (NSW)
The Sun (Sydney)
The Sunday Sun (Sydney)
The Sunday Times (Sydney)
The Sydney Mail and New South Wales Advertiser (NSW)
The Sydney Morning Herald (NSW)
The Sydney Wool and Stock Journal (NSW)
The Tasmanian News (Hobart)
The Telegraph (Brisbane)
Truth (Sydney)
Tumut and Adelong Times (NSW)
The Worker (Brisbane)
The Yass Courier (NSW)

Online sources

Australian Senate, *Debates*, 9 Apr 1902, https://parlinfo.aph.gov.au.

Australian Senate, *Debates*, 10 Apr 1902, https://parlinfo.aph.gov.au.

Corpolongo, J.M. 'Refuse, reform, and reversal: The environmental history of the Chicago River, 1830–1910', PhD thesis, University of Oklahoma, 2020, https://shareok.org/handle/11244/324294.

Hautzinger, D. 'From the archive: Marshall Field's Christmas windows', WTTW, 1 Dec 2017, https://interactive.wttw.com/playlist/2017/12/01/archive-marshall-fields-christmas-windows.

Jack London State Historic Park, California. https://jacklondonpark.com/.

Mitchell Marks, P. 'Maverick, Samuel Augustus (1803–1870)', Texas State Historical Association, 2023 [1952], www.tshaonline.org/handbook/entries/maverick-samuel-augustus.

The National Archives (UK). 'The Suffragette Collection', 2024, https://shop.nationalarchives.gov.uk/collections/suffragettes-collection.

The Nobel Prize. 'Jane Addams: Speed read', 2024, www.nobelprize.org/prizes/peace/1931/addams/speedread/.

Rae, A. 'The 1906 earthquake survivor who fought for San Francisco's homeless', KQED, 28 Jun 2021, www.kqed.org/arts/13898345/the-

1906-earthquake-survivor-who-fought-for-san-franciscos-homeless-population.

RootsWeb. 'Laurel Susannah FRANKLIN (1892–1903)', 2020, https://freepages.rootsweb.com/~hanhorg/genealogy/ind_narrative/ind799.html.

Women's Suffrage. 'Miss Zelie Passavant Emerson', n.d., www.suffrageresources.org.uk/database/1823/miss-zelie-passavant-emerson.

Kerrie Davies is the author of *A Wife's Heart*, which created national discussion about the iconic poet Henry Lawson and his marriage. She has appeared at the Sydney and Brisbane Writers Festivals, and the National Folk festival, Canberra. A former journalist for *Vogue* and *The Sunday Telegraph*, Kerrie is Senior Lecturer at the School of the Arts & Media, UNSW Sydney, a 2024 Visiting Fellow at the State Library of New South Wales, and writes for *The Conversation.*

She lives between the North Coast of New South Wales and Sydney with her husband, Oliver, and two dogs, Ursa, a Samoyed, and Loki, an enormous husky shepherd cross.

★

'Captures a wonderful sense of Miles as a person. A fascinating page turner.'

Gillian Armstrong AM, director of the movie *My Brilliant Career*

'*Miles Franklin Undercover* examines Franklin's fears, frustrations and fierce determination to speak her own truth with intelligence and compassion. How I wish I had known her. Davies' riveting book is the next best thing. I feel I know her intimately.'

Jane Caro AM, Walkley award–winning Australian columnist, novelist, feminist

'Evocative and richly drawn, this sparkling book shows us a side to the great literary heroine that is darker and even more interesting than many Australians know. Kerrie Davies draws a textured picture of early 20th-century literary Australia, and sharply conjures the creative struggle of the woman-artist, torn between social expectation and a yen for adventure. I loved it.'

Jacqueline Maley, journalist and author of *The Truth About Her*

'The inspiring account of a woman whose name we all know but whose life has remained a mystery to many of us. Heartbreaking and heart-warming in turn, *Miles Franklin Undercover* is a triumph of enthralling storytelling, painting a picture of a woman of incredible courage and resilience that led the way for every Australian female writer to come.'

Sue Williams, author of *The Governor, His Wife and His Mistress*

'A captivating read—Miles comes alive.'

Brigitta Olubas, author of *Shirley Hazzard: A Writing Life*